AF413662

HOW TO KILL A LANGUAGE

Power, Resistance, and the Race to Save Our Words

SOPHIA SMITH GALER

CROWN
An imprint of the Crown Publishing Group
A division of Penguin Random House LLC
1745 Broadway
New York, NY 10019
crownpublishing.com
penguinrandomhouse.com

Published in Great Britain by William Collins,
an imprint of HarperCollins Publishers Ltd.

Library of Congress Cataloging-in-Publication Data
Names: Smith Galer, Sophia author
Title: How to kill a language : power, resistance, and the race to save our words /
  Sophia Smith Galer.
Description: First edition. | New York, NY : Crown, [2026] | Includes bibliographical
  references and index.
Identifiers: LCCN 2025055079 (print) | LCCN 2025055080 (ebook) |
  ISBN 9798217086979 hardcover | ISBN 9798217086986 ebook
Subjects: LCSH: Language obsolescence | Endangered languages
Classification: LCC P40.5.L33 S65 2026 (print) | LCC P40.5.L33 (ebook)
LC record available at https://lccn.loc.gov/2025055079
LC ebook record available at https://lccn.loc.gov/2025055080

Hardcover ISBN 979-8-217-08697-9
Ebook ISBN 979-8-217-08698-6

Manufactured in the United States of America

1st Printing

First US Edition

The authorized representative in the EU for product safety and compliance is Penguin Random House Ireland, Morrison Chambers, 32 Nassau Street, Dublin D02 YH68, Ireland, https://eu-contact.penguin.ie.

For Mum and Nonna,

Pür i cantarèin dla Sèrra,

Bòn a cantà.

Sperum ca sum stat brav

A la tò storia cuntà.

CONTENTS

You will notice when reading this book that words in other languages besides English are not italicized. This is because these words needn't be highlighted as being distinctive or other, and languages needn't be compartmentalized from one another. In this book, the words all belong to the multilingual speakers I interviewed, and they represent the only point that I really want to emphasize: that all languages belong to all of us.

INTRODUCTION

Upstairs, a language is dying. Nonna is in bed—al lett—and we are in the living room, waiting for the swelling in her legs—i gamb'—to go down. Mum and I rushed here from the other side of London when Nonna called us, worried. She is 93, a matriarch, and the youngest of eleven siblings. She is also the only one of them still alive, living over 1,300 kilometers away from her birthplace.

Modern medicine, and my mother's dutiful care, keeps her with us in a terraced house in north London near Holloway Road, a time warp from the 1950s with an avocado-green bathroom and a linoleum floor in the kitchen that I used to slip on if I ran too fast in my socks. I spent what feels like half my childhood there. My nonno, who died ten years before I was born, laid down the terrazzo out front, a mosaic of quartz-like pinks and grays that stands out against the dull pavement of their neighbors. Their house was my Italy, with tomatoes persevering on vines in the back garden and ragù always on the stove. But the tomatoes have not grown there for years now, and the last time Nonna ate ragù I had cooked it, spending hours on a batch like hers—frying the soffritto, spicing the beef with cloves—that was brought in a foil tray to her bedside.

Whenever I visit her with my mum, she speaks to Nonna in her mother tongue, which they call al dialët. I've always thought it sounds more like a kind of angry French, with strong nasal twangs and words that end abruptly, not like Italian with its ever-flowing vowel sounds. If they speak to people outside our family and not from our parts, their language effortlessly changes to standard Italian—not that I realized this growing up. As a child, I heard what I perceived to be variations on Italian spoken around me but not to me. Nonna would sometimes ask Mum if la fiöla wanted something—meaning me, the girl—and Mum would reply in English, saying, "Ask her, Mam', she's right there," gesturing at me. I didn't need the translation, but Mum and Nonna always spoke to me in English, and spoke to each other in dialët when they had adult things to discuss. In fact, I could understand a great deal of their language. I just couldn't *answer* in it.

Similar to most of my other schoolfriends from immigrant backgrounds, I did not speak my family's old language, just their new one. My school didn't offer Italian, and so I learned it neither at home nor at school. I felt a lot of shame about my inability to speak it. But I took to French and Spanish in class with ease, and I relished learning about the world and the different languages spoken in it, an appetite that eventually took me to get a degree in Spanish and Arabic and a career in international news reporting. These languages gave me new perspectives and pleasures, like the chance to read my favorite book in its original language (Gabriel García Márquez's *One Hundred Years of Solitude*) or to successfully negotiate a cab fare with a Beirut taxi driver. In journalism, being multilingual gave me first access to stories, scoops, and interviews. Eventually, as I grew older and more confident in my adopted languages, I started to wonder about the language that had gotten away. If I could learn languages like Spanish and Arabic, I started to think, how could I not learn the language my own mum and nonna spoke?

My curiosity began to grow, leading me down internet rabbit

holes about people like me who had grown up hearing and understanding, but not speaking a language. One day, while I was reading about Italian, I came across a page that changed everything: a list of all the languages spoken in Italy. There were dozens, including some near the valley Nonna is from, which were allegedly *not* Italian. All my life I'd been telling people Mum and Nonna spoke Italian and that that was the language I felt like I'd "lost my chance" with. But in reading this, I realized I'd gotten it wrong. Words like la fiöla weren't a kind of Italian as I'd assumed; they were from a whole other language.

This meant that they spoke *both* the Italian they'd each learned from school lessons and another language at home—one called emigliän, if my map was right, although my family called it dialët. Emigliän is only one of almost thirty indigenous languages in Italy—so why had I never been told about them? In these long evenings, paled by the blue light of my laptop, I learned that Italy glittered with a mother lode of language diversity and that Vulgar Latin sprouted into many new forms across the peninsula in the Middle Ages, from the alps to Etna, as ancient Romans became the subjects of new empires and rulers. This is not a country of Italian, bordering Spanish and French, but of entangled languages, great and small, crawling around and into each other: Occitan, Vèneto, Lombard, Furlan. But there was a catch: This linguistic wealth was fast disappearing. As I read more about it, my vocabulary began to darken with new phrases like *language death*, *endangerment*, *vitality*; words that are assigned to the status of a language's existence in the world, as if they are rare plants or pandas. And that is when the penny dropped. Deep in the long list of Italy's endangered languages lay Nonna's.

In the next one hundred years, up to half of the world's languages will die.[1] That is how many people talk about languages: They might be abstract systems of communication, but we want to give them lives, sentience, personalities. We connect them to people and places; we describe their groups and histories as family trees. Of the rich seven-thousand-plus body of thoughts, feelings, vocabularies, and grammar systems that exist today, well over three thousand languages will go. No funerals will be held; no cemeteries will fill. Some languages will leave behind dictionaries, novels, hours of radio; others will leave nothing save for a relative's turn of phrase someone still remembers with affection.

Many linguists and language activists believe we shouldn't call a language's annihilation "language death" because it's distressing for the last speakers to see their great cultural bank, intimately connected to their ethnic identity, receive a death sentence. You can also argue that it's wrong; languages can, in theory, be revived and respoken. But what has happened in my own family, as well as in many others, has taught me a hard truth. It is simply a reality that some languages we love and identify with will never be spoken again, in our homes, our communities, or, in the most severe cases, anywhere else on our planet. Some call that death—others call it sleep, extinction, or dormancy. Whatever you want to call it, it is not the norm across human history for languages to disappear so rapidly. Many of these endangered languages are probably varieties you've never heard of, but others that are definitely critically endangered include Irish, Otomi, Breton, Ainu. Linguists are unanimous that languages are disappearing at an unprecedented rate; the UN Assembly president has said that one indigenous language disappears every two weeks.[2] A conservative estimate places the number of all the languages we've ever had at 31,000; a middle-of-the-road estimate puts that figure at 140,000. In the twenty-second century we will be fortunate to have 4,000 still with us.

Our ancient ancestors comfortably navigated their lives changing dialects and languages every few kilometers and enjoyed varying degrees of multilingualism. A language could signify who and what you were as much as where you lived, and a language's fate would be tied to its speakers' ability to survive in the face of war, disease, famine, and whatever other ancient misfortune plagued our forebears.

The vast majority of the world's languages were, and are, spoken and not written, defying most attempts to estimate and record them, but we can still get some sense of our abundant history today in certain parts of the world. Ghana, which we will visit later in this book, holds more than eighty spoken languages. Papua New Guinea has the highest linguistic diversity on the planet with more than eight hundred. China, which you may have thought of as a country that speaks Mandarin and a little Cantonese, hosts more than three hundred. Language diversity of this level is actually *normal* in the grand scheme of human history, as is language shift and change; English and Hindi, once upon a time, shared a single common ancestor. Monolingualism—and the assumption that people might speak the same language over hundreds of kilometers, forever—is as man-made as the book you are reading these words in. It is increasingly normalized by a global internet that bids us to all participate—at least, if you speak one of its main languages. Forty-nine percent of the world's top ten million websites are in English.

So why does this matter? If you stop speaking a language, surely you just speak another one instead? And what is the use of speaking a language that only sixty other people know? Well, if you're a native English speaker, and there were just fifty-nine of you left, would you leap to Spanish, Russian, or Japanese without a second thought when a government or an occupying power told you to? Or because your parents and your teachers are convinced your old language won't get you a job one day? For native speakers of other languages, this is not an intellectual exercise but a reality that they or their ancestors had to reckon with. Leaving a language behind is heartbreaking for any language's speaker, regardless of their community's size. A language is the way your parents spoke to you; it is every memory of your childhood. It roots you to your ethnic identity and values, informing all our life choices.

We lose far more than a bunch of grammar rules and words when we lose a language. We also lose the wellspring of information that flows from it—its sayings, its means of identifying and perceiving the world, its character. Languages aren't dictionaries, but encyclopedias, containing entire worlds of often irreplaceable information. Prostratin, an enzyme found in the mamala tree in Samoa, was discovered to help treat HIV only because Paul Cox, an American ethnobotanist, was also a Samoan speaker. He learned about the tree's healing properties from a local tribal healer who knew all about it, because it had been passed down to Samoans for generations. Many such conversations like this are yet to take place, especially in an equitable way that benefits both indigenous peoples and foreigners like Paul. In 2011, scientists estimated that 86 percent of the existing species on earth and 91 percent of species in the ocean still await description, meaning that they exist in nature but have not yet been formally observed, studied, or named by scientists.[3]

This knowledge can be the key to studying the natural world, where Western science's monolingualism has caused mistakes and delayed discoveries. Indigenous Americans living in the Columbia Plateau and speaking a language called Sahaptin, for example, have always distinguished two different tubers from each other—the mam ī n and the sasamit'a. The different words reflected their practice of commonly eating the first while avoiding the second, which was only eaten by animals.[4] Western scientists had lumped them into the same species, but upon further examination the elders were proved right— these were two distinct tuber species.[5] Linguist Nicholas Evans, who has documented the Iwaidja language in northern Australia, tells a similar story. He was once sitting watching a PowerPoint presentation about local animal species, alongside other linguists and Iwaidja speakers. One of the slides showed the Australian snubfin dolphin, which had only recently been recognized by Western science as a distinct dolphin species. One of the Iwaidja men present, Khaki Marrala, casually commented that Iwaidja has always had a different word for this dolphin anyway—manimuldakbung. The snubfin was the first new dolphin species to have been acknowledged in fifty-six years, but if scientists had bothered to speak to the Iwaidja people, or learn their language, many years earlier, they needn't have been so ignorant. The Iwaidja may know much more, but with fewer than two hundred speakers left, time is running out to ask them. The world's biodiversity hotspots, teeming with the greatest variety of flora and fauna, also host more than 70 percent of the world's languages. We risk losing the information that may help us preserve such places if we fail the speakers who have long been their protectors.

Along with knowledge, we also risk losing countless intangible cultural artifacts: folklore, food, songs, traditions. In the present, we feel impoverished by the loss of Sappho's work, which we largely know about from what the great poets said of her rather than what she herself produced; we only have one complete poem from her. We are poorer without her complete work, and we are poorer still when we prevent the Sapphos of today from recording the poems they carry. Their work might be some of the only proof of a specific time and place—it could very well represent a knowledge, command, and art that will help our descendants adapt and learn, just as we do now. We may only try to understand the lost Scandinavian language of Scotland—Norn, spoken in Shetland and Orkney and brought as Old Norse by the Vikings—because we have the Hildina-kvæði, the ballad of "Hildina," a song that a young Scottish clergyman wrote down after he heard an old farmer called William Henry singing it in 1774. This is the language these islands spoke for hundreds of years, abandoning the Pictish they used before for the language of their new Viking overlords; by the time William Henry was singing, Scots had in turn long substituted Norn in daily life. Yet people still wanted to sing in Norn; they were still drawn to Norse fatalism, with tragic heroes and untimely yet inescapable demises, known as urðr—doom. The ballad of "Hildina" is a tale of avenged romance and bloodshed, and the Norse nobility embroiled in it, gives us a window into these islands' history and way of life where no other extant source can.

Finally, languages are crucial to our sense of identity—and, by extension, to our well-being. Groundbreaking research in Canada from the 1990s and 2000s revealed that communities where indigenous peoples could, in the majority, hold a conversation in their Aboriginal language experienced low to zero youth suicide rates. In communities where fewer than half could speak their language, suicide rates were six times higher. This isn't surprising; a language's health is part of self-continuity, symbolic of whether that community has also been able to hold on to their land, or access health care, education, and legal rights. In other words, languages are bellwethers of enfranchisement. This manifests in the vocabulary of indigenous groups around the world, where the Western binary of mental and physical health is challenged. For the Māori, there is an inseparable link between someone's health and their community's health called taha whānau—family health—which encompasses an individual's belonging to a community and the resilience that this provides, in addition to spiritual health.[6] In Australia, a government inquiry in 2012 looked at how indigenous languages could contribute to addressing disparities in health and life expectancy, and the committee concluded that they were so important in closing this gap that Aboriginal and Torres Strait Islander languages should be recognized in the Australian constitution. Their recommendation has still not been ratified by the Australian government.[7]

In short, language diversity is one of our most potent weapons against the diminishment of deep knowledge, the homogenization of culture, the erasure of history, and even some of our health crises. And yet it has never been more imperiled.

We need to understand how we became so profligate with our abundant language resources and lost sight of the need to protect them. Many of us take the world's unfathomable linguistic diversity for granted, and assume that losing a couple of languages isn't the end of the world. But each language *is* a world—and we're not just losing a couple. We're set to lose at least half. So, if thousands of languages have existed on our planet for thousands of years, why are they disappearing faster than ever before?

The short answer is that something is disappearing them.

■ ■ ■

When you consider a mass extinction event, you probably think of dinosaurs and comets. You may have seen a fossil in a museum, a skeletal face peering at you eyelessly from behind glass. You may have seen films with scenes of spasming lava, roaring *T. rexes*, the colossal, unthinkable devastation of a prehistoric time that gave way to our own life on earth. But you needn't bother going to a museum if you want to see a mass extinction event today, and you needn't think of big reptiles. You only need to open your mouth. Say something. You probably speak one of the world's mega languages—you could be one of 400 million first language speakers of English or the 1 billion who speak it as their second. More than half of the world speaks 23 out of the 7,000+ known languages today. Most of these 23 languages have become dominant thanks to their colonial histories and written traditions; French didn't become an official language in more than 20 countries by accident.

Just as history is written by the winners, languages often tend to be spoken by them, too.

Schoolchildren in Ireland and Wales in the nineteenth and twentieth centuries were forced to wear tally sticks around their necks, notched for every time they spoke their native Celtic languages, before they were hit at the end of the school day for how many notches they had accrued. The story of English is not just about Beowulf and Shakespeare; it's also about those children being smacked daily by their teachers. It's about colonial administrations, such as that of Whig politician Lord Macaulay, who said he wanted a class of imperial subjects in India to be English-speaking so that they could be "a class of persons Indian in blood and color, but English in tastes, in opinions, in morals and in intellect," who, as interlocutors, could "refine" the multilingual Indian population. These words, spoken in support of a law that would eventually be passed, allowed the British East India Company to begin teaching an English curriculum instead of a traditional Sanskrit and Persian one, a decision that would eventually lead to the cultural prominence English enjoys in India today. In a postcolonial world, such transparently racist edicts may be less commonplace. But my research into linguicide, the systemic erasure of languages, has found that not only are decisions made a century ago still having catastrophic consequences today, but that far too little is being done to reverse or even decelerate them.

In the 1980s, the Finnish linguist Tove Skutnabb-Kangas developed the idea of linguicide to highlight this. Lingui*cide*, she and her partner and linguist Robert Phillipson argued, was part of the "taxonomy of policies which a state can adopt toward minority languages." For them, linguicide was not only the outright killing of a language. Letting a language die, or not supporting its coexistence, was, to them, covert language murder with similar results to *overt* language killing—perhaps a little like comparing manslaughter and murder. It is, of course, clear to see how a war, a genocide, or criminalization may end a community's language and even the community itself. But it can be more inconspicuous when a language disappears from school lessons, or political rhetoric, or watercooler conversations in offices, losing prestige in society until it's spoken only in the privacy of homes, at kitchen tables and between loved ones. Some languages are considered more valuable than others, even in societies where we would never dream of saying one person, or culture, is of more value than another.

The delay in recognizing the severity of this loss makes a little more sense when you realize that linguistics itself is a young area of science; it took about two centuries even to get close to today's estimation of seven thousand–odd languages. Conversations unpicking how nation-states or empires have been responsible for linguicide, or how indigenous communities may reclaim lost modes of expression, are similarly barely decades old in some countries. It has unsurprisingly been the international body that safeguards intangible cultural heritage—the United Nations Educational, Scientific and Cultural Organization (UNESCO)—that has declared this decade as the Decade of Indigenous Languages (2022–32) in a rapid awareness-raising campaign. Yet many countries fail to support multilingualism, regardless of whether that multilingualism is indigenous or the result of flourishing migrant populations. It took Italy until 1999 to create a law to care for its minority languages, managing to miss at least twenty-five of them in the process; both Gaelic and Scots were only made official languages equal to English in Scotland in 2025. Languages and linguistics degrees at universities are increasingly in decline, undersubscribed, their departments understaffed, and their research underfunded, at the very moment when we need their work more than ever.

Many of the world's vulnerable languages are in their final generation of speakers, lingering for a little while longer before a policy, a natural disaster, or an autocrat sweeps them away. As a journalist I can see, and hope to unravel, the brain behind linguicide in this book, the engines of marginalization and monoculture that are literally taking the words out of our mouths. But as a granddaughter and daughter, listening to what could be the last months and even days of a language that has formed the soundtrack to my life, I hope also to show you linguicide's great cruelty and the broken hearts it leaves in its wake. Emigliän is critically endangered, and the variety of it that my nonna speaks with native proficiency comes from an even smaller speaker set, from one specific valley in the Piacenza Apennines. This language will last a little while in my mother's generation, and it will disintegrate not long after mine—in north London and in northern Italy, in the dense woodland where church bells ring through ever-emptying valleys.

I have traveled around the world in an attempt to expose this linguicide, charting where and how and why languages are being rubbed off the map. Each chapter uncovers a different weapon of linguistic murder, from military invasion to neglect, and in most cases I have traveled to meet speakers myself. Security challenges prevented me from going to Ukraine, Kurdistan, and Israel, with all three places caught in conflicts and atrocities that are tightly linked to linguicide. The protagonist languages of these chapters are not all endangered, but they have all at some point been victims of linguistic hurt or discrimination, in itself revealing how practically any language, no matter how widespread, can suffer great harm.

In these chapters, I find that linguicide can take myriad complex and even opposing forms. In the UK, I've witnessed in my own British-Italian family how languages disappear in diaspora (Emigrate), with speakers struggling to maintain their languages past a second generation as their nation disperses. Conversely, in Oman, I witnessed what can happen when a nation coalesces around just one language (Build), leaving the rest of its people's linguistic diversity to wither on the vine. Between Ukrainian and Ladino, I saw the linguicide that can happen when a domineering power either tries to force itself into your territory (Occupy) or exiles you from it (Expel). With both the Karuk tribe in California and the Kurdish population, I saw what happens next: the gross abuse (Exploit) and persecution (Criminalize) of a community. Down the line, some of the longer-term weapons of linguicide emerge in Kichwa and in Hebrew, languages that have been ousted from daily speech when they lost (Shame) or gained (Sanctify) cultural cachet, respectively. In Ghana, I saw how languages can be overlooked (Ignore), and how that neglect, coupled with the climate crisis, will cost us our languages. And, finally, I went to Italy several times, praying I could find somebody who could solve the mystery of my family's language (Remember). Is it really a variety of emigliän? Will I ever find out what happened to it?

This is not just a book about language loss or death; it's a book about life in the face of destruction. After all, this isn't a lost fight. So much can be documented, studied, and saved this century if we give communities and linguists a chance. I speak to many language activists throughout this book, all with their own frustrations and tragedies, but also—crucially—with their own solutions. A language's fate is not predestined, but constantly reshaped by the forces that surround it, including the communities who are finding new, if different, lives for their languages. New learners and even speakers are being created every day in languages you have probably never heard of, so there must be hope for me in learning my family's languages.

The choice is mine, because that is the scenario I was left with. No policy, no funding, and no awareness about multilingualism or language loss penetrated my nonna's life, my parents' lives, and indeed my own life until my late twenties. I hope that, after reading this book, at least the latter point will have been addressed; that you will leave it understanding what you can do on a personal level to celebrate the loud and abundant linguistic diversity of where you live, acknowledge what has happened to it, and discover what can be done to protect it. This book offers ample models of how to counter linguicide, which must begin now, not in ten or twenty years. It will be all humankind who suffers for it, if we delay addressing our planet's unprecedented rate of language loss. The medicine will come too late. The scientists, linguists, and language activists will lose their race against time.

And what will we all lose when a language disappears? What does a community or person lose?

What have I lost already?

HOW TO KILL A LANGUAGE

THE STORY OF ITALIAN

> **qualunquismo:** political disengagement,
> literally "whatever-ism"

The final chord was played, and Neil, my accompanist, kept his foot on the pedal, letting the notes hover in the air a moment longer. Then, total silence. He raised his eyes to mine and looked at me expectantly.

I turned toward the examiner, a man in his fifties with the same impenetrable facial expression they all seem to have. He was still writing, which meant I had a moment to gather my thoughts. Singing exams always made my throat dry up, as if someone had wrapped kitchen paper around my tongue. I took a sip of water and felt the adrenaline begin to smooth out. "I will now perform my folk song," I said. "It is called 'Vola colomba.'"

I was fourteen, and singing "Vola colomba" was the first time I had ever really needed to produce Italian. Exams like these punctuated my teenage years, back when I dreamed of becoming an opera singer. Vocal training was regular, disciplined, and demanded that I pronounce Italian, German, and French like a native. Mum would sit with me at the kitchen table, running through the lyrics of arias I'd been given to make sure I pronounced the Italian properly. I was regularly wrong; at school I had learned Spanish prosody, the stress and rhythm of a language, which in Iberia punches out like a ricochet. Italian words are more irregular, delivered with a wider pitch range that, like music, lilts words up and down expressively. The vowels are so similar between the languages that I'd frequently cross-contaminate my consonants, releasing the salivating hiss that creeps through the Spanish *s* like a pressure valve into a poor, unassuming Italian word, like la musica. "That's Spanish!" Mum would wince, as if I'd scraped a fork across a plate. But I'd never had an Italian lesson. I didn't know any better.

Moments like that were painful reminders of my distance from Italian, my accent betraying my total Englishness and now the other languages I was adopting, too, and I felt like a fraud. But at my nonna's house in Holloway—where I had first learned "Vola colomba"—my Italianness went unquestioned. She had heard the song as a young woman; it had been written about Trieste, the Italian city split in two during the Second World War, and in it the singer tells a dove to fly down and speak to their beloved, who is praying desperately at church for their return.

"Diglielo tu che tornerò / Dille che non sarà più sola / E che mai più la lascerò"—tell her I'll come home, that she won't be alone anymore, and that I'll never leave her again.

Nonna knows all the words to "Vola colomba" and sings it with a descant harmony in her high soprano voice, which she learned from singing with her siblings, none of whom had any formal musical training. Long after that singing exam, Nonna would grin at me from her sofa with a glint in her brown eyes, and I knew that this would probably be followed by a request to stand up and sing our song. For the first time in my life, we were speaking Italian together— it just happened to be sung. There is a video of me, Nonna, and her sister, Zia Elvira, singing it in Zia's garden from more than a decade ago, with Zia and me on the same line and Nonna soaring above. It has entered family folklore. And even though it is about Trieste, none of us think of Trieste when we sing it. When I sing it, I think of my nonna; and when Nonna sings it, she thinks about her Italy, hundreds of miles away from Trieste, and the childhood of which she is the last remaining witness.

Tell her I will come home.
Tell her she needn't be alone any more
And that I'll never leave her again.

Emigration may well be one of the greatest causes of linguicide in the world. In just three generations, and sometimes even two, most emigrant families will lose the language that connected them to their place of origin. For Nonna, that's an old brick farmhouse in the middle of nowhere in the mountains of Piacenza, in Emilia-Romagna. I have only been there once; there is no electricity, no running water, and no inside toilet. Nonna's childhood in poverty—la miseria as it is called in Italian, which feels far more evocative—was worlds, and languages, away from my privileged upbringing in north London. It's an upbringing her grandchildren would probably never have had, had she stayed. Such economic progress usually demanded the sacrifice of one mother tongue for another.

The Italian American poet and translator Joseph Tusiani said that from the day in which a son says "Mother" instead of "Mamma" and "sky" instead of "cielo," there's a "separazione spirituale che lo studioso di linguistica non può catalogare"—a spiritual separation that even the most studious linguist would struggle to explain. We understand that language is one of the ways in which we pass our identity and heritage down to our children, and yet many families seemingly let go of their heritage languages, perhaps by what they feel is choice or necessity. Language planning policies from governments, both at home and abroad, often fall suspiciously quiet when it comes to the continuity of emigrant languages.

When we talk about linguicide, we're often talking about minority languages in their own countries; languages like Basque in Spain or Māori in New Zealand, which predate the nation-states they went on to precariously find themselves in. Stories like this dominate our understanding of how languages are erased. But the truth is that many countries are not only hostile to the competing indigenous languages that may belong there, but also to foreign languages that resettle, just like people do. In a couple of generations, emigrant families can go from being pockets of linguistic hyperdiversity to total monolingualism in a rapid language shift, the term given by linguists to the sublimation of one language into another.

This new reality is sometimes celebrated as integration. But not only does this ignore that *bi*lingualism is just as effective a means of integration, it passes over the seismic personal cost of language loss in migrant families. The cost to the country is just as significant; according to one economist, the willful monolingualism of a country like the UK—a stereotype so famous, there is an entire Wikipedia entry about it—costs us £48 billion a year through lost business opportunities alone.

In this chapter I'll use Italian—the emigrant language I've watched slip away from my family in the UK—as a test case to examine how emigrant language loss happens and who might be responsible. This was a responsibility that, growing up, I always assumed to be mine and my mum's. When I was younger, I can remember complaining to Mum that she didn't send me to Italian class after school, like Nonna did for her. "You didn't want to learn Italian!" she still says today, as if my fate had been sealed long ago by my errant child self. I'm sure she's telling the truth, even if I don't recollect it. Given that Italian was never offered as a subject or a club at school, I'm not sure how much information I ever really had on it; my parents, similarly, were never told about the benefits of retaining heritage languages.

In one of their essays on linguicide, Tove Skutnabb-Kangas and Robert Phillipson talk about this—the mass loss of heritage languages in Western countries with high immigrant populations, where children can't access lessons in the languages their parents and community speak at home. The linguists do not mince their words: The lack of "immigrant minority education in these countries" equates to "linguistic genocide, as defined by the UN," they write.[1] They do not blame people like my mum or my nonna for not passing Italian on. They blame our government.

■ ■ ■

"I love the language, that soft bastard Latin," Lord Byron wrote in his poem *Beppo*. Italian, for him, "melts like kisses from a female mouth, / And sounds as if it should be writ on satin." In contrast, English was "whistling, grunting guttural, / Which we're obliged to hiss, and spit, and sputter all." Hundreds of years later, Italian still holds a certain allure. The language learning platform Babbel ran a poll in 2024 searching for the world's sexiest accent, and the six thousand people they surveyed placed Italian at the top of the list. Linguists over the years have speculated as to why Italian consistently holds this position; is it its purring, rolling *r*, its undulating pitch? Or is it because of our often positive association with Italy and the values we place on that culture—the food, the music, the way people look—as inseparable from its language?

The same survey, reported in the *Daily Mail*, contains a clue: German was considered the most direct language and English the most polite. Anyone who has met either a German or an English person knows that this is hardly their language's fault; these are cultural values that are expressed through their language and actions. When it feels like people have different personalities in the different languages they speak, this is part of the reason why; we are acculturating, speaking like native speakers not only in how they form sentences, but in how they behave. I swear more in Spanish and mention God a lot more in Arabic. Byron himself couldn't avoid this: *Beppo* is written in a specific meter typical of epic storytelling in Italy at the time, which he presumably knew only because he'd become an Italian speaker and was beginning to write like an Italian, too. Regardless of how beautiful everyone from Byron to Babbel survey respondents think Italian is, or how they came to those conclusions, you'll find it taught in just 1 percent of British schools.[2]

On a personal level, people's preferences for certain languages over others are aesthetic and plagued with a few social biases, like Byron's. On a state level, what schools are told to teach is informed by all of those personal views plus political agendas, history, and trade. Inevitably, it's also directed by the government's view on immigration. Donald Trump won a second term on an anti-immigrant platform in which he complained that foreign languages were "coming into our country" and that illegal immigrants "have languages that nobody in this country has ever heard of. It's a very horrible thing." His executive order to make English the official language of the United States suggested that English was the only language to take seriously if you wanted to be a US citizen in Trump's America. Such decisions trickle down into education systems for both children and adults, as well as the litany of public services that require language support. At the time of this writing, the move seems to have been more of a statement than something that's actually led to legislative change, but whether or not these are hollow threats, they indicate a broader disregard for America's many languages besides English, and a value for English monolingualism over multilingualism *with* English.

In the 1980s, a linguist called Richard Ruíz took a broad look at language planning—how governments influence language use and education—and charted three different approaches that a country could take toward its diverse population: language as a problem, language as a right, and language as a resource. His view was that languages were absolutely resources "to be managed, developed and conserved," viewing "language-minority communities as important sources of expertise."[3] Although he believed the languages also deserved protections in the forms of rights, he was skeptical about the success of this approach, acknowledging that just because something is allegedly protected by law, that doesn't necessarily mean it is protected in practice. The US itself, with a Civil Rights Act that technically protects linguistic minorities but a president who seems eager to condemn them, is one example.

The languages that governments deem resources rather than problems for children to learn are highly politicized, informed by history as well as trade partnerships and modern diplomacy. In the UK, we prioritize French, German, and Spanish. French is there because it was the first foreign language *and* the language of prestige, introduced to the courts of England by our sophisticated Norman invaders, and has enjoyed first-mover advantage ever since. German stepped in as another royal language, this time of the House of Hanover in the 1700s, as well as a language of the Enlightenment. It went unchallenged until 2001. Twenty years after the introduction of GCSEs (the exam that schoolchildren take at age sixteen), more Brits took a GCSE in Spanish than they did in German. This probably happened because of lobbying around Spanish as an easier language to learn from culture and trade organizations, as well as increasing numbers of Brits purchasing holiday homes on the Costa del Sol.[4]

Non-European, and non-colonial, languages are suspiciously absent from this trio, as are immigrant languages. When the UK wants to invest in a new language within the curriculum, it is almost always for diplomatic reasons, which is why one of the latest developments has been the Mandarin Excellence Program, teaching the language to eight thousand pupils across England to make the UK fit for purpose, in the words of then Foreign Secretary David Lammy, in the face of "global war and the huge pressures we have with competing superpowers." Languages aren't studied only because they're perceived to be beautiful; they're also studied because of the maxim *know thy enemy.*

All of this is to say that the languages of emigrants tend to be absent from curriculums. And yet in so many of my interviews with second- and third-generation children in my position, it is extremely rare for anyone to blame their school for language loss. I don't think anyone is expecting a single school to teach fifty different languages to an advanced level, but many manage to teach students any of fifteen different musical instruments or coordinate with local schools to provide specific classes or training to wider groups within a region. Nor do second- or third-generation descendants ever seem to place blame on the wider education system or government. Instead, we blame ourselves. We ask: Why can't I speak Italian? Why didn't my mum speak to me in Italian, when it's what Nonna did with her? Why didn't Mum send me to Italian school, like the one she went to? In absolving our governments of responsibility to maintain heritage languages, we shift the blame to the grassroots system that replaces them: our parents.

According to Malwina Gudowska, a Polish Canadian writer and linguist who researches multilingual mothers and how they may raise multilingual children, blaming mothers in particular is a gendered, even sexist response to this problem. She wrote a marvelous book called *Mother Tongue Tied* about her own attempts to raise her son and daughter in London as Polish speakers alongside their English. It is a language she "alone was responsible for," in her own words, between her and her monolingual English husband. Mothers' traditional caregiving roles end up meaning they can have, as one study found, "at least double the impact on language exposure than fathers."[5] Is it double the impact because of something inherent in mothers—or because many of us have collectively decided it's not a father's job to contribute their own equal-sized input? I suspect I know the answer. She writes that gender inequality in both society and the home can make mothers feel uniquely responsible as guardians of their children's multilingualism, "killing" it if they don't do their job properly. She describes it as a paradox of scrutiny and praise—"invisible mothers performing invisible work until it is time to assess their success or, especially, their failure."[6]

I told Malwina about my Italian, and my mum, over coffee in north London. "I totally understand why your mum didn't speak to you in Italian," she said. "There's not enough support systems. You've said there was no Italian at school. I don't know about your dad?"

No one had ever mentioned my dad before. It occurred to me, for the first time, that my dad had as much say in my possible bilingualism as Mum, but that I'd levied all the pressure, just as Malwina describes, onto her. Dad, who met Mum while working at an Italian bank, has a smattering of Italian, but he wouldn't have been able to understand the vast majority of what Mum and Nonna say to each other and could have said to me. I think he would have felt alienated; the easier route to take was, of course, always to speak in English at home. Malwina nodded as if I had confirmed her suspicions. Even though her husband was supportive and has even learned Polish himself, she struggled: "It's just emotional and physical labor and it would be so easy to speak English to my kids. It's not that I want to— but it would be so easy."

It's also what a lot of multilingual parents wrongly get told to do—to speak to their children in just English or whatever the language of the country they're living in is. Malwina can remember a nurse coming to visit her and her son when he was two years old, and who chastised her for teaching him Polish. "You should really wait till he can speak English stronger," the woman had told her, suggesting that multiple languages this early on would confuse him. This is a pervasive myth told to parents, sometimes with the additional untruth that learning more than one language delays their speech development. Early bilingualism is not only fine, but grants a child all the multilingual benefits that this book will elucidate. Malwina had the benefit of linguistics expertise to ignore this advice; many do not.

Bad guidance like that is all the more damaging when you consider the enormous inputs a child needs in a language in order to get good at it; if you think children can become perfectly fluent just by speaking to their parents at home, ask yourself why you probably had to sit through over a decade of learning your country's dominant language at school. We understand that if a child is to speak a language *well*, they need immersion at home as well as *beyond* the home. The idea that they are "sponges," able to take in languages as a plant absorbs light, has most memorably been challenged by Carmen Muñoz, who, as a language researcher at the University of Barcelona, shows an image in her lectures of a sponge on a table and some water on the opposite side. It's all well and good that there's a sponge and some water, but if no one actually picks up the sponge and puts it *in* the water, it's not going to soak it up. Starting to learn a language very young, when the nervous system is still growing, and *maintaining* this for a long time as their brain develops and matures, is what grants children the "native"-speaking proficiencies that older language learners cannot imitate, rather than some innate "sponge" power. The health visitor who spoke to Malwina was giving advice that would actively hurt the child's chances of becoming bilingual in the future.

When we met, her children were seven and ten, and Malwina described them as very capable Polish speakers. But she wasn't relaxed; her efforts to continue their language learning were ongoing between lessons, trips to Poland, and day-to-day conversations. "You could leave it there," I said to her, thinking about how much work she had already done—work that had earned results in her children's apparent fluency—and how it wouldn't be long before her eldest was a teenager. "At some point, it will be up to them to decide what to do with Polish, right?"

She sighed, unconvinced. "I don't want it to end with me," she said.

■ ■ ■

What does Malwina mean by "it"? Is it her Polishness she is worried about ending? Or is it how she has experienced the world, an experience that, for her, is inextricable from the language she lived it in? Either way, "it" is easily lost. The three-generation cycle of emigrant language loss gets to work incredibly quickly. In a 1998 survey of five thousand second-generation students from Hispanic and Asian communities in south Florida and Southern California, well over half of them had already lost their parents' heritage language. This appeared to depend on the parents themselves; teens were more likely to still speak a language like Spanish or Mandarin if their parents had stayed married, had spoken the language at home, and were "high status" (translation: rich enough to put children through a high-quality education). But that very variability itself demonstrates that a child needs support and infrastructure beyond their home environment if they're going to maintain a language. "The key ingredient is the community. It's not about your parents," a woman called Carmen Silvestri told me.

Carmen rarely has any free time. She pivots between a research career in applied linguistics and over a decade as an Italian teacher in Damascus, Rabat, and, now, London. She has been so active here that she even set up her own language school in south London for Italian families, something that's often known as a complementary school, one to be attended in addition to a normal school. Although she tells me that she's trying to focus on her academic career now, I get the sense that she's finding it hard to fully leave the teaching life behind. Only last year she agreed to run a class for non-Italians— people like partners of Italian speakers who couldn't speak the language, but now found themselves married to Italians or parenting mini-Italians. When she started seeing the names build up on the registration list, she noticed, quizzically, that all the surnames were Italian. When she met these new students for the first time, she realized they were all Italian-heritage Londoners in their mid-twenties. "We ended up with a whole class of heritage language speakers," she said. Not parents, and not necessarily partnered, either, but all of them with the same problem. They had signed up because they all felt like they couldn't speak Italian. "Some of them had struggled even to get to A1," she said, her eyes widening; A1 is the most basic beginner level in the European grading system.

It is likely that these Londoners were like me, growing up going to schools where we were often the only Italians, or where all the young Italians didn't speak their parents' languages. Perhaps that is why the same US survey from 1998 observed that 40 percent of the Latin American students had managed to maintain their heritage language, compared with just 10 percent of Asian students. Apart from the obvious advantage Latin American students have of a shared common language across the different countries they come from, the researchers believed that peers reinforced the groupthink of the ethnic background they came from. The higher the proportion of Asian students in a school, the lower the knowledge of parental languages would be—almost as if their monolingualism was contagious. The opposite was true of schools with high Latin American populations, where students seemed to benefit linguistically from being around one another. The researchers theorized that a common language was a more key value for Hispanics than it was for Asians, who prioritized other factors in their community building. Maybe Italians in the UK were more similar to the Asians in the US, considering their language an optional part of their ethnic identity.

In her class, Carmen could feel the longing of a generation that had already lost a firm link with Italian. "'Why is it that my surname is Rossi but I have no Italian in my repertoire?'" she said, imagining herself in their shoes. "While it's happening, it's hard to notice it's happening. It's a cliché—you know you love her when you lose her." Sociolinguist Joshua Fishman called it the Three-Generation Shift Model, in which the immigrant grandparents are the native speakers of their heritage language and usually acquire limited proficiency in the new language of their host country. The second generation act as bilingual brokers between their families and the country they were born in, ultimately becoming dominant in the language of the recipient country instead. By the time they have children, the language shift has become so total that it is likely they will speak mostly mono-lingually at home. Similarly, in the US, first-generation immigrants experience increased language shift to English over time—meaning that their English begins to replace their original language more and more in daily life—and also that the younger an immigrant child is when they learn English, the more likely that the language of the entire household will shift to English as they grow up.

But Carmen has observed another three-generation cycle—the one that brought the Britalian Londoners to her class, and the one that has motivated me to write this book. Knowing what we have lost—perhaps Malwina's elusive "it"—we are desperate to bring it back. In an essay entitled "The Problem of the Third Generation Immigrant," written all the way back in 1938, a historian called Marcus Lee Hansen in the US proposed Hansen's Law: "What the son wishes to forget the grandson wishes to remember." Language loss *is* a loss of connection; if we need that connection to establish identity, then third-generation immigrants can find themselves rud-derless.

This is reinforced by the outside world. Italians online will regu-larly mock Italian Americans for their inability to speak Italian, marking it as one of the many reasons they're not really Italian re-gardless of whether they carry citizenship or not. I've been told it myself. That we might share a heritage, myself being a *British* Italian and the online commenter being an *Italian* Italian, doesn't seem to matter; for people who refuse to accept dual identities, I don't fit the bill.

This is leading to an uncomfortable linguistic division, and even a social media trend, in the US with Spanish. The amount of Span-ish being spoken in American homes has gone down by at least 10 percent in the last forty years as immigrants settle and have their children; 68 percent of Hispanics there are now US-born. Accord-ing to the Pew Research Center, 78 percent of US Hispanics say it's not necessary to speak Spanish to identify as Latinx—but a new term that has emerged online suggests language loss is not universally accepted. Young Latinx who do not speak Spanish have found themselves increasingly labeled as "no sabo kids." Saber, the verb meaning "to know" in Spanish, is misconjugated by many young Latinx who say no sabo for "I don't know" instead of the correct no sé, something they would only do if they didn't speak Spanish well. There is a little discussion online of young people wanting to reclaim being a no sabo kid, but most uses of the phrase are memes, performed by fluent Spanish speakers, in which they stereotype monolingual Latinx. It is linguistic shaming that labels them, accusingly, as an outsider to their own culture.

Latinx who are monolingual in English internalize being a no sabo kid even if they aren't directly labeled it. Take Glenn, a young father I spoke to who was raised in a Mexican family that spoke only English at home. Other than his dad, stepdad, and grandparents, there was very little Spanish spoken around him, to the point that he not only felt like an outsider when he heard Spanish, but also when he saw "a baile or quince," he said, referring to the traditional Mexican fifteenth-birthday party. When Glenn's link to the language was severed, he also lost his identification with customs and traditions he associated with that language. Now Glenn is learning Spanish and visiting Mexico as an adult. "It's a long, hard, but rewarding journey to learn our language and culture for the first time," he told me, adding that he is still so used to getting things wrong in Spanish that he will feel pangs of imposter syndrome even when he gets something right. I relate powerfully to Glenn, feeling like I'm letting an imaginary birthright down every time I make a mistake in Italian and still doubting myself when I've made no mistake at all. If you can't build a robust linguistic self-esteem in which every mistake is a chance to improve rather than an instant failure, then your pursuit of a language is cut abruptly short; research on Mexican Americans has identified that speakers with low proficiency, suffering from the weight of expectation, can have such a negative self-perception that they abstain from Spanish use altogether.

There's no equivalent term for no sabo for Italians—but we do have "no sapo" children, too. There is a slender amount of research that has been done on Anglo-Italians and their languages, such as Siria Guzzo's work in Bedford, a town outside London with a community of more than ten thousand Italian residents. Most second- and all third-generation Bedford Italians maintain what Siria describes as "a passive competence in Standard Italian and dialect" but also "an extremely strong sense of ethnic Italian identity." Margherita Di Salvo, who investigated Italian communities in Bedford and Cambridgeshire, found that as Italian proficiency plummeted in both communities by the third generation, other markers for Italian identity emerged. For the first generation—the grandparents—speaking Italian meant being Italian, and they equate the loss of the language with a rupturing of their Italian identity. The second generation in interviews told Di Salvo something my mum has said to me a lot—that she isn't considered English here, nor is she considered Italian in Italy. For them, it was their values that made them Italian. Their parents were more strict than English counterparts, compelling their children to observe traditions and behaviors that were important to them like church and religious festival attendance and marrying within the culture. Elements like religion, their bloodline, and even their hair color and facial features were now becoming markers of Italianità that were as significant as their language.

But by the third generation Di Salvo was noticing a new linguistic crisis. Some grandchildren were so ashamed about their poor Italian that they refused to visit their grandparents' hometowns, preferring instead to holiday in tourist destinations where they could speak English. In Bedford, in particular, grandparents who had stayed in the UK so that they could be close to their grandchildren instead experienced a chasm of communication, with no common language. This is known as Shared Language Erosion—the combination of immigrants' low proficiency in English with the poor language skills of a child or grandchild in their family's language.

Shared Language Erosion has wide-reaching and little-known consequences. In 2021, US researchers studying migrant Latino communities argued that parents' and adolescents' inability to communicate effectively with one another may contribute to declines in physical, mental, and behavioral health.[7] They suggested that such communication gaps can lead to "increased parent-child conflict, reduced parental competence, aggravated preexisting flaws in parent-child attachment, and increased adolescent vulnerability to deviant peer influences." In their analysis, more than 40 percent of Latino immigrant adolescents reported high levels of misunderstanding with their parents. Not only does this sound generally misery-making, but it may also be harming immigrants' health: The authors propose that Shared Language Erosion could help explain the well-documented health gap in which second- and third-generation immigrants report worse physical and mental health than those in the first generation. More research is needed to probe this theory, but it is one that all my second-generation friends fervently agree with.

My nonna's English is good, but collapses if she is stressed or worried, as she understandably is when in the hospital. Luckily, with my trilingual mum, there's no chance of Shared Language Erosion as she triages effortlessly between the medical staff and Nonna. Mum's fluency in Italian and dialët ensures Nonna isn't only understood, but that she can communicate with someone she trusts about things she feels are too private or intimate to share immediately with a stranger. Nonna still gets nervous reading her post, asking Mum or me to help make sure she's understood. Now, every morning, Mum rings Nonna to make sure she has taken her tablets and asks her questions to test her memory and monitor what we fear could be cognitive decline. At the end of the day—and it is every day now that Nonna requires care—Mum is exhausted, having shouldered an interpreting burden that the NHS would, plainly, not be able to meet. There must be countless other mums like mine, deploying their language skills to keep those they love healthy. If something happened to my mum, I'd have to become the language broker, which I'd barely manage with my Italian and would utterly fail to do with the dialët that comes more naturally to Nonna. Emigrant language loss can cost individuals connection to an ethnic identity—but for their relatives, it could cost them something as fundamental as access to health care.

This usually thankless language brokering is part of the invisible labor keeping society functioning. There are some oft-cited health benefits to bilingualism—delaying the onset of dementia, helping children demonstrate more self-control, helping adults demonstrate more creative thinking *and* logical decision-making. Social ones, too: the new job opportunities; the increased connections we make as we travel and live in other countries. But when we look beyond the seemingly self-serving benefit to the bilingual brain, and consider the people around them, the benefits multiply much further. For all the relatives we love who express themselves more confidently in their heritage language, our ability to maintain that heritage could be the difference between happiness or hardship; between dignity or disappearance in a system that never looked out for such languages, or their speakers, in the first place.

But speaking a heritage language is as much about generating joy as it is about coping with challenges; even if Nonna could speak English as well as her dialët, she would face fewer challenges, but I would still be shut out of half of her world. It is the jokes you can laugh at, the compassion you can share, the passwords to acceptance and membership. Speaking a family language has been directly connected to identifying with ethnic identities across Armenian, Vietnamese, and Mexican youth in the US. Researchers have also found that speakers of a second language enjoy a positive boost to their self-esteem, which provides us with innumerable benefits far beyond our linguistic repertoire. Far from thwarting assimilation, aligning with an ethnic identity enables migrants and their children to articulate who they are in multicultural societies, fostering community cohesion so that they can share the knowledge, traditions, and gatherings that make a community something to belong to in the first place. This is cultural resilience—one of the many invisible immunities against loneliness and alienation that a society can offer someone, one that is so invisible that we have almost completely failed to acknowledge it.

The findings from Bedford reveal heartbreaking stories of broken family relationships, as well as a severance of ties between countries. Among my own friends, in Italian diasporas and others, I see them repeated again and again; not going to an event for fear that you don't belong, not attempting to pronounce a word or phrase for fear that you're going to be mocked. Emigrant language loss is the sacrifice of knowledge that should be passed down, love that should be experienced and cultural memory that should be recorded—all because of the imagined benefit of a "true" British identity that accounts only for English. An overwhelming number of grandchildren in this position say they had parents who prioritized English above any other language so that they could better assimilate. How myopic this is—well intentioned and understandable, but shortsighted all the same—all to help our children win the opportunities in life we feel we were denied. One in four of us in the UK regret never learning a second language, and I wonder how many of us feel this way because there was another language once, cradled with care, by people who dreamed of a better life in our near memory. And when we call out for it, our hands outstretched, we are met only with silence.

■ ■ ■

I pressed my thumb into the corner of the envelope and tore it, pulling out another envelope inside that contained five colored papers, folded into neat squares. Referendum Popolare, it said, 8–9 Giugno 2025. There were several more sheets of paper explaining how the vote worked and my right to do it as a registered elettore italiana residente all'estero—an Italian living abroad. For a referendum in Italy to work, at least 50 percent of the nearly sixty million Italians need to turn out for it, including the nearly six million like me who live abroad. Citizenship in Italy is passed by *iure sanguinis*, the right of blood, an often unjust rule that benefits individuals like me, who have never lived in Italy, over migrants who have. Two out of every three Italian-born children with parents from other countries are still denied full citizenship rights.

Along with a number of labor reforms, this referendum proposed halving the residency required before a citizenship application, taking it from ten years to five. As I read through the brightly colored ballots and pulled the lid off my Biro, I could only make sense of it because of my Italian, born in the ambient sound of Holloway but solidified in the many attempts I have taken over the years to try to turn myself into a speaker. There will be many third-generation Italians in the UK who would not have been able to complete this vote, for which no English version was provided, and a month later a British Italian newspaper ran with the headline "Referendum-flop," declaring that only one in every four Italians living in the UK had voted in it. The vast majority of those of us who had voted had voted yes; unsurprising given those opposed to what were progressive policy changes only needed to stay at home in order to make the referendum redundant. Party politics aside, you would think that Italy might be invested in its citizenship-wielding diaspora-speaking Italian in order to engage with democracy or to spend some of our foreign cash back home.

This is pressing because there are now two substantial Italian communities in London: the historic one, pre- and post-war, which brought my grandparents here, and a contemporary one following the 2008 financial crisis. Not even Brexit put them off: Six hundred thousand of them applied to settle here after Britain left the EU. But despite being such recent arrivals, people like Carmen are already noticing emigrant language loss seep through the cracks. She was motivated to set up a complementary school in her local area because, as a linguist, she could sense that the lack of a space to learn Italian would become a problem in the future. Young parents from this aspirational new wave started to ring her up, all telling the same story: one parent was Italian, the other wasn't. Their child could understand Italian well, but they spent their life in English-dominated spaces, they didn't learn Italian at school and weren't confident speaking it.

We don't know how many complementary schools there are in the UK, because no one seems to have bothered tracking them or building a database of them. What we do know is that they teach anything from a language class to folk dances from back home to religion lessons. Estimates put the number anywhere between three thousand to five thousand, all generally run by the community themselves and rarely for profit.[8] "It's not a business," Carmen told me as if the memory of running it exhausted her. "You're not making enough money for it to be less stressful. I never made enough money to pay myself." When Mum was a teenager, a local parent ran Italian classes for teenagers like her in Islington; while she sometimes felt she couldn't be bothered, she is very grateful now for the grounding it gave her in Italian, which she went on to use in jobs in London's Italian Hospital and a Roman bank, neither of which exists any longer.

Such schools often have to pay rent to mainstream schools for a chance to use their classrooms and learning facilities; if they can't afford that, they'll make do with church halls or even teachers' houses. The Italian government does contribute funds toward the learning of Italian across the UK; in fact, it often makes up for staffing gaps. In 2024–25 twenty-seven schoolteachers in London, the South of England, and Wales were paid for by the Italian Ministry of Foreign Affairs and International Collaboration. On the one hand, it looks like there's lots of provision: Nearly €600,000 has supported the running of Italian lessons in British schools, reaching more than 8,508 pupils with no additional cost to parents.[9] But when it comes to after-school and extracurricular clubs—the kind where heritage learners are offered specific support—the ministry has covered only 40 percent of the costs, with families paying the rest of the fee.[10] The likely conclusion, then, is that more of their funding is going toward supporting non-Italians with learning a language that could boost Italy's soft power than toward the people of *iure sanguinis*. Heritage learners like me are, to put it bluntly, less profitable in their eyes. Squeezed to the margins of a child's learning day, the end of a parent's bank account, and the stretched capacity of overworked teachers like Carmen is where learning Italian as a heritage language has wound up for most families.

It needn't necessarily look like this. Sweden is globally recognized for its robust legal and financial defense of heritage languages. Mother Tongue Instruction—modersmålsundervisning—is offered through the national school system. Every child who uses a language that isn't Swedish with at least one caregiver at home is entitled to it, as long as there are four other children who are interested in joining in the local area and there is a teacher available to teach it. This was Sweden's response to an increasingly diverse population, as well as to lobbyists from Finnish, Estonian, and Jewish communities who campaigned for the right to education in their own language. It is not without its flaws—57 percent of children who are eligible actually take the classes—but, compellingly, the grade that the children achieve within it can improve their overall final grade that year, yet cannot decrease it (in case they under-perform).[11] In a world in which so many of us are persuaded to see only certain languages as valuable, this is a remarkable way of making sure that nearly any language, with a community surrounding it, is recognized for what it has already granted you, and what it holds in store for you as you grow up and move into the working world. And, if you find language-learning tough, as many do, then you aren't shamed with a grade that says you didn't do well.

To introduce the above mechanism to a country's curriculum feels increasingly radical in a world where political parties win votes by scaremongering about immigrants. The UK would be starting almost from the very beginning if it were to inject more languages into schools; in England, just three schools in every five hundred have whole-school policies that address foreign languages, English usage, and integrating students who speak English as an additional language.[12] Without much interest from the UK government, and varying levels of interest from the heritage country's government, maintaining an emigrant language in diaspora is essentially a game of rigged roulette. If you're lucky enough to live with a thriving local community, with funded language lessons, with two happily married parents (preferably from the same place), *and* you've only ever been around people who support multilingualism, then, yes, you may maintain your heritage language. Fail to tick one of these boxes and your fate may already have been decided.

I am so lucky that I have had the disposable income, the time, and the privilege of a language degree to enable me to be my own pushy parent, my own overworked teacher, to take the soft clay of Italian I was raised around and try to turn it into something hard, practical, and usable in the Italy in which I travel and work today as an adult. It is a work in progress that brings me simultaneous pleasure and pain, reminding me of what I belong to and what I will be forever somewhat alien to. That feeling of exclusion will follow me my entire life, and it will, despite all my efforts, be the reason that many will believe I have no entitlement to the heritage my nonna passed to me. It is hard to quantify what emigrant language loss costs, but, for many, it was the right to *be* Italian, and for me for many years the right to better look after my nonna, understand my mother, exercise my democratic right to vote, and maintain a link between London and the villages of northern Italy we come from. It is true that I do not need to speak Italian day-to-day in the UK, but that does not mean that I do not need to *have* it, for other, deeper, reasons.

And without Italian it would be impossible for me to take the next, crucial step in my journey. After all, Italian is only half of my family's linguistic capital. Al dialët—the language Nonna increasingly pivots to, the language Mum has always spoken to her before any other—lies somewhere on Italian's linguistic border. It is a total mystery; I don't know its name, its identity, how it came to thrive where my nonna once lived and why, now, it languishes on an endangered list. The only resources for it exist in Italian and the only way I'm ever going to be able to read and understand them is if I keep learning it.

In the meantime, I'll also need to learn something else: If mother tongues really do mean so much to who we are, our health, and our well-being, how is it that we can disregard them so casually? It's one thing to see a language disappear when it's displaced. It's quite another problem entirely when it seems to be eradicated by the very community that cradled it in the first place. For the rest of this book, that is what we'll see—languages that are being lost between grandparent and grandchild, even though all three generations have been born in exactly the same place.

This is because languages do not die only in diaspora; sometimes they're killed in their own home.

THE STORY OF ŚḤEHRĒT

yəšɔ̌š: to bring water from afar[1]

"Come, have a look at this," Arif said to me, gesturing toward his small orange tarpaulin hut. He disappeared for a moment before emerging with an iron pole that had a chunk of cement stuck on each side. I was confused; what's a big stick like that got to do with camels? Then he began to lift it with one arm, his deltoid bulging out from the top of his cargo waistcoat, and I realized it was a makeshift dumbbell. "This is my gym!" he said, smiling. A few moments later I could understand why he had it. When he handed me a bowl of milk, frothy and filled to the brim, that he had retrieved for us from about five camels, I nearly dropped it. It must have weighed at least eight kilograms.

We had driven for hours to reach Arif's place of work, until the roads stopped running and dirt paths and camel herds appeared instead. He's a long way from Salalah, which is where most of his family live. One brother is an engineer, another is in the army, and Arif, as the youngest, has been left with the responsibility all the others rejected: raising the family's livestock. Camel milk and meat are considered local delicacies, and their milk especially has been associated with health properties since the Prophet Muhammad's time. Arif certainly looked very healthy; his muscular build, his carefully manicured mustache and curled crop of jet-black hair set him apart from some of the other herdsmen I had seen. Hundreds of cows and camels depend on Arif every day, and when he called for his camels to come and eat, they pried themselves away from their socializing to answer his call. They know him by voice—and he knows them by name, each and every one.

Earlier that week I had met two Omani women, Wisal and Nour, seasoned travelers who train herders like Arif as tour guides. Wisal told me that she was once struggling to explain the meaning of "anxiety" to a herder who was not familiar with the term in Arabic, their second language. But when she began to describe what it felt like, he told her, "Yes, I know that feeling. I have it when my camel gives birth." When another couldn't fathom why Nour likes to spend money on foreign mountain-climbing trips, she explained that her love of climbing was like his love of camels and therefore worth the money. Instantly, he understood; camels, too, are worth everything you can give them.

This affection comes through in Arif's language. In Ṣḥehrēt there are two words for shelter depending on who is in it: one, stɔrtá, is specifically for people; the other, dĩs̆áf, is intended for livestock.[2] It is bad luck to ask how many animals someone has for fear you will give them the evil eye; as a result, Ṣḥehrēt holds a system for counting them as "under five" or "between fifty and a hundred."* I can think of a lot of people who'd appreciate a similar system when asked how old they are.

Arif spends what could be a thousand dollars every month tending his camels, far outstripping the value they would have on the market if sold. In the long run, selling them would probably be cheaper, but his family would be distraught if the camels went, so

---

* I am writing these words in Latinized script, which is as I found them in the word lists and academic research available to me; many of these were based on work done long before Ṣḥehrēt had its own writing system. Speakers of this language today would use an Arabic-based script to write them, which I'll be getting to shortly.

he's in a catch-22 of caring for them. It's not his *whole* life; when he's not up in the mountains, he's down in the city winning volleyball matches, which he plays competitively. I ask him if he'd like to play internationally; he'd love to. But then, he asked, who would look after the camels?

Adam, my fixer, was looking at Arif's gun. Most Jibbali herders I have seen carry rifles, and all Omani men as a general rule also own a khanjar, a small ceremonial dagger. Both are brought to any formal or community events where there is an expectation to turn out smartly. "Russian?" Adam asked, pointing at the rifle. Arif nodded. I wondered how many times he had fired it. Arabian leopards and wolves, as well as the striped hyena, lurk between the mountainside and the low, sparse shrubbery here, threatening his precious camels. When I told Arif that I was in Oman because I wanted to learn more about its endangered languages, he was nonplussed. "Everyone speaks Jibbali here," he reassured me. "It's safe."

I looked back at the gun and I thought: *Is it?*

Measuring the vitality of a language is a complicated business. For example, you might be surprised at how long a comparatively "small" language can survive. The South Pacific island of Vanuatu has a little under three hundred and fifty thousand people, yet more than one hundred living languages. That means each language, if their speakers were distributed evenly, would have an average thirty-five hundred speakers. Of course, the speakers aren't distributed evenly, which means that many have survived with far fewer speakers for centuries. Vanuatu has been this way for a very, very long time, reminding us that a language needn't be endangered just because there aren't many speakers. The difference is that a small language *today* is a lot less likely to survive for very long than it was two hundred years ago.

The Śḥehrɛ̄t language, Arif's first, is spoken by at least thirty thousand people and perhaps as many as eighty thousand people in the mountains of southern Oman in a region known as the Dhofar.

It borders Yemen and nurtures a variety of languages other than Arabic that belong to the family of Modern South Arabian Languages, including Mehri, which has many more speakers than Śḥehrēt, and Bathari and Hobyot, which have far fewer. This is the only part of the entire Arabian peninsula that has preserved the Semitic languages that existed here before Arabic spread with Islam and Arabization. Semitic languages, most famously Arabic and Hebrew, are distinctive for their trilateral root systems, where almost every single word comes from a three-letter root from which you can then make more than a dozen new words and verbs. When I read Arabic at university, studying these verb systems felt like playing Wordle every day. Take d-r-s, which, when written as a Form 1 verb, simply means *to study*. Turn it into another form—say, Form 2, where the r is doubled, and you have d-rr-s, literally *to make someone study*, which unsurprisingly gives us the verb *to teach*.

Although Śḥehrēt and Arabic are both Semitic languages, they aren't remotely mutually intelligible, and I can't understand any Śḥehrēt when I listen to it. But I do hear a familiar sound system, with a mix of long and short vowels clamped by strong consonants and glottal stops. Beyond Oman, these languages are little known, and this collective ignorance is not an accident, but, rather, a product of politics, funding, and bureaucracy. Not only is there little material in the West about these languages outside of academia, but the language is almost entirely unwritten and its own speakers are divided among themselves about what to actually call it. The names used are either Jibbali, which is the Arabic adjective for "of the mountains," or Śḥehrēt, the language's own adjective for the same thing. Another name, Shehri, is also strongly linked to the name of a particular tribe— the Al-Shehri—who speak this language in the Dhofar, hence why people *outside* that tribe may prefer Jibbali as a more inclusive term. But researchers in the UK prefer to call the language Śḥehrēt, which they say is supported by their indigenous collaborators. So, even though I had to dart between calling the language Jibbali, Shehri, and Śḥehrēt in Oman depending on who I was speaking to, for ease of understanding I'll refer to it exclusively as Śḥehrɛt for the rest of this book.

The Modern South Arabian Languages are believed to be the oldest Semitic languages still spoken today. They contain remarkable linguistic fossils of the Semitic past; for instance, unlike Arabic, they preserve a lateral sibilant, an "s" sound where the air comes down the sides of the tongue rather than the middle. It's a sound I never have to make when I speak Arabic, and if you're a monolingual English speaker, you have probably never used it either. This particular consonant is so old it is considered *Proto*-Semitic, and the closest Arabic sound today I can think of is the shim, like the English "sh," as if I'm telling someone to be quiet. But this Śḥehrɛt "sh" I'm talking about is very different. Janet Watson, a leading British researcher of such languages, compares it to the Welsh "ll." She points out that Mehri, an indigenous language neighboring Śḥehrɛt, has the word śəff, "to want," which is not to be confused with šəff, "to fart silently," which uses that English "sh" sound. I can't decide if the latter word is onomatopoeic or not. Either way, the languages in these mountains have an unusually high presence of *s* sounds that add a flinty rush of air to their speech. Śḥehrɛt has more consonant sounds than all the other languages in the region, sitting at a mighty thirty-six. In comparison, English has twenty-four.

Perhaps, as a result, their words are capable of packing in an impressive amount of meaning in a small package. There is just one short expression for "to leave food to burn"—ħlkʼ aħlekʼ—or "to make someone greedy"—tʼmʕ etʼmaʕ.[3] I could even, in one word, "put someone in a dangerous position"—hlk ɛhlek—and husbands may not be surprised to learn that in this language there is a verb "to anger someone's wife"—nɣm jnuɣum. We don't know how long Śḥehrɛt has been spoken here, but we do know that a thirteenth-century Arab merchant, Ibn al-Mujawir, visited the mountains of the Dhofar where Śḥehrɛt is spoken. He described the people he met as "having their own language which none can understand but they."

The reason we aren't entirely sure how many people speak Śḥehrēt—I've seen numbers that vary by sixty thousand people—is because the data hasn't been collected in the first place. Estimations really are guessing games because of the lack of greater surveying or census information. Although Arif told me that Jibbali is a widely spoken language, he conceded that he is aware of some people in the city who are raising children like me: young people who are exposed to their family's language, but can only answer in the country's dominant language. In Oman's case, this means that Arabic has become not only many Jibbali people's first language, but that they're no longer bilingual *with* Śḥehrēt. It is the kind of rapid shift to monolingualism that we saw with emigrant language loss, within the walls of one country. It means transmission between Śḥehrēt-speaking parents and their children is starting to collapse, which is one of the most significant moments in a language's vitality, when its status crosses from the vigorously alive to the threatened.

Faced with this difficulty of assessing a language's health, several researchers and institutions have tried to develop measurement systems. UNESCO has a six-level scale of endangerment; Ethnologue, an encyclopedia of the world's languages run by an American Christian nonprofit organization, has one with five. The most granular framework, however, comes from the linguist Joshua Fishman, who helped build a way to measure language endangerment. Since the 2010s, it's been slightly expanded by other linguists to help build the table on the next page: the Expanded Graded Intergenerational Disruption Scale (EGIDS). As will become apparent throughout this book, linguists mean well, but they don't always give things the snappiest titles. I invite you to read it in full, especially to decide where the languages you know may rank within it. It was designed for spoken languages; signed languages can be endangered, too, and an adaptation of the EGIDS Scale exists for them as well. But this spoken language chart progresses from the liveliest of languages, used internationally and by all ages, to languages that get smaller and

EGIDS TABLE

LEVEL	LABEL	DESCRIPTION	UNESCO
0	International	The language is widely used between nations in trade, knowledge exchange, and international policy	Safe
1	National	The language is used in education, work, mass media and government at the national level	
2	Provincial	The language is used in education, work, mass media and government within major administrative subdivisions of a nation	
3	Wider Communication	The language is used in work and mass media without official status to transcend language differences across a region	
4	Educational	The language is in vigorous use, with standardization and literature being sustained through a widespread system of institutionally supported education	
5	Developing	The language is in vigorous use, with literature in a standardized form being used by some though this is not yet widespread or sustainable	
6A	Vigorous	The language is used for face-to-face communication by all generations and the situation is sustainable	
6B	Threatened	The language is used for face-to-face communication within all generations, but it is losing users	Vulnerable
7	Shifting	The child-bearing generation can use the language among themselves, but it is not being transmitted to children	Definitely Endangered
8	Moribund	The only remaining active speakers of the language are members of the grandparent generation and older	Severely Endangered
8B	Nearly Extinct	The only remaining speakers of the language are members of the grandparent generation or older who have little opportunity to use the language	Critically Endangered
9	Dormant	The language serves as a reminder of heritage identity for an ethnic community, but no one has more than symbolic proficiency	Extinct
10	Extinct	The language is no longer used and no one retains a sense of ethnic identity associated with the language	

smaller, used only in particular places by older generations and not passed on to children. Such languages are not long for this world.

Śḥehrēt is 6b, threatened; only some of the child-bearing generation are transmitting the language to their children. To Arif, it would be inaccurate to say that this is representative for everybody. Almost everyone *he* knows only spoke Śḥehrēt at home as a young child and then learned Arabic when they began to attend school. He is right: Śḥehrēt is still widely spoken in the Dhofar. But no schools teach it, no one learns how to write it, and Arabic, the only official language of the country, is increasingly, as one linguist has put it, "the language that is needed to fit into the bigger community, to get education, and to have better jobs and social status."[4]

If linguists are so certain that a language like Śḥehrēt is under threat, why would one of the language's own speakers be so adamant that it's alive and well?

■ ■ ■

I had arrived in Oman three weeks earlier, for an Arabic refresher course in Nizwa, the historic capital of Oman. It is the most important city in the country's interior, where gravel and sand desert are split only by motorways, the odd village, and large, Mars-red hills that, millions of years ago, constituted the ocean floor. Archaeologists still dig up remnants of pre-ancient shell beds, dotted with fossilized coral and bivalves. Nizwa is blanketed by date palms and is as hot as 45°C in the summer when I was there, the kind of heat that hits dry and deep in your chest, forcing you to breathe deeply as if you're in a sauna. As my taxi driver took us down to Nizwa from Muscat, we soon noticed cars appearing on the other side of the road covered in mud. "They're coming up from Salalah," Abdullah said in Arabic, pointing at them. "They will be stopped—you can't see the number plate."

The Arabian Gulf is more commonly known for sand dunes and

scant rainfall, but not the Dhofar, and *especially* not the Dhofar in August during the khareef, the monsoon season, which had covered these number plates in muck. The region is a subtropical cornucopia of ecological zones: a coastal plain, foothills that peak into mountains, cliffs, and a dry, flat expanse that gradually yellows into full desert. During the khareef, it's laden with a mist that hovers over you like a sort of cooling gauze. In London, we would find it mildly annoying, yet another type of rain we could do without. In the Gulf, it is paradise, a miraculous respite from the heat, which nourishes verdant life. Nestled in the Dhofar are forests, waterfalls, and springs that in Arabic are given the same word we give our eyes—'aiyun. I don't know whose eyes they are supposed to be; is it the earth, peering out to us? Or is it us who are looking in?

The fact that so many different geographies are packed in next to one another means that various parts of the Dhofar host their own individual microclimate, which over the millennia have puckered the terrain with alluvial fans and river terraces, lagoonal deposits, and limestone caves. With the Arabian Sea on one side and the mountains and desert on the other, it is easy to understand how the Dhofar remained insular, as inward-looking as an island. The desert, which becomes the Rub' al Khali, or "Empty Quarter," is the largest continuous sand desert in the world. But the shifting politics and changing borders of Oman also allowed the Dhofar to remain distinctive for many hundreds of years; culturally, it continues to share much more with Yemeni mountain communities across the border, just a few kilometers away, than with Muscat, which is more than one thousand kilometers north. Roads were only built for the first time in the 1970s; if it takes twelve hours to drive up to Muscat today, I can't imagine how long it used to take. Ibn Battuta, the epic medieval traveler from Tangier, visited the Dhofar in the 1300s and recorded that the journey from Aden took a month across the desert. At that time, Salalah was part of Yemen. He said the market was "one of the dirtiest in the world," quite a claim given how extensive Ibn Battuta's travels were, and that it was "desolate," without villages or dependencies. Yet trade thrived; Thoroughbred horses were exported, Indian rice was imported, and fat sardines and coconut palm honey were sold to a healthy flow of ships' merchants.

After 1750, the Dhofar formally came under Omani rule, absorbed into a powerful maritime empire that also included Balochistan and Zanzibar. Still, it was left relatively autonomous; Oman had always been somewhat divided, and the Dhofar was far closer, both geographically and often culturally, to Yemen. Power was split between the central state of Oman, governed by an imam, and the Sultanate of Muscat, which ruled the coastlines; the "interior" as it was known, with its capital Nizwa, was more inward-looking and Arab than the trade-focused, multicultural coast. The Dhofar, all those kilometers away, was treated like a dependency, sustaining itself with its own cultural identity and indigenous languages. It was when the British Empire—covetous of Indian Ocean trade routes and then suspected oil wealth—got involved that things started to shift. As rival empires scrambled for dominance on the seas, the British supported successive Muscat sultans with treaties and loans in a bid to swell their power over Oman. They were especially close to one of the sultans who was central to Śhehrēt's story: Sultan Said bin Taimur.

The country that the sultan took hold of in 1932 when he came to power looked unimaginably different from the Oman of today. There were only ten kilometers of paved road in the entire country, and an infant mortality rate of 75 percent. It has been the discovery and exploitation of oil wealth that has since transformed the region's fortunes in less than a century, but that discovery would only take place about thirty years into the sultan's rule. Before that, Said bin Taimur had taken over a state that was in debt and completely reliant on the British to defend it from resistant tribes. His solution for his perilous finances was to block development projects, a decision that dragged Oman behind in comparison to the modernization of other Gulf neighbors. Resentment began to brew and, with it, Said bin Taimur's paranoia.

A slew of policies were introduced to quell insurrection. Citizens were largely prevented from leaving the country, and sometimes their own region, throughout his rule. They were forbidden to listen to the radio. Sunglasses were banned in case people took advantage of disguise to spread rebellion. And Oman was already a deeply hierarchical society. Chattel slavery was legal long after it had been banned in other Gulf states. It is said that Said bin Taimur used to shoot at the fish in the pool of water beneath his palace's balcony, which would sound fairly innocuous but for the fact that he also had some of his slaves swimming in it at the same time. His lack of interest in developing the country was probably also rooted in suspicion of what such progress would grant his subjects, and he once told an adviser that the British had lost India "because you educated the people."[5] Of all of Oman, Salalah and the Dhofar suffered most acutely; as if its geography didn't isolate them enough, they also had an isolationist sultan restricting opportunities for growth and development. Tribes in the Dhofar responded to such draconian rule by deciding that enough was enough. They formed the Dhofar Liberation Front and so began the Dhofar War.

I heard little of the war when I was actually in Oman, aside from the odd hushed conversation with locals who alluded to it. "It's a land of secrets," one said to me, raising an eyebrow to suggest they weren't going to say anything else on the matter. The Dhofari rebellion quickly turned into an ideological proxy war against Arabian monarchies, attracting outside interest. The Soviet Union, South Yemen, China, Cuba, North Korea, and Iraq all supported the Dhofari cause, building a fearsome Marxist guerrilla movement. A former SAS officer—the British version of a Navy SEAL—said that the insurgents, known as the "adoo" (the enemy in Arabic), "were the most heavily armed fighters we were up against since the Korean

War." Guns like Arif's, almost certainly inherited from a grandfather who fought in the war, are a vivid reminder.

Said bin Taimur's paranoia about losing control was later justified; incapable of thwarting the insurgency, the British shifted their support to his son, Qaboos, a British-educated modernist who Said bin Taimur had kept under house arrest. They helped him stage a coup against his own father and end the war. Neither Oman nor the Dhofar would be the same again. "My people, I will proceed as quickly as possible to transform your life into a prosperous one with a bright future," Qaboos said in his first speech. "Yesterday it was complete darkness, and with the help of God, tomorrow will be a new dawn on Muscat, Oman and its people." A country without enough hospitals or schools blossomed into a modern state; in fact, in 2010 Oman was ranked as being the fastest mover on the HDI— the Human Development Index—globally in the last forty years. Qaboos, who died in 2023, luxuriated in the same adoration and patriotic pride for his efforts that Queen Elizabeth II enjoyed in the UK; many endearingly call him their father, Baba Qaboos, or mahbub—beloved.

Qaboos understood that a new national identity could be built if he unified the ethnolinguistic groups of Oman that had for so long been separated from one another. He was also uniquely placed to achieve this, given that his mother was Jabbali. Adopting Arabic as a standard language conveniently lubricated these social divisions within the country and established Oman as a power player within the wider Arab world. Whether you are from arid Nizwa or fecund Salalah, this tribe or that one, you are, today, an Arabic-speaking Omani. Countries don't *need* official languages—England, for example, does not have one at the time of writing—but in 2011 the sultan made sure to decree Arabic's status. This was an explicit move in a nation in which Arabic had already long implicitly been not just a lingua franca, but a power language. Said Al Jahdhami, a linguist, wrote that "some parents wittingly do not pass their ethnic group's language to their offspring so that their children harness to the Arab identity instead of the ethnic group's identity."[6]

It's difficult to get a precise breakdown of Oman's demography: The intelligence department allegedly keeps records about every Omani citizen and their ethnic background, but these statistics are classified and inaccessible to the public and to researchers. But clearly Oman is a melting pot, and its multiculturalism—with many different immigrant populations from Asia as well as indigenous groups—is simultaneously celebrated as an Omani value and carefully contained. My two Arabic teachers in the north of Oman told me that they were not allowed to marry outside their tribe. Neither of them described such a custom as restrictive; rather, they saw such marriages as an important part of social cohesion within Omani diversity. I did not get the impression that many really break the rules here, at least not publicly; privately, I heard stories of everything from premarital sex to a black market for pork. Much is done to preserve stability here—and, in nation-states, language ideology is wielded very carefully by its architects.

When people reach for examples of linguistic nationalism, they don't mention countries like Oman. They more commonly think of China's policies to promote Mandarin. Since the year 2000, the government has passed laws standardizing one written and spoken language in a country of more than three hundred languages, with committees in every province policing the use of Mandarin. They might think of Narendra Modi's India, where Hindu nationalists prioritize Hindi above all other languages, ignoring the regions of India where other languages are more dominant. They may even think of Italy, and the spread of the standardized Tuscan language variety that became Italian throughout the land, displacing all regional languages. These are all countries that have been vociferous about their intentions to create one nation speaking one language, perhaps as a direct result of the high number of languages they contain and the rebellious threat that their associated identities have posed. Omani politicians, by contrast, have never had to be so vocal; with many of its languages tucked away in an isolated region, the linguicide that emerged from Omani nationalism was a comparatively silent killer.

Less than half of the population knew how to read or write before Sultan Qaboos took power. Illiteracy has now dropped in Oman to 2.7 percent, and with it horizons have broadened. There is no doubt that the ascent and officializing of Arabic have achieved this; all members of a society benefit from a lingua franca. But we need to think about the languages people know how to read and write *in*, and whether multilingualism stands a chance within this context; a lingua franca needn't be the *only* lingua someone knows. As the modern Omani nation-state was created, and as the Dhofar emerged from the isolation it had known for centuries, the country's language-planning policy began to take effect within this new nation of literate Omanis that, by and large, has only made room for Arabic and, if there's a second language, English. In 2021, researchers spotted that greater road density and more years of schooling were both more associated with the loss of language diversity than any other variables, and Oman, now with its roads and literacy, is a textbook case.[7]

Everyone is now taught how to read and write in Arabic, but there is no education in any of the Modern South Arabian Languages for speakers from those communities. None of those languages enjoy co-official status with Arabic, and none of them have a literary tradition. Modern Standard Arabic—the universal register of the Arabic language used by governments and broadcasters across the Arab world—holds prestige in every domain, be it religious, political, or personal. It is not that Ṣḥehrēt is actively outlawed or persecuted; it is that it is not even mentioned.

As a result, Ṣḥehrēt goes unwritten and untaught. One day, this could mean it also goes unspoken; if it's to survive for future generations, something has to change. It is a change that would alter the

very nature of the language—and how its speakers communicate—
forever.

▪ ▪ ▪

Said Baquir can still remember the feeling of the laryngograph
around his throat, his fingers closing around his neck as he speaks to
me in a café near Salalah's coast, where a mist loomed over an invisible sea. "You need to know more than how to collect a word," he
told me, if you wanted to document a language.

Said, in his early twenties and with bright, curious brown eyes, is
an accidental linguistics assistant; as a baby, he was once cradled in
the arms of the linguist Miranda Morris, a friend of his parents.
Fifteen years later he was recruited by her for research at the University of Leeds' Center for Endangered Languages. Said speaks four
languages: Śḥehrɛt and Hobyot—another local language here—
from his parents and community, on top of Arabic and English,
from school and wider Omani society. His first linguistics gig was as
a transcriber of sound files that had been recorded of Śḥehrɛt-
speaking elders telling stories. "It was very difficult to transcribe," he
remembers. "Sometimes people have a problem pronouncing. Old
people don't speak clearly." But eventually he got there, with a pile
of successful transcriptions and an altered mindset. The stories he
heard from the speakers made him realize what had already been
lost between his parents' generation and his.

Another year, as part of his work with Leeds researchers, he had
two electrodes placed on either side of his throat to capture the
sounds he made through his larynx. In the past, linguists without
modern technology had to rely simply on their own ears and eyes to
work out how words were pronounced. But Professor Janet Watson,
one of the renowned British linguists who has worked with Modern
South Arabian Languages (MSAL) like Śḥehrɛt, has upped the ante
with whatever she can get funding for to accurately capture how

Śhehrɛ̄t is spoken. The laryngograph, which measures vocal fold activity and breath, revealed that Śhehrɛ̄t uses breathed and unbreathed sonorants, challenging the wider understanding in linguistics that such sounds—vowels and consonants like *m, n, l,* and *r*—are either voiced or unvoiced, with or without vibration from the vocal folds. Try saying "mmm" in English and then try making the same sound, but whispering. Your whispered mmm, almost as if you're blowing air out of your nose, is a completely separate sound in Śhehrɛ̄t from its unwhispered counterpart.

All Śhehrɛ̄t sonorants use no voice, but they do use air that, if you tried listening to them, would not be audible; such pre-aspirated consonants had only been found in southern America and some places in Africa. Now, because of Janet's work, we know they have also emerged in the Arabian peninsula. This is what much of linguistics is: not only studying languages we already know about, but living in a community for months or even years on end to document languages that we *don't* know about. Such knowledge has two benefits. The first is that we have a better understanding of how human language has developed over thousands of years. The second is that, if in years hence the Śhehrɛ̄t language was moribund, there would be enough material for a learner or a child to understand how to aspirate these otherwise silent sounds.

Another tool that Janet has used with speakers—electropalatography—monitors a speaker's tongue and its contact with their hard palate; the device looks like an orthodontic treatment and has to be molded to the speaker, which has meant Janet has had to fly speakers to the University of Leeds to observe them. These studies revealed that speakers are using consonants at the ends of words, a fact that listeners without prior knowledge would not be able to detect. "These words have an *l, m,* and *r* at the end," she told me, before launching into a flurry of Śhehrɛ̄t words. As hard as I tried to focus, I couldn't hear any of the consonants she had mentioned. "You can probably *see* them," she said, gesturing to her mouth, and she was right; I could see her tongue move, and her lips purse slightly. "Why do people go to the effort of producing these sounds when there is nothing to hear? They're typically face-to-face languages—if you can't hear a sound, but you can see it, that's enough."

We will never quite know how other words were pronounced in the languages that we do have a written record of but which were lost before anyone was able to make audio recordings or conduct this kind of study. This is because writing systems alone don't always give us enough pronunciation information; despite all of their hieroglyphics and the West's centuries of fascination with ancient Egyptian, for example, we still have to make intelligent guesses when we reconstruct how it was pronounced. It did not occur to the civilization responsible for pyramids, papyrus, and advanced embalming methods that it might be handy to include any vowels in their writing system, known as an orthography. Śḥehrɛ̄t, on the other hand, has a completely different problem: It is an unwritten language, and so anyone trying to faithfully pronounce or learn it when there are fewer fluent speakers around is going to find the task even harder.

Śḥehrɛ̄t isn't unusual in this sense. Most of the world's languages aren't written, and only about a hundred of them have produced a significant literary tradition.[8] For anthropologists, a writing system almost behaves like a metric for civilization: How else could knowledge be communicated, a society be organized, or a history be documented without one? Few civilizations managed to build complex states, urbanization, and economies without written recordkeeping, although there is quipu, the Incans' system of knotting color-coded strings, which would be better described as early data visualization. Writing is associated with education, and education with wealth and power; the historically written languages of today all have national and international influence, and most of the unwritten languages are spoken by small minority groups. As Arabic creeps further and further into different domains in Oman, the vocabulary and associated knowledge of Śḥehrɛ̄t will disappear, too, and if they aren't written down somewhere, they won't even live on as archival reference points. They will disappear forever.

As the Dhofari population grew more and more literate from the 1970s onward, people began to write to each other in Śḥehrēt with their nearest available tool, the Arabic script. It is better than nothing, but the number of consonants is far lower than the full inventory Śḥehrēt uses, meaning that speakers have to be proficient enough to use contextual knowledge to help them understand what has been written. Written, and widely accessible, rules about Śḥehrēt would give the language a permanent record, as well as the beginnings of textbooks that could be used in schools; Śḥehrēt's rich oral tradition has been so well nurtured that Śḥehrēt speakers have never *needed* to write in it, but now, as the language begins to disappear, linguists argue that it won't be able to withstand Arabic's dominance if left unwritten. When linguists like Janet are welcomed into communities and invited to help research unwritten languages, they often have a decision to make: Do we create a completely novel writing system, or do we adapt one that already exists? Sometimes writing systems go beyond faithfully representing how a language is pronounced, and are also developed specifically to help a language stand out from its neighbors and establish a distinctive identity. Armenian, created in the early 400s by the cleric Mesrop Mashtots, is an excellent example of this, with a bespoke orthography crafted for its speakers and not used by any other language. But it's incredibly difficult to launch a brand-new writing system from scratch. In the case of Śḥehrēt, the linguists decided that, since practically all MSAL speakers under fifty had been educated to some degree in Arabic, they should simply *add* to it.

It took years, but that is exactly what has happened. Śḥehrēt, which, fifty years ago was primarily spoken by illiterate mountain communities and was almost nowhere to be seen on a printed page, may now be messaged on a smartphone using a modified Arabic keyboard. Janet's team looked at ways that Śḥehrēt speakers were already writing their language with underspecified Arabic letters and then adapted them using Unicode, the text-encoding standard that supports the different symbols used by languages across the world. Said showed me an example of this script in a book he has been writing about traditional cosmetic practices in the Dhofar. In the Mehri language, children's books are being produced with this script, too.

Still, only a minority of speakers appear to have adopted it, something that doesn't bother Janet. "We get used to writing with poor orthographies," she said. "Just look at English." It is true. English has something called a deep orthography, an elegant way of saying that the way we write words gives us incredibly confusing information about how to pronounce them, "dough" and "rough" being two such examples. Arabic doesn't provide enough phonetic information in it for Śḥehrɛt either, but the main thing is that people are writing in Śḥehrɛt full stop, regardless of the writing system. And, crucially, in the spaces where the language *is* being authoritatively documented, it is being faithfully represented with Śḥehrɛt rather than Arabic consonants.

Writing down a previously unwritten language is a way to document it, but it is not a way to safeguard it. Just because a writing system exists does not necessarily mean that all of a language's words are being reported, by speakers or by linguists. Miranda Morris, a colleague of Janet's, fears that Śḥehrɛt's beautifully specific language around livestock raising and local fauna could be rapidly disappearing, and hopes to see word lists created in the future. She gathers and publishes these lists herself, and at the moment is focusing on the most extremely endangered languages in Oman, like Bathari, which is spoken by fewer than a hundred people today. Bathari is "a language of the sea," she says, spoken by a people pushed onto a strip of desert beach with little more than a few goats. In the seventies, she saw them hunt sharks on inflated goat skins. "Their language is really detailed on sea matters: winds, mist, tides. Some Jibbali speakers know absolute minute detail about a certain type of goat, or camel, or agriculture. The trouble with the lexicon so far is they don't show this enormous expertise."

In a glossary of more than three hundred terms that have already been collected, I learned that Śḥehrēt has a different word for cow dung compared to the dung of other animals, as well as specific words to differentiate liquid from solid cow dung, which presumably gives herders information about the well-being of their herd. Diverse words, without the need for adjectives as in English, determine what direction wind is coming from, and there are two words for "there"—one if you can see what you're pointing at in the distance and another if you can't. We have long since stopped using a similar word in English—yonder. There are also eight different verbs for "to go," depending on what time of day you're setting off between dawn and twilight. A language's words reveal to us what a culture values; for a people who have long lived a seminomadic life raising livestock in the mountains, the times of day and the direction of the wind carried far more importance than they do for many of their descendants now working nine to five in Salalah.

A language that loses these terms, Miranda says, grows impoverished. In some cases, the specific words become substituted for more general words. The MSAL all have a single word for home, but once upon a time different words were used to specify if they were nighttime or daytime living quarters, or if they were a hut or a cave. In other contexts, they are being replaced by Arabic; the evil-eye-defying livestock-counting system has seen its word for "close to a hundred"—máḥber—replaced by the Arabic mi'a, which means "one hundred."

If you speak a language every day, it can be hard to introspectively monitor these changes, never mind care about them. The linguist David Crystal, who has written extensively on the death of a language, describes this as the cloud of living "inside a language" where you're less attuned to what makes it distinctive. He uses the following thought experiment: Imagine English was endangered, and you had to rapidly gather what is most essential to preserve for our children. You might instantly think of English's great literary canon, the works of Shakespeare, Austen, Dickens. But what about famous speeches? What about the words to "Happy Birthday"? Or the obscure one-hit-wonder of a band that defined your adolescence?

After I left Arif, I visited the National Museum in Muscat, which made no mention at all of Oman's formidable indigenous languages, fizzing with ancient consonants and age-old practices in the green mountains. I thought about Arif, the only son in his family to stay in the hills, as the rest of his brothers descended to the lure of a good salary and a comfortable way of life. I thought about my nonna, who left her own mountains, too, of how little I know about them and how little I would have known even if my family had stayed put. The prosperity of a nearby city would have pulled us away from the rural lives and knowledge bases that sustained us for so long, as it had scattered Arif's family. How quickly, it seems, that a language, withdrawn from its natural habitat, begins to wither.

■　■　■

I knew I couldn't leave Oman without seeing one of its national treasures, a frankincense tree. In Salalah, I had walked through the markets at sunset, where men and women were selling frankincense oils, creams, perfumes, petroleum jellies. A triangular wooden incense holder, called a bukhoor, waited for buyers who would then use it to burn frankincense under their clothes and hair, weaving its smoke into every fiber of their clothes and bodies. My fixer Adam would inspect unprocessed frankincense—frankincense tears, as they are called—and, with the seller's permission, would pick one up and chew on it, like gum. In one store, a man squeezed some oil into a bottle of water and gave it to me to drink for the day. It is a fragrance I associate with the swinging of the incense at church—sanctity and awe that I couldn't touch, let alone eat. But in Oman, and especially in Salalah, this is a tree that has provided so much more beyond religious symbolism. Its harvest and trade were part of what made Oman's early history so rich; the industry is now a shadow of its former glory. Raising livestock is not the only profession that many Omanis have left for more lucrative, oil-funded work in the cities.

Dr. Amir Azad Al Kathiri, a linguist, has worked hard to preserve local frankincense knowledge because he believes that to maintain a language "you need to preserve the lifestyle." Funded by Oman's culture ministry, he has produced a book[9] documenting knowledge about frankincense direct from the communities who have so long tended to the trees. To carry out such work, he interviewed sixty-three Omanis across four language varieties—Śḥehrēt, Mehri, Bedouin Arabic, and urban, standardized Arabic.

Many of the words tied to the harvesting of frankincense are not Arabic. Hallún marks the period in which harvesters would make incisions into the frankincense bark, returning weeks later to cut out the scar and then make a new incision on the exposed wood. Only then does the tree weep. Workers were given a fair distribution of areas to harvest in a system called the ārbaʿ, a word Śḥehrēt speakers still use today to distribute camel meat or beef fairly among a group of people. When the cutting is over, the final resin is gathered in a period called kashm, before moving on.

Amir was keen for me to know about the many uses of frankincense, including as a tea and even as a source of light. In the past, during Eid, beads of frankincense would be set alight on rooftops as beacons for mercantile or nomadic relatives returning home. This tanwīr custom is no longer practiced, and frankincense is mainly used for incense, cosmetics, and even dripped in water to aid digestion. There are people here trying to revive its harvesting and trade, encouraged by government support, although more than one person in Oman has also told me about the illegal harvesting of wild trees that seems to have been allowed here with little policing and how rash cuts to their bark have left many trees tearless. But the elders remember the poems, and a time when frankincense prospered, passed down to them from their ancestors.

At the end of the book, Amir and his colleagues note, with sadness, that since they began writing it three elders had already passed away. "They were elderly people who preserved very important narratives describing the human element and the folklore of the Dhofar frankincense community," they write, adding, "the narratives were collected in various languages and dialects, all of which are threatened with extinction according to *The UNESCO Atlas of the World's Endangered Languages*." Without linguistics, the elders' language and memories, and without Amir's interviews, this rich compendium of frankincense folklore would not have been written. But he is keen for his work to stretch beyond the page.

Taking out his phone, he showed me a video of a tourism project he has helped to set up in the Dhofari mountains, named after the menzelt sites where families used to harvest frankincense trees. The sites needed natural caves in which to store the frankincense as well as easy access for the camel caravans that would carry the stocks to their eager merchant sellers. "Tourism can help preserve cultural heritage," he told me. At the site, you can witness how Oman's frankincense families once lived and how they would have worked on the trees. He hopes that as Omanis and foreigners flock to enjoy the Dhofar's khareef season, they may also find the time to come and visit these caves. Tourism creates jobs and affords a way for someone like Arif to stay in the mountains and get the benefits of globalization—profit, education, health care, and multilingualism—without having to leave his family's home. Workers at the site will be able to learn the old words about the frankincense trade, and recount them to curious visitors. I was excited to hear that heritage projects in Oman could start working with linguists like Amir and amplifying indigenous languages. Maybe bringing the business incentive of tourism would enable those who are eager to prosper in life *and* who are proud of their local language to live and speak well. But it is ultimately a clever solution from an entrepreneurial team; it would be a lot more powerful if the government gave the kind of funding, investment, and schooling to its indigenous languages that it has given to Arabic, and recognized both as a vital part of the Omani nation.

Amir's site was a few months away from opening when I visited, which meant I was still in search of a frankincense tree to admire. We took a trip to an orchard that has been granted special permission to create the first frankincense farm in Oman. It was out in the wilderness, just before the land peters out into desert. There were no cooling caves here, just the remains of a camel's pelvis, centipedes, and a stoic guard in uniform who looked surprised to see anyone. The trees bore necklaces with QR codes on them, an attempt to track their progress and their tear production. I saw their scarred bark, and I thought about the trees that get scored so deeply that they never weep again. In Oman's indigenous languages, they say that each frankincense tree has a manṭaf, a spot that is like the heart that should never be hurt.

I thought about Amir's work, and how his knowledge of linguistics had helped sustain not only language but nature, folklore, a way of life. And I wondered whether Ṣ́hehrēt, alive but scarred, has a manṭaf, too.

THE STORY OF UKRAINIAN

надолужити (nadolúzhyty): to make up for what was missing;
literally to restore something to wholeness again

Oryna can still remember her old passport: dark blue, with a golden tryzub on the front, the three-pronged trident and emblem of Ukraine. Within it lay her two selves.

Ukrainian passports always listed names in both Ukrainian and Russian, and in Russian, Oryna was Arina. And Arina was the name she preferred to use; it felt like no one else in Dnipro, a city once founded to be a southern outpost of the Russian Empire, was ever called Oryna. Arina made sense with everything else in her life—the Russian she spoke at home, the Russian she spoke at school, and the Russian she would probably speak at university.

When Ukraine ditched their domestic passports for ID cards, her passport page in Russian was lost and Arina was now Oryna, at least on paper. While she continued to be called and to call herself Arina everywhere in her life, the rest of her country was changing. The Maidan revolution in 2014, in which more than a hundred protesters were killed, had ousted pro-Russia President Viktor Yanukovych, sending him into exile. Russia had annexed the Crimea, the peninsula surrounded almost entirely by the Black Sea. By 2018, a law that had once been introduced to protect Russian as a regional language in Ukraine would be declared unconstitutional; a new law would give the Ukrainian language priority in more than thirty different spheres of public life. A comedian who was eyeing his country's presidency was spending his lunch breaks with a Ukrainian tutor, eager to speak Ukrainian properly following a Russian-dominated youth spent in the same region Arina is from. Although little was changing in Russian-speaking homes like Arina's, a lot was changing in the Ukrainian government, where the Ukrainian language's importance was surging. And Vladimir Putin wasn't particularly pleased.

The Russian language was "under attack," Putin wrote in a 2021 essay[1] about the "historical unity" of Russians and Ukrainians. The Kremlin decided to publish the essay in English, too, evidently trying to persuade readers beyond the Russo-sphere. Putin brought up language sixteen times in the piece, portraying Ukrainian as a vernacular dialect enriching the literary language of Russian. He described the throne of Kyiv, the first east Slavic state from the late ninth century, as a shared historic legacy, and Russians, Ukrainians, and Belarusians as mutual descendants of ancient Rus'. For many years already, Putin had spoken about the threat his compatriots were under in Ukraine, who were not just Russians but русскоязычные, russkoyazychnyye—"Russian speakers." "They may not necessarily be ethnic Russians," he said in 2014, "but they consider themselves Russian people."[2]

Putin was right that many in Ukraine have grown up more confident speaking Russian than Ukrainian, particularly in the regions closer to their shared border. But to suggest that this was because of a common cultural ancestor, and that Ukrainian was simply a variety of Russian, was a savage leap of the imagination, one that emboldened Putin to invade the country. In his supposed venture to "save" Russian speakers, Putin made a decision that killed many of them, displaced ten million people from their homes, and caused up to a million casualties at the time of writing. The very night he launched the invasion—February 24, 2022—Arina made her own decision. She was no longer going to speak the language of the aggressor, regardless of the fact that it was her mother tongue, and she was going to give up her name. Arina became Oryna—*just* Oryna. And she has barely spoken a word of Russian since.

Even if you aren't Ukrainian, it is still likely that you also took part in a small language revolution after the invasion of Ukraine. A lot of us altered our pronunciation and spelling of the Ukrainian capital city Kyiv following February 24, after news outlets rapidly published explainers recommending we call the city Kyiv, not Kiev. "Kiev" transliterates its Russian name and pronunciation, ending in more of an "eh" than an "ee." In the twentieth century, Soviet power and delicious chicken Kievs ossified this pronunciation for most of the Western world, and this, Ukrainians argue, is textbook Russification, the ongoing attempts of the Russian government to acculturate Ukrainians into its Russo-sphere.

Even though the Ukrainian government had long attempted to change this exonym with the Twitter hashtag #KyivNotKiev, it was the assault of Russian tanks on Ukrainian soil and our television screens that gave the West the most convincing impetus for word change. All of us who have pronounced Kyiv correctly since have fired a shell over the linguistic frontline—even British supermarkets, which renamed the classic dish a chicken Kyiv. In the meantime, Russia has steamrollered through Ukrainian sovereign territory with an unparalleled destruction of its language; wherever it has occupied since 2022, it has dismantled Ukrainian-language road signs, imposed Russian as the language of instruction and public life, and has even seized and destroyed Ukrainian books. Ukraine has reacted to this viscerally, from ordinary people all the way up to the top of government. This ongoing conflict reveals not only how languages become weapons of war, but how an occupied country may respond when it has its language as well as its nation to defend.

The Russia-Ukraine war is not the first time that languages have become a pretext for which to invade or kill. In 1956 in Sri Lanka, then Ceylon, an Official Language Act was passed to replace English with Sinhala as the country's sole language, despite Tamil being the first language of several minority ethnic groups. The Tamils saw this as discrimination, which fueled riots and ultimately spiraled into a civil war that lasted twenty-six years. More widely, if there is an ethnic dimension to a conflict, there is almost certainly always an ethno*linguistic* element to it, too. In Guatemala's thirty-six-year civil war, the government conflated indigenous Mayans with leftist insurgency groups. Bilingual educators teaching both Spanish and Mayan languages to children were often singled out as guerrilla organizers and executed.[3] During periods of war and conflict, language diversity becomes another vector of risk, a nuance complicating the clear distinctions propagandists try to draw between enemy and ally, vanquished and victor.

War also has lasting, damaging effects on a state's language choices long after the battles on the ground have ended. By the time Yugoslavia broke apart in the nineties, so, too, did the Serbo-Croatian language into Bosnian, Croatian, Montenegrin, and Serbian, not because they were different languages to linguists, but because nationalists needed them to be different as they started to carve out their own identities. Years later, in 2017, two hundred linguists, writers, and activists from around the region came forward to declare that they did, in fact, all speak the same language,[4] albeit allowing for many varieties, to stall increasing nationalist divisions that threatened to repeat history. Language planning can stop war as much as it can start it. Canada's official languages are French and English because, centuries ago, both the British and French empires vied for control in the region. Once the British seized power, they had to placate culturally French colonies that risked uproar if they couldn't hold on to their Catholic faith or French law. Respecting both languages' existence, and citizens' right to access public services in both of them, gave us the bilingual country we know today, but it also probably prevented a lot of bloodshed, and expense.

This particular language battle is not new for Russia or Ukraine.

It has been a long and protracted war of attrition, with parts of Ukraine controlled by the Russian Empire for centuries before it became part of the USSR; the medieval kingdom of Rus that once ruled from Kyiv broke apart to be governed in various parts by Poland, Lithuania, and Austria until most of today's Ukrainian lands came under Russian control in the 1600s and 1700s. Freedom from the Russian Empire was short-lived before the USSR took hold in their stead. Linguicide as a phenomenon is far better known in the Ukrainian-speaking world than it is in the Anglosphere where it generates barely four pages in a Google News query; a search for лінгвоцид (linhvotsyd), Ukrainian's word for the term, retrieves more than double the number of results. There is even a linguicide memorial that was erected a few years ago in Kyiv, and it is one of the only monuments in the world exclusively designed to remember the killing of a language.

Valentyna Merzhyievska, who created it, was inspired by a similar memorial she had seen in Berlin: eighty double-sided aluminum signs hanging off streetlights, each one telling the story of the exclusion and disenfranchisement of Germany's Jews. Today, in Kyiv, there are thirty-eight signs positioned around the city in a similar manner. Each bears a year and an illustration, as in one street in Old Kyiv that has a drawing of a bird trying to sing while a rope is being fastened around its neck. It marks the 1784 prohibition of Empress Catherine II, which stopped churches from being able to deliver services or print works in Old Ukrainian. A few streets away, the figure of a man is trapped in flames marking the year 1978, when the dissident Oleksa Hirnyk set himself on fire protesting Russification. In a note written before he died, Hirnyk said, "My protest is about the ordeal, the torture, that the Ukrainian people have endured."

The intention isn't only that people happen upon them while they're getting on with their day, but that they might be persuaded to join one of the walking tours Valentyna has helped develop with linguists and experts. A fifty-minute tour around the neighborhood of Podil takes you to a series of buildings such as Pyrohoshcha Church, to contemplate how local literature was condemned by the Russian Orthodox Church Council in 1690, or to a local school to think about the banning of Ukrainian primers in 1769. At the end of the tour you reach a publishing house and a sign that gives the year 2022: "Destruction of Books by the Occupiers."

To justify these acts, Russian statesmen have long devalued Ukrainian, arguing that it isn't its own language and that proper education and citizenship therefore meant speaking the proper language—Russian. One minister as far back as the 1800s actually said "there was not, is not, and can be no distinctive Little Russian language," referring to Ukrainian.[5] To see Ukrainian as "Little Russian," and not a language in its own right, is the same powerful misconception that Putin has reiterated in his own rhetoric. Being close enough to be dialects of each other doesn't prevent separate national languages (hence the existence of Bosnian, Croatian, Montenegrin, and Serbian). But in the case of Russian and Ukrainian, it isn't even true. Linguistically, they are aunt and niece, and linguists certainly do *not* consider them to be varieties of the same language.

Both are descended from a common ancestor, Proto-Slavic, which by around 1000 CE had already morphed and splintered into lots of different varieties as its speakers expanded throughout Europe. Old east Slavic eventually gave birth to Russian and Ruthenian, the name given to the language of the early modern Polish-Lithuanian Commonwealth. It is out of Ruthenian that both the Belarusian and Ukrainian languages emerged. Ukrainian and Russian have had significant linguistic differences for hundreds of years regardless of their shared distant ancestor. Ukrainian has engaged in years of contact with other languages throughout its history because its territories were once part of the Austro-Hungarian Empire or the Polish-Lithuanian Commonwealth as well as the Russian Empire.

A common misconception is that the languages are similar because Ukrainian speakers understand so much Russian, but the lack of reciprocity here—the fact that Russians can't understand Ukrainians—reveals that this is actually because Ukrainians have historically been forced to learn Russian and Russians have never been forced to learn Ukrainian. A 2004 survey by the Kyiv International Institute of Sociology found that Russian was spoken at home by 43–46 percent of the country's population, with majority Russian speakers predominant in eastern and southern regions of Ukraine. This has nothing to do with the bare mutual intelligibility between the languages and everything to do with the last two centuries of Russian colonialism and policies compelling Ukrainians to learn their language. While lots of words share similar roots and might even look the same, some 38 percent of Ukrainian vocabulary is different from Russian, almost the same as the difference between French and Portuguese, whose speakers would be justifiably appalled if you tried to convince them they spoke the same language. Even the shared words Ukrainian and Russian have can hold diverse meanings, such as the Russian word for "week" being Ukrainian for "Sunday." The biggest similarities can be found in the words that Ukrainian's and Russian's shared ancestors would have needed to live day-to-day like the word for grain, зерно, which is identical in both languages. But even many of these are different, like the word for morning, which is ранок (ranok) in Ukrainian and утро (utro) in Russian.

Ukrainian has been shaped by its other neighbors' languages, too; the names for months of the year, for example, have nothing to do with the Latin calendar, which is how most European languages catalog them. It is an unusual feature that Ukrainian shares with Belarusian and Polish; instead of the months being connected to ancient Roman gods, the months bear information that would have been far more relevant to agrarian societies. The word for December, грудень (hruden'), comes from "clod of the earth," referring to the frozen soil at this time of the year. липень (lypen') comes from the word for the linden tree, and so marks the month of July, when they are in full bloom.

Their accents are also different, as is pronunciation. Take the example of паляниця (palianytsia), a round loaf of bread that is so distinctively Ukrainian that it has appeared on postage stamps. In February 2022 the Ukrainian media published stories that the army had been using this word to identify Russian reconnaissance groups because it contains several letters that would be mispronounced by a Russian and not by a Ukrainian. Such a distinctive word that marks someone as belonging to a certain group is known by linguists as a shibboleth. Several letters within the Cyrillic alphabet that they share are different, too. This is why Kyiv (Київ) is Kiev (Киев) in Russian. The Ukrainian writing system has been systematically stripped of its status throughout the twentieth century. Under the Bolsheviks in 1933, the letter *G* in Ukrainian, Ґ, was removed from the Ukrainian alphabet by the Communist Party, which argued that it was a recent linguistic corruption, conveniently ignoring the fact that it was used in the Peresopnytsia Gospel, a handwritten Bible from the 1500s that, today, Ukrainian presidents swear their oath of office on. The ostracized letter wouldn't be formally reintroduced until new spelling rules brought it back in 1990.

Under Stalin, dictionaries throughout the countries of the Soviet Union were purged of local terminology. Gradually, any Latin-based alphabets across the USSR, such as those for Uzbek or Tajik, were replaced with Cyrillic, and between 1938 and 1994 Russian was required in schools, often from the first grade. Bilingualism with Russian shot up, and the number of non-Russians professing fluency in the language began to form the majority. Other languages across the USSR slipped quietly out of education systems. Where in the 1960s there had been schools in forty-seven non-Russian languages across the bloc, by 1982 that number had plummeted to just seventeen.[6] In Ukraine, Stalin made more than one hundred and fifty changes to

Ukrainian between 1928 and 1946, altering elements of its writing systems, morphology, and grammar to make them more Russian. He had Ukrainian-language writers and poets murdered in what has since been termed the "Executed Renaissance," eradicating an entire generation of "Ukrainianizing" intellectuals, including those who had compiled Ukrainian dictionaries.

Such restrictive policies were still being pushed up until the final years of the Soviet Union. In 1978, a government directive ordered that particular subjects in technical schools and universities should only be taught in Russian and that additional Russian resources and teachers be sent to schools in rural Ukraine. In 1983, new funding in schools meant that an educator who taught Russian would be given a 16 percent salary increase. Ukrainian language teachers did not receive the equivalent.

Even Valentyna's Linguicide app, which I was able to access in English, is also available in Russian. "There were many internal debates within our team," she remembers. Finally, they decided that it should be available in Russian. "There are still many people in Ukraine—especially among the older generation—who have spent their entire lives here but do not have a strong command of Ukrainian. If someone lived in heavily Russified regions, avoided Ukrainian media, and never had to use the language professionally, they could go their whole life without fluency. For such people, reading or processing information in Ukrainian requires additional effort—something they might only do if they are already motivated to learn more." To win people over, you sometimes have to speak to them in their own language.

It's not that Ukrainians ever stopped speaking Ukrainian; it was devalorized out of public life. Thanks to Russian intervention, it increasingly became associated with a rural rather than a literary and cultural life, an attitude that has lasted into the present day. All the Ukrainians I have spoken to who are in their twenties and from Russian-speaking areas say that, had they spoken Ukrainian at school, they would have been bullied. Ukrainian was only made a state language in 1989, and Ukraine was declared independent in 1991 after the fall of the Soviet Union. Ukraine barely had a chance to recover from past Russian linguicide by the time Russia annexed the Crimea in 2014; now, in the middle of a full-scale war, lives are at stake as much as language is. The rules, however, have changed since the Soviet era. Ukraine is independent—and it, too, is armed and ready for a language war.

■ ■ ■

When it comes to language protection, and the inevitable strictness that accompanies it, the classic example is France. The Académie Française, born in seventeenth-century literary salons and eventually emerging as a formal council, is comprised of forty members who unironically call themselves "the immortals." It certainly takes what can seem an eternity to elect one of them; at the time of writing they still have three vacant seats that have been empty for years because they can't achieve a majority vote on any of the candidates. When Daniel Rondeau, a writer and former diplomat, was inducted in 2019, he wore robes designed by Givenchy: a navy wool gabardine and black silk tailcoat and cape, with an aureate-embroidered lining of green and gold olive branches.[7] It took the atelier sixteen hundred hours to make, and along with the other embellishments, such as a ceremonial sword, new members spend tens if not hundreds of thousands for the privilege of joining what many think is the language police. The novelist Amin Maalouf, who chairs the group under the title of "Perpetual Secretary," has publicly admitted that he had to raise nearly $230,000 to cover the costs.[8] If this seems bourgeois, that's no accident: The Académie Française has never seriously pressured itself to represent all of France. In 2008, they opposed the French government's proposal to recognize and protect regional languages. Of the seven hundred forty-two immortels, only eleven have been women, and in the current roster there is just one

Black member, Dany Laferrière, hardly representative of the modern Francophone world. It is estimated that more than half of the world's French speakers live in Africa.

Globally, the Académie is notorious for furiously defending the French language with its prescriptivism, which is when rules are imposed on how a language should be used. The opposite of this is descriptivism, in which a language is analyzed for how it is already spoken. In recent years, French prescriptivism has most heavily targeted Anglicisms; this is not necessarily a bad thing, and it is a challenge that many languages around the world, particularly those with far fewer speakers, are right to resist. But recommendations issued in 2022 highlight how out of touch they are. They argued that French words needed to be used in video game jargon, not Anglicisms; so "streamer" should be "jouer-animateur en direct" and e-sports should be "jeu video de competition." Who would want to use those?

Ukraine has not so much a language police as a language antivirus, led by Taras Kremin. He was wearing a half-zip, bright blue fleece when I saw him—no robes or regalia, just an enormous Ukrainian flag hung up behind him. He sees the Académie Française as his French counterpart, a comparison he also extends to Germany's Goethe Institute and the UK's British Council. Together, they are all members of the European Federation of National Institutions for Language, which has thirty-nine member organizations across the Continent. While the British Council does promote the English language worldwide and pushes British soft power, it doesn't act as a language watchdog; in fact, the English language doesn't have a language police, and it tends to be lexicographers who document language change for the Oxford English Dictionary rather than any government body officiating standard use. Kremin counters that he's not laying down the law, either. "I want to underline—I am not a policeman. We collect this information for the next steps."

Long before Kremin was a politician he was a university professor, with a PhD in Ukrainian literature and philology. Before that he was a poet, like his father, Dmytro, a significant figure in post–Second World War experimentalism who was determined to teach children Ukrainian and who engaged with his friends in samvydav, the publishing of books forbidden by the Kremlin. I learned about him from a beautiful translation of one of his poetry collections by Svetlana Lavochkina. "Kremin means 'flint' in Ukrainian," she writes in its introduction, pointing out it's a real name, not a nom de plume or nom de guerre. "Flint: a fire starter, a hunting spear tip, a blade—all precise metaphors for Kremin's work." Apparently Dmytro Kremin's early poetry, which he wrote when still a teenager, was criticized for being foggy, to which he retorted: "If the readers think my work is foggy, it needs to be clarified whose brain the fog has befallen, mine or theirs." He frequently appeals to the traditions that surround him—the Bible, ancient Greece, Slavic mythology—to cast Ukraine as a crucified, long-suffering nation. Occasionally his flint comes out: In one poem he declares that "Ukraine will never kneel, / Unless for prayer."[9]

Dmytro Kremin died in 2019, never seeing the current invasion. When I asked his son what poetry *he* likes to write, he immediately said: "About Ukraine. My Mykolaiv region, the Black Sea region. My parents, my wife, my daughter. And about our Ukrainian victory!" Like father, like son. He owes his Ukrainian language skill to his father, as his region and education was, in his words, entirely "Russified." Following the Maidan revolution in 2014, when he became a Member of Parliament, he immediately focused on education, particularly "enforcement of the right to education for persons residing in the temporarily occupied territory." And since 2020 he has held the position of State Language Protection Commissioner, the second person ever to hold that title.* He is not a civil servant, and acts independently of government.

---

* As of July 2025, Kremin's term has come to an end, and he has been succeeded by Olena Ivanovska.

The state language law that created Taras Kremin's job was only introduced in 2019. It was a broad revitalization program for the Ukrainian language, pushed hard for security as much as cultural reasons. Kremin doesn't spend every day wondering which new Anglicism to berate. He's too busy enforcing the complex state law. Without going into all forty-nine pages of it here, it ensures that all Ukrainians are taught Ukrainian at school and asks that everyone in Ukraine become proficient in the language. New Ukrainian citizens will be expected to demonstrate an appropriate proficiency in Ukrainian, either immediately or within a year of acquiring citizenship.

An enormous number of professions require proficiency in Ukrainian, including that of the president and all politicians across Ukraine and specifically in the Crimea, as well as military officers, bank staff, anyone in state education and medicine, and all lawyers. Cultural and artistic announcements and posters must be produced in the state language, and foreign language shows must always offer a Ukrainian translation. Publishers are obliged to produce at least 50 percent of their titles in Ukrainian, and websites registered in Ukraine must also carry a Ukrainian version along with any other languages they may support. Foreign websites that serve Ukrainians must load in Ukrainian by default on their browsers. The law also preserves the right for people from indigenous groups and national minorities to be guaranteed the right to study their native language via schools or cultural societies. Tatar and minority languages recognized by the EU are examples of language communities that may benefit from this; Russian does not benefit, having had its status as a protected language removed.

Kremin's duty is to determine whether or not these language laws are being abided by. He is obliged to make annual reports and to present them to the public, as well as forward his concerns to other commissions and administrations who may then conduct internal investigations or discipline people for violations. In 2021, he produced a long report on the violations documented in the Crimea,

Luhansk, and Donetsk after Russia's 2014 takeover of those regions. In Sevastopol, the Crimea's largest city, the number of pupils studying Ukrainian at school had plummeted from more than twelve thousand to just two hundred fourteen in 2020, with just one school left in the region teaching the language. In 2019, the International Court of Justice ordered Russia to ensure the right of Ukrainians in the Crimea to be educated in Ukrainian. Nothing changed.

Ukrainian newspapers, television stations, and websites in the region were still shut down or blocked, and human rights groups reported that occupying forces were forbidding musicians from singing in Ukrainian on Crimean radio stations. A Ukrainian cultural center set up shortly after the occupation found their staff repeatedly detained, interrogated, threatened, and fined. Larysa Kitayska, an activist who was arrested for "spreading hatred and enmity," told Ukrainian media that "the oppression of the Ukrainian language in Crimea can now be seen in everything. If you communicate in Ukrainian, some people laugh, others look at you with disdain, especially visitors from Russia." When she appeared in court, they wouldn't give her a Ukrainian interpreter, a violation of her rights under Article 74 of the Geneva Convention.[10]

In Donetsk and Luhansk, Russian was declared the state language soon after Russia occupied the territories in 2014, and by 2017 all schools had their language of instruction switched to Russian. Without Ukrainian language skills, the students graduating from Donetsk and Luhansk high schools will now not be able to enter Ukrainian universities, keeping them from reintegrating into Ukrainian society; many learn it on the side with private teachers or using YouTube. Svitlana, a woman in Luhansk, told Deutsche Welle[11] that the only way for her children to study Ukrainian at their school would be to attend a class at 7 a.m., which only lasts twenty minutes, obviously scheduled at a time to deter most learners. "The children themselves say: rather than learning Ukrainian like this, it is better not to teach it at school at all." She added that her daughter was now teaching herself. "She said it is better than treating the language so negligently and humiliating it."

Kremin generally finds himself busiest not with these regions but with disciplining Kyiv. Year after year, Kyiv is the city that marks the most language law complaints, which are generally made either by citizens, human rights organizations, or the police. Ukraine's open data service shared a report in October 2024, listing the number of violations in the year so far, and Kyiv made up 39 percent of the complaints. Kremin called it a "problem city," receiving citizens fleeing from the war in Donetsk, Luhansk, Kherson, and Mikolaiv, where Russian is likely to be their first language. "Next is Odesa and Kharkhiv," he told me, with 326 and 149 complaints respectively. Although Kremin doesn't identify as a policeman, sixty-four fines were issued in the year up to October 2024 for violations, the vast majority of which consisted of websites not being accessible in Ukrainian.[12] Considering Russia's considerable disinformation machine, Ukraine is right to be worried about Russian-only websites that are trying to post online within Ukraine. In 2024, the Reuters Institute for the Study of Journalism reported that Ukrainians get more of their news from social media than any of the other twenty-four European countries cited in the report.[13] Digital and grassroots media could adapt quickly where traditional channels, disrupted by war and having their own TV towers bombed by Russia, had to defer to the online world to get information out rapidly. Reliance on the internet for news is wonderful for accessibility, but it becomes a major vulnerability in an information war.

With all of these complaints and violations collected in one place, Kremin is hopeful that his reports will support Ukraine's international human rights claims and help prove "language genocide," as he puts it. There is no international crime of linguicide, but evidence of linguistic discrimination may help the Ukrainian government build their argument for genocide against Russia. At the time of writing, many of these cases are active, including two interstate cases between them. In June 2024, the court found Russia guilty in one of them of systematic violations of human rights in the Crimea "beyond a reasonable doubt," something the country has repeatedly denied. Russia is no longer a member of the European Convention on Human Rights (ECHR), nor does it have a remotely positive track record of responding to such rulings with meaningful change. However, the ECHR can still have an effect in dealing the kind of reputational damage that worsens sanctions and further deteriorates international relations, even if it cannot legally enforce what it has prescribed. Cases can be brought by individuals as well as by states, and as of February 2025 there were 9,264 individual applications against Russia from citizens in the Crimea and other occupied or war-ridden areas. Similarly, the investigations of the International Criminal Court have already culminated in the release of an arrest warrant for Vladimir Putin. But rights continue to be violated, and territory continues to be occupied. The war has not stopped and so Kremin has to keep documenting violations.

Take Mariupol, for example, which has been occupied by Russian forces since 2022 following a three-month siege. It didn't take long for pro-Russian separatists to begin tearing down Ukrainian road signs and replacing them with Russian ones. This translation, Kremin said, made "a great difference for Ukrainians. This is about our sense of identity. Our realization of our language law in all the spheres of Ukraine—our cities, our squares, our names." Along with a switch to Moscow's time zone and Russia's school curriculum, the Avenue of Peace has become Lenin Avenue, and Azovstalska Street, which shares its name with the fortresslike Azovstal steelworks from which Ukrainian forces defended Mariupol to the very last moment, has been renamed to instead acknowledge Tula, a Russian city.[14] The UN estimated that 90 percent of residential buildings in Mariupol were damaged or destroyed during Russia's siege; the almost blank canvas has enabled Russia to refashion the city in its image. Human rights defenders fear that Russia will obfuscate its war crimes with such rebuilding, but if linguicide were counted among those crimes, they are doing nothing to hide it. Oleg Morgun, the head of Russia's administration in the occupied city, has said, "In liberated Mariupol, we honor and remember the true history of our country."[15]

Well, in liberated Ukraine, they honor and remember the truth, too. Two languages can play at *that* game. In recent years, Ukrainian place names have been hugely "derussified," along with the names of squares—agoranyms—and streets—hodonyms. In 2023, derussifying place names became a legal requirement, with a new law—On the Condemnation and Prohibition of Propaganda of Russian Imperial Policy in Ukraine and the Decolonization of Toponymy—forbidding toponymy associated with Russia. By September 2024, 327 settlements had been renamed according to Visit Ukraine.[16]

Rust marks on the sides of walls that once bore old street signs are often the only clue in Ukraine that a street was ever known by another name; and now, where a lone Ukrainian flag stands waving in the middle of a square, it is likely that it is a recent addition, replacing a statue of someone like Catherine the Great. An analysis of Kyiv in its two main renaming phases—first following the invasion of the Crimea and then following the beginning of the full-scale invasion in 2022—has revealed that about 17 percent of the capital's street names have been changed. It is primarily Soviet nostalgia that has been erased from Kyiv's geography; names commemorating revolution, civil war, or state leaders like Lenin. Symbols have also been pried out of toponyms, especially anything beginning with the word *red*, as well as names of famous Russians like Dostoevsky and Tolstoy.

Instead, in the central city of Cherkasy, a street that previously honored a Soviet war hero was renamed Zakhysnykiv Ukrainy, "Defenders of Ukraine" street, in 2023. Another street, which had been renamed after the classic Russian summer home, the dacha, was returned to its original name, after a zaton, meaning a creek. "Soviet and pro-Russian names should disappear forever from the map of Cherkasy," said Serhii Tyshchenko, the first deputy mayor and the chairman of the Toponymic Commission in the city. Sometimes, residents make special requests for a street's new name; in the neighborhood of Bortnychi, renamed streets now focus on the art of beekeeping, which was once the most important occupation there, so there's Vulykova, "beehive" street, and Medonosna, "honey-bearing" street.

You don't necessarily need a war to decolonize place names. In Wales in 2024 Eryri National Park formally switched to Eryri and Yr Wyddfa as official names in all their communications. These are the Welsh names for Snowdonia and Snowdon and have always been used by Welsh speakers to describe their landscape, but English speakers have long used words from Old English for them instead, after snāw and dūn, meaning snow hill. Restoring Māori place names was part of New Zealand's founding Treaty of Waitangi, the treaty between Maori chiefs and the British Crown signed centuries ago. These name changes are still occurring, with many places now adopting bilingual names that refer to both the English and the original Māori name that it was once called. Even New Zealand itself is now becoming commonly referred to as Aotearoa New Zealand, revalorizing its Māori title "the land of the long white cloud." New Zealand's indigenous people looked to the skies, where colonizers looked to the seas; New Zealand comes from the Middle Dutch for the antonymous *sea land*. Making such names visible recenters and legitimizes them. Far from merely being aesthetic changes, they often function as symbols that reflect wider, more deeply rooted efforts at language reclamation.

These laws and name changes are how Ukraine has responded to Russian linguicide from the top down. But from the bottom up, the Ukrainian public's response to its domineering neighbor has also heralded an incredible reversal of fortunes for the Russian language in the country. Laada Bilaniuk, an anthropologist at the University of Washington, can remember interviewing a woman in the

2000s from a central southern area who told her that she would never date a man who speaks Ukrainian because that would mean he's a "country bumpkin." "So even after a decade of independence and Ukrainian being official, it's really hard to lose those connotations," Bilaniuk told me. But as Russian interference in Ukrainian politics grew, she began to encounter the opposite attitude; she has seen street conversations move from Russian only to a mix of languages and, now, increasingly monolingual Ukrainian chats.

Following the invasion some people, like Oryna, as we have seen, changed their language overnight. Ukraine's Content Analysis Center gathered more than a million online posts from Ukrainian social media users, and the trend is clear: We're seeing a decisive move toward posting in Ukrainian rather than Russian. Only 15 percent of the content of private individuals was in Ukrainian in 2020, but by 2023 it appears to have risen to 51 percent. Instagram, above all, has seen the most dramatic shift in Ukrainian language posts—90 percent of content posted out of Ukraine is now in Ukrainian there—and in almost all regions of Ukraine their content analysis seems to show clear "derussifying." This is far slower, grinding to a halt or even rolling backward, in Russian-occupied areas of Ukraine. In 2023 the center observed that posts in Ukrainian geotagged to the city of Kherson seem to have dropped by 5 percent. The report also acknowledges that if Russian social networks are included, then every second post in Ukraine is still written in Russian; users on these banned networks predictably have little interest in pushing for Ukrainian.

But for those who do support the Ukrainian cause, speaking Ukrainian is part of a wider cultural boycott of everything Russian: No more Russian cars, no more Russian music. In a 2022 ARTE.tv documentary titled *Ukraine: Language Wars*,[17] a young Ukrainian tells his interviewer: "When someone arrives from Kyiv and speaks Russian to me, I don't want to talk to them anymore. I can't do it—it kills me." People still want to speak a second language, but now it's English. One woman says: "When Russia falls, the Russian language will not be so widely spoken. English will be the most popular language." Her friend quickly adds: "Because soon we will be in the European Union, and our most important task will be to know English." As the Russian language's presence wanes, so, too, does its influence. Deciding to switch the main language you speak in, however, is not easy, and if a language is someone's mother tongue, is it their responsibility to stop speaking it just because another speaker decides to use it irresponsibly?

Bilaniuk, who has studied the organic bilingualism of many Ukrainians, often had her work criticized as Ukrainians began to coalesce around the Ukrainian language, as if bilingualism was not a historic legacy but "tantamount to a legitimation of the role of Russian in Ukraine, since for so long that role had been to undermine and replace Ukrainianness," as she wrote in her book *Contested Tongues*. Even language mixing with Russian, long occurring and accepted in Ukraine, is still sometimes seen by Ukrainian nationalists as encroaching on the purity of their long-suffering language. Ironically, this parodies the Russian anxieties of a century ago, when the Soviets were worried that non-Russians, especially peasants, were speaking incorrect Russian—except that they were worried because they were busy trying to eradicate, rather than protect, Ukrainian. What these people in the countryside and in the borderlands were really doing was speaking Russian with gaps that were filled with their native Ukrainian. This combined language, a pidgin, was christened surzhyk—the name for a blend of wheat and rye that was considered low grade. Pidgins, like dialects, are often not given the respect they are due, a great shame given that the spontaneous language improvisation that forges them shows off some of the greatest communication skills we as humans are capable of. Belarus also has a Belarusian-Russian pidgin—trasianka—which, again, referred to a mixture of hay and straw. You can hear in both names how this linguistic mixing is seen as making a low-rate mess of both languages rather than creating a third, legitimate language.

There are many kinds of surzhyk; as pidgins go, it is an especially flighty one, representing how amorphously Ukrainians have had to adapt themselves over the last one hundred years. Pidgins form when two groups of people are in frequent contact without a common language. The Ukrainians who, pressured by Soviet language planners in the early USSR, started transplanting Russian words into their everyday speech, spoke surzhyk in order to negotiate this very sudden language change. Over time, Ukrainians moving to Russian-speaking cities like Kyiv or in the east started to speak surzhyk as they transposed their lives from rural villages to urban jobs. Now, post-independence, the trend is reversing: Native Russian speakers in Ukraine are trying to get better at speaking Ukrainian, and the two languages are mixing in a different way. All three scenarios produce different kinds of surzhyk, unique to each individual's needs. Today, if surzhyk is heard, it is often spoken by people like Oryna. She has found it challenging to pivot to Ukrainian even though she learned it in school and believed that she spoke it fluently. Sometimes, she said, she speaks surzhyk, which she thinks is a little like Spanglish, to help her get by. "The main challenge is to start speaking freely. Sometimes you can say a Russian word with a Ukrainian accent. That is the main challenge—to speak more accurately, with a hundred percent Ukrainian vocabulary."

Bilaniuk likens some of the old feelings around surzhyk to historic attitudes about languages such as African American English. Both have been dismissed as "lesser" forms of language when really they're just as valid as any other; now, surzhyk is frequently spoken in feature films. "It's realism, this is how people talk," she said. The reality is that surzhyk, as much as Ukrainian, is a language of resistance, defying the "pure" Russian that emperors and governments tried to force through the Ukrainian education systems for centuries.

It might be a pidgin born of contact with an occupier, but regardless of that, it's a home-grown language. Kateryna Ustiuhova, a writer who has been a refugee in Scotland since 2022, recalled that she called her brother one day, speaking in fluent Ukrainian even though they only ever spoke surzhyk at home. He replied: А ти можеш просто по-нашому, по-человечески? "Can't you just speak normally, humanly, like we do?" But it's difficult to speak normally in a country where two languages are pitted against each other, and where their pidgin is either ignored or chastised. Surzhyk reminds Ustiuhova of her hometown and of the rural women who raised her, kneading bread for Easter and joking in their warm mixture of idiomatic Ukrainian and Russian-inherited vocabulary. "For me, surzhyk is the realest thing in my homeland. In that Ukraine of mine, which is not polished for tourists, not nightingale-laden from the pages of a textbook. Instead, it is the one that is simple and ancient like the rough skin of grandma's hands."[18]

Ustiuhova's perspective reminds us that intellectual distinctions between languages can often be irrelevant to our core, emotional relationship to what we speak, and what we need our language to actually *do*. Every day, millions of Ukrainian refugees FaceTime and Telegram message their loved ones still at home or fighting on some frontline in whatever language comes, unconsciously, to their mouths and fingertips. I thought about them as I sat in a taxi in the spring of 2025, looking out of the window at English meadows I'd never seen before. I was heading to an undisclosed location with a team from NATO, who were hosting a site visit to see Ukrainian soldiers receiving combat training from the British army. I knew that most of them probably didn't speak English; I also knew that the Brits were hardly likely to speak any Ukrainian.

When I first arrived they were taking a short break, and one of the Ukrainian soldiers had his jacket off, revealing a substantial gut. He had a Coke in one hand and a cigarette, from which he drew deeply, in the other. He looked like he was in his forties, maybe fifties;

by this point in the war, most of the volunteers had signed up long ago, and most of the men who were now being sent to the UK to train were conscripts. Fourteen different NATO allies send Ukrainians here, speed-running soldiers through the drills and skills they'll need to stay alive on the frontline. Some arrive looking for refresher training, but most have never been on a battlefield or only have the survival instinct they've learned on the job as partisans defending their cities.

One young man, who spoke excellent English and looked a natural in his khakis and flak jacket, told me he was from the west of Ukraine and grew up speaking Ukrainian; for him, his biggest worry about the Russian language wasn't that people in Ukraine might speak the language, but, rather, that they might *read* in it. "If you speak Russian, you might watch a lot of content from Russia," he said. I asked him if he meant he was worried about Russian disinformation, and he nodded. "There is obvious disinformation, and tactical disinformation that's maybe ninety percent true and ten percent a lie. Given the small lies, people eat them, and they change their understanding of the war." In Ukrainian, that's what happens to lies—they get "swallowed." Ukrainian also has a standard verb for "to consume," as we have in English, but to swallow a lie feels more visceral; we digest it and it becomes part of us. This is, of course, where Kremin's commission tries to break through—thwarting disinformation before it has the chance to nourish news-hungry Ukrainians.

I watched a group of them practice a forest battle scenario, where Brits played Russians, hiding in the undergrowth. About fifty meters to my right, special effects technicians were firing off blank mortar shells—the reason I was wearing earplugs—to accustom the soldiers to the sound of war, and I could smell what seemed like rich, dark honey, like the newly named streets of Bortnychi, probably something to do with the pressure or heat of the projectiles. A lone woman, with a high, dark brown ponytail and dressed all in black, was darting between the soldiers as they crouched, shot, and sprinted. The British officers would bark orders and she would echo them. She was translating everything he said into Ukrainian, studying all the faces around her as she kept up with the marauding troops.

The young Ukrainian soldier told me afterward that this woman and her colleagues do a lot more than just interpreting. "They're not only interpreters," he said, "they know the army subject deeply, they can add something," providing explanations as well as the direct translation. In fact, everybody here calls them linguists, as though they are trying to acknowledge the wider expertise that they are sharing beyond straightforward translation. The gender breakdown was almost the inverse of the all-male unit I had been watching; bar one young man who had moved to the UK a couple of months before the war broke out, every single linguist was a woman. Some are here as refugees, others as migrants, but they all have people they love fighting back home. One of them told me that Ukrainian is the main language spoken here, but that, yes, surzhyk is present, too. This is their war effort—using their Ukrainian, their English, and their inevitable fragments of Russian in the hope that it helps a soldier save his own life, his comrade's life, and the future of their country. Perhaps, in decades to come, Russian words will fall into disuse in Ukraine, because they will no longer be needed in a long-established sovereign state. But for the time being, they'll stick around, pieces of shrapnel from a bygone language war.

The loudest, and most historic, of language stories from the invasion of Ukraine will be about the great "derussification" and re-mapping of a country whose enemy is very much contemporary, terrifying, and aiming for linguistic annihilation. Russia is intent on the same linguicide that many of its tyrants have endorsed for centuries, except this time the world is watching and even helping Ukraine's linguistic defense. It will not be the last time language is used as a weapon of war—and now each country that finds itself its victim can turn to Ukraine's Language Commissioner as a blueprint for self-defense.

But, on an unseasonably warm day in late winter in rural England, I witnessed a more complex story of a language, and its speakers, at war. Here, it's not so important if a Russian word creeps in. This is not misinformation or colonialism, but a helpless love child of language contact who did not choose its own parents. And in the areas of occupied Ukraine where Russia insists on cultural hegemony, long memories of past linguicide may prove an effective weapon for Ukraine to remind young people of what was hard-won, what was taken from them, and what may—with a lot of effort, and maybe even a little grain and rye—one day come home.

THE STORY OF LADINO

> **desmazalado:** "unfortuned," similar to ill-fated

My day began with a quest: "Go to the church past the Rotonda." It wasn't the easiest instruction to follow in Thessaloniki, a northern Greek city with at least twenty churches, but I made my way there, weaving between the traffic and passersby. History juts out at you from every corner, each chapel and tower tempting you to examine it. I even passed an archaeological dig. The men and women in their T-shirts and dusty jeans peered up and smiled at me, but I was interested in a different exhumation. One that had just happened at this mysterious church I had been told about, which had uncovered a piece of history that many in Thessaloniki would probably prefer to forget.

Eventually I found it. The Church of Acheiropoietos is a rounded, fifth-century basilica that nestles below street level, which meant I could look down into its gardens from above. And there, slumped on the ground, was what I had been searching for: a slab of white-gray rock, resting under the shelter of an olive tree. It was a tombstone, or what was left of one. On three of its sides were the marks where it had been torn away from its greater parts, and on the other were the beginnings of three Hebrew inscriptions.

What are broken Jewish tombstones doing in a Greek Orthodox church? Thessaloniki's Jews were never buried here. From the fifteenth century onward, five hundred thousand people were buried in a vast Jewish necropolis, which today lies on the site of Aristotle University. The journey that their tombstones had taken, removed from the cemetery and stacked in a pile in a church garden a kilometer away, was part of the reason I had flown to Thessaloniki.

This was once home to the largest Jewish community in Greece, and its members were Sephardic, as are their descendants living here today. This means that, unlike the Ashkenazim of Eastern Europe, the overwhelming majority of Thessaloniki's Jews can trace their ancestry back to the Iberian peninsula, which they have always called Sefarad. Sefarad is so old that a prophet in the Hebrew Bible—Obadiah—mentions it as a refuge for exiled Jews following the ancient sack of Jerusalem, half a millennium before Christ. One day, he said, the children of Sefarad would return to inherit the lands the Babylonians had taken from them.

But a different exile, and expulsion, awaited the people of Sefarad. Around the world, you may come across surnames like Lopes, De Cordova, and Toledano that still carry the ancestry of Spanish and Portuguese Jews who were expelled from the Iberian peninsula following its bloodthirsty Reconquista, led most notably by Spain's "Catholic monarchs," Isabella and Ferdinand. The Christian victory over the region's Muslim rulers culminated in the 1492 Alhambra Decree that commanded Jews either convert or leave. The Ottoman Empire, where Jews were recognized as Dhimmis—non-Muslims entitled to legal protection—offered a safe haven in the Mediterranean, away from the violence of medieval Western Europe. Soon, new synagogues sprouted in Thessaloniki, known under the Ottoman Empire as Selânik and Salonika by the families who had left Iberia. This port city had hosted a Jewish population of varying sizes since Roman times; now, a new community grew up, founding places of worship that carried the names of the homes they left behind: Lizbon, Aragon, Katalan. Many would have country- or island-hopped to get to Salonika, picking up words along the way, which is why their language sounds and reads like fifteenth-century Spanish, peppered with words from Hebrew, Arabic, Turkish, Greek, and Italian, as well as many other language varieties long disappeared. The resulting language is a time capsule, rich in Jewish tradition and alive with five hundred years of European history in exile. It is known by many names: Judeo-Spanish, Ladino, Judesmo, or Haketia, depending on where you find it or whether it is spoken or written. In this chapter, I will call the language Ladino, by far the most widespread and most frequently used name for it today.

The tombstone I was looking down on was one of only three occasions I would find Ladino written anywhere in Thessaloniki. Yet less than a century ago more people spoke it here than Greek. The story of Ladino—and particularly the variety of it spoken here in Thessaloniki—will show us what happens to a language when its speakers are in exile. In many ways, the language is a marvel, a testament to the survival instincts of a language that, like its people, finds life in every new home it creates. But its lifeline depended on a time where people lived within walking distance from their synagogue, ensconced in a neighborhood where they knew they could find the kosher food they needed and work to pay their way. The Ottoman Turks had no word in their language for "minority,"[1] yet they had many millets, autonomous religious communities in charge of their own, local responsibilities like internal security or taxes. Modern nation-states are not so relaxed about allowing communities to self-organize or about nurturing linguistic diversity either. There are similarities here to emigrant language loss—languages plucked from their homes and battling against the odds in diaspora—but with a major difference to emigrants like my grandparents: Refugees do not choose to leave their homes, and stateless refugees can hope for no support from their place of origin. A language in exile survives only for as long as its community of speakers is protected. Without a powerful nation-state to defend it, the only people who Ladino speakers in this city could ever really rely on were themselves. Just a handful still live here, in the city once called la madre de Israel.

I took pictures of the tombstone shards and then turned back toward the busy streets again. I had another quest to pursue now—to find the only man left in this city who could decipher them.

■ ■ ■

It is very tempting, in the world of endangered languages, to be drawn into the search for the "last speaker." Countless news articles have been written about these quasi-mythical individuals believed to be the last native speakers of a dying language. Obviously, it's unlikely to be an identity someone has willingly chosen, and they're even less likely to be happy about it, particularly as they presumably no longer have anyone to speak with. A few around the world are memorialized by their tombstones, including in the UK, where a stout obelisk in a Cornish churchyard reads

> Here lieth interred Dorothy Pentreath who died in 1777, said to have been the last person who conversed in the ancient Cornish. The regular language of this county from the earliest records till it expired in the eighteenth century in this Parish of Saint Paul.

Not long after her death, at least six other speakers appear to have emerged, though by the end of the century they, too, would pass. This is why the search for a last speaker is often a futile one: It is very difficult for linguists to confirm whether someone really *is* the last speaker after all. In a village in northwestern Turkey, another tombstone remembers Tevfik Esenç. It reads:

> *Tevfik Esenç*
> *Recite a Fatiha* [the first chapter of the Qur'an] *for his soul*

Who immortalized the Ubykh language,
the last Ubykh who could write and speak this language.

Ubykh has a similar origin story to Ladino. It was born in the Caucasus, then transposed to the Ottoman Empire as its Muslim speakers fled imperial Russian persecution in the nineteenth century. Esenç had worked with linguists for decades before his death in the nineties, allowing them to catalog Ubykh's whopping eighty-three consonants and just three vowel sounds. Besides Africa's "clicking" languages, this is one of the highest consonant inventories on the planet, and had French linguists not found Esenç in time, in 1930, we would have little record of it. Georges Dumézil, who interviewed him, wrote that Esenç "is aware that the language will be lost" and that it gave him pride "to record the funeral of his ancestors' language on tape."

Another linguist called Meral Kafa, of Ubykh heritage herself, wrote in 2020 about the last time she visited Esenç. He told a story from his sickbed that she could only half understand. She could not hold back her tears. "Twenty-eight years ago today," she wrote, "I witnessed the end of a language, moment by moment, and listened to the last sounds of my ancestral tongue." In Esenç's final tape, he pleaded that if there was another Ubykh speaker out there and they heard mistakes in his recording, they should provide their corrections. Though there are those who wish to revive Ubykh, it seems as if linguists were accurate in identifying Esenç as its last native speaker, as no one has come forward since. "This is how I end Ubykh," he said. "May God grant you goodness and beauty! The Ubykh language ends here."

The Ubykh language, like its people, found a refuge for the last one hundred years of its life in the country that became Turkey. Sephardic Jews, on the other hand, came to the Ottoman Empire and wider Mediterranean much earlier, following their medieval expulsion from Iberia. Forced conversions, and the policing of heresy, had meant that anyone seen avoiding pork or even relaxing too much on a Saturday could find themselves at the sharp end of an interrogation, expropriated of their assets, or worse. Three hundred thousand Jews are believed to have been forced to convert, flee, or die at the hands of the Spanish Inquisition. They found several cities in which to flourish, like Venice, Amsterdam, and Ferrara in Italy, where the Ferrara Bible was published in 1553. It was a word-for-word translation of the Hebrew Bible, written specifically for Sephardic Jews who had lost literacy in Hebrew but were more than capable of following along in their own Hispanic language. At the time it was simply named Biblia en Lengua Española—"Bible in the Spanish Language." Conducting such a translation—bringing a non-Romance language into a Romance one—was known as fazer el ladino, "making it Latin." The name Ladino for the language itself probably derived from this practice, one that would have been incredibly active for a population now living in diaspora and attempting to reconnect with their Jewish roots. They took to publishing prayer books, grammar books, and even plays in Ladino. The same happened in the Ottoman Empire, where, in order to encourage the learning of Hebrew, Hebrew-Ladino glossaries accompanied an explosion of printing in Ladino works of science, ethics, and philosophy.

The languages, skills, and experiences that exiled Jews brought with them did not escape the notice of contemporaries. A French geographer from the 1500s, Nicolas de Nicolay, wrote that European countries lost out when its Jewish communities left, because the Jews brought everything they knew to the enemy Turks instead, like "divers inventions, crafts and engines of warre" as well as "printing, not before seen in those countries, by the which in faire characters they put in light divers books in diverse languages as Greek, Latin, Italian, Spanish and the Hebrew tongue." Salonika became one such city, transformed by Sephardic creativity into a new Jerusalem. A Toledan sailor, Diego Galan, who traveled to Salonika in the late

1500s, said that the city's Jews spoke "Castilian as fine and well-accented as in the imperial capital" a century after they had been expelled.

When I first heard Jacky Benmayor's voice, I thought something similar; I recognized my Spanish in Jacky's djudeo-espanyol, as he calls it. We had no problem understanding each other, which was great news as he was the person I had been looking for, the only one in Thessaloniki who could give me more information about the tombstones. In 2022, the *Greek Herald* newspaper wrote that Jacky Benmayor was "the last speaker in Greece of a Jewish language close to extinction." I'm not sure how true this is; when I went to interview David Saltiel, the president of the Central Board of Jewish Communities in Greece, he proudly told me *he* spoke Ladino, too. Either way, one thing is fairly certain. While Jacky may not quite be the last person left who can speak and understand Ladino in Thessaloniki, he's certainly the most learned, and he is absolutely *one of* the last heritage speakers of the Salonikan Ladino that thrived here a century ago. He is, at the time of writing, seventy-seven years old. When I met him, he did not look his age—he was tall and tanned—although he was laboring with a great wheezing cough. Sometimes he took lengthy pauses before he spoke, as if he were riffling through his mind to find what he was looking for.

Jacky can trace his family's direct presence in Salonika to the nineteenth century, but based on his surname he suspects they are descended from the Jews who were expelled from the island of Majorca in the 1400s. Ben—Hebrew for "son"—is combined with mayor—Spanish for "older"—and good recordkeeping in Thessaloniki's synagogues shows Benmayores among the members of the two Majorca synagogues. Jacky has lived in the same apartment I met him in with his wife for more than thirty years, and it overlooks the same sea his ancestors crossed hundreds of years ago. When I first contacted him I wrote to him in Spanish, and he replied to me in Ladino. His emails glittered with *k*s, a letter alien in Spanish, but a staple of his espanyol. "Me plaze su enteres por la lingua djudeo-espanyola i sto disposto a enkontrarmos i rakontarle la mia esperyensa kon esta lingua, un poko de su storya i su situation en el mundo i spesyalmente en Saloniko oy." Without consulting a Ladino dictionary, I understood it: "I'm happy about your interest in the Ladino language and I am ready to meet and tell the story of my experience with this language, a little on its history and its situation in the world, and especially in Thessaloniki today." But some of Jacky's words escaped me; he wrote that he was unsure whether he would be able to have me round to his flat as the boyadjis were over. "I could have said 'painter' to you," he said when I met him, beginning to laugh, "but I wanted you to look it up!"

Ladino preserves the Latin "f," which, in today's Spanish, has since changed to a silent "h"; you can see that in the word "son," which is fižo. In Spanish, it's hijo, with both words deriving from the Latin filius. Even so, most words are familiar to me unless the domain switches to anything connected to Jewish ritual or culture, where the lexicon becomes Hebrew, although a lot of them have been Spanishified; jérem, the Hebrew for excommunication, has been turned into the verb enjeremar in Ladino. Jacky's boyadjis is a Turkish acquisition, as are lots of words that refer to state administration or public life, like a court—jukyumét—or askyér—army. At one point in our conversation Jacky quoted a poem that had the word fustaan in it, which I recognized from Arabic, meaning dress. French, too, gave Ladino many loan words as it was a prestige language within the Ottoman Empire: A shower became duš, a young mademoiselle a mamazél.

Ladino's magpie charm, collecting words here and there, has formed a formidable Mediterranean lingua franca. I felt sad when it occurred to me that maybe languages like this don't really exist anymore because English and French have become European lingua francas instead, and that for most European languages loan words are ever heavier loads of Anglicisms rather than being from a wide variety of their neighbors' languages. I took my phone out to show him the photos I had taken of the broken tombstones, but he wasn't able to make anything of them: They were too fragmented to read. He was able to show me photographs of other shards he had been sent by the Central Board of Jewish Communities, and began reading a large stone segment, the only one of its size that seems to have been recovered from the church. He read a long phrase in Hebrew that I didn't understand, followed by the phrase "edad de ocho años."

"Eight years old!" I translated. It was exactly like Spanish.

"Yes," Jacky said, and continued to read. "Ayum . . . that is Hebrew again, for 'today' . . . they died in 5676 . . . that's the beginning of the twentieth century."

Jacky needs both his Ladino and the Hebrew he studied to read these tombstones—the year he is referring to is from the Hebrew calendar—and this combination of languages is rare in Thessaloniki. He has told the local press that he has had to transcribe and transport so many tombstones, discovered all over Thessaloniki, that he no longer feels emotional about it. Clearly, neither does the Greek state nor the media: The discovery of the tomb shards that I saw received no coverage in the Greek press. I only found out about them because the Central Board had told me about it in passing.

The reason the tombstones are scattered across the city, far from their first resting place, is because the original Jewish cemetery—a necropolis that once held five hundred thousand bodies—was razed to the ground in 1942 during the Second World War, when the Nazis occupied the city. With the support of local Greek authorities, they destroyed one of Europe's largest Jewish cemeteries. Really, however, they finished off what the Greek government had been trying to do for years without success; throughout the early 1900s, modernization and new urban planning were being introduced around Greece to "deturkify" the country following the collapse of the Ottoman Empire. When fires destroyed much of Thessaloniki in the 1910s, the authorities took advantage of the damage to rebuild the city in the country's new national image. In 1929, a part of the Jewish necropolis was singled out by the Ministries of Welfare and Agriculture for expropriation. All graves were to be transferred, regardless of religious doctrine, and a university was to be built on the land in their place. In Jewish law, a burial ground is sacred, and graves must remain undisturbed in perpetuity. Sephardic newspapers—there were around eight published in the city—were furious at the decision, which one editor called "an irreparable disaster for Sephardi Jewry . . . a true national catastrophe."

Years later, under the fascist regime of Greek dictator Ioannis Metaxas, it was decided that thirty-three thousand hectares would be given over to the university. The government would be responsible for excavating the tombstones, collecting the dead, and transferring them to another part of the cemetery; the length of time this would take would also allow for a full survey of the tombstones and inscriptions, thus helping to preserve their historical value. But this didn't happen. Slow progress, and the state's reluctance to build a new cemetery for Jewish burials, meant that the cemetery continued to expand. Without knowing it, Ladino speakers were burying their dead in the same place they had done for six hundred years, for what was most likely the last time.

On April 6, 1941, German troops entered Thessaloniki. A team studying "world Jewry" was deployed to scour the city, plundering its libraries and synagogues. They were perplexed by Thessaloniki, with one Nazi asking where the ghetto was; in the city that had welcomed thousands of Jews centuries ago, there had never been a need for one. Heinrich Himmler warned Hitler that Thessaloniki's Jews would pose a threat to German security in the city, and by the following year all male Jews aged between eighteen and forty-five were ordered to present themselves for registration so that they could be used for forced labor. Nine thousand Jewish men waited in queues for hours, forbidden from eating or drinking, and bullied into a circus of gymnastic exercises by Germans.

After several months of this torment, the community managed to pay a ransom to the Germans to free them, but there was a catch: Now that the community had their working men back, they could start transferring all of the necropolis's graves and build a new Jewish cemetery. When the chief rabbi said that this would be impossible to do so quickly and that they would need to begin work after the winter, the municipality ordered the cemetery's immediate demolition. One survivor described the devastating rush of family members to their relatives' tombs; his own went to recover the body of his twenty-year-old brother who had died on a trip to Rome. His coffin was opened, where "my poor brother appeared in his smocking and his pointed shoes as though he had been put there yesterday. My mother fainted." They removed what bodies they could. Without a full survey, and without the consent of the community, the necropolis was obliterated.

But it was not only a city of the dead; it was a city of words, with many of the tombs bearing Ladino script. When the cemetery was smashed to pieces by workmen, so, too, was the most visible presence of Ladino in the city. The broken shards of the tombs, and the disembodied words that they carried, were looted by Greek authorities and turned into building blocks for their new, modern city. The Greek Orthodox Church I had been directed to was one such beneficiary, which had evidently used these stones to rebuild following the war. A shared belief in God—the same shared belief that had once granted the Jews protection in Thessaloniki under the Ottoman Muslims—was not enough to influence the Christians' treatment of the Jewish dead.

Think for a moment about the many other monuments in Greece that have been preserved in the name of cultural heritage, including the cemeteries of ancient Greeks. What was it that made the Jewish necropolis less worthy of preservation? There was no international outcry in the chaos of war over its annihilation, no alarm sounded over this early sign of genocide. Salonika's Jews were untethered from a Jewish nation, a Spanish nation, or, apparently, their own Greek nation. This is the fate of a persecuted minority and all that they carry, including their language; if they can only rely on themselves, they have little defense when a dominant culture decides it's time to eradicate their presence or history.

To date, the community has never been compensated for the expropriation of their land and the destruction of their burial ground. All you will find in Thessaloniki is a memorial that stands in the middle of the university grounds, established in 2014 after years of campaigning, with signs in multiple languages, including Ladino, detailing what happened there. Te topas en lugar santo, it says in Ladino—you're stepping on sacred ground. But it doesn't only document the destruction of the cemetery, for there was worse to come. Soon the inscriptions, the dictionaries, the newspapers, and the whole teeming life of Sephardic thought and language would come to a terrifying halt.

■ ■ ■

Imagine a guitar and an accordion accompanying a delicate soprano voice, rising up a scale. "Un dia de Saba amanesyo," the voice starts to sing, to the tune of 1939's popular German tune "Bel Ami": "at the break of dawn one Sabbath."

> No savemos lo ke akontesyo
> La djuderia ya fue asserada en los ghettos de la siudad.[2]

> We don't know what happened
> They locked up the Jews in the ghettos of the city.

I am listening to a collection of songs that have been exhaustively gathered, researched, and performed by Greek soprano Mariangela Chatzistamatiou. She is not Jewish, but was asked several years ago to give a performance of Ladino songs at a Hanukkah meal in the

Greek city of Volos. The concert went so well that more and more invitations from Jewish clubs started pouring in, but with her popularity came a challenge. Mariangela realized that she was singing the same repertoire over and over again, and that she wasn't clear which were Sephardic songs from elsewhere in Europe and which were songs that had actually been written or sung in Greece. I met Mariangela in the library of the Jewish Museum of Thessaloniki, where she has studied among its dense wooden shelves for years, poring over books for any musical reference to the songs that were once commonly sung here. She hoped she would gradually be able to grow her repertoire and better serve the communities asking her to sing. Instead, the journey has ended up taking her a lot deeper into Jewish musical history and much farther away than Thessaloniki. All the way to Auschwitz-Birkenau.

In "Un dia de Saba amanesyo," the singer recalls the events of the Nazi occupation when Thessaloniki's Jews were sent to a ghetto in the western quarter of the city. It ends the last verse burning with rancor: "a la fin lo van a gumitar," "in the end they will rue what they have done." This was before they were ordered onto the train and a journey that most would never return from. "Bel Ami" is quite an uplifting tune, and the lyrics can feel incongruous with the melody. Perhaps the rousing music was a call to action. Mariangela, who played me this song from a CD player in the empty library, thought so, too. She said, "We have several cases of people who were able to survive through music. Either because they played or because they sang, or because they could get some courage and some strength to last another day."

By the time Ladino-speaking Jews were composing songs in the camps, the lyrics deepen in their despair. "Padre mio mi keridoi," wrote David Haim, who survived Auschwitz and emigrated to Israel. "Kyen te lo iva dezir ke veniryias kon tu ermano / Il rekmatoryo de Aushvits." "My beloved father. Who would have told you that you would come, together with your brother, to the Crematorium of

Auschwitz." It was sung to the tune of a Turkish melody—another contrafactum, a new song using the music of an old one—and is one of the only examples we have of music from a Holocaust survivor and composer. The Sephardic musical tradition is enormous, and was in fact my first contact with the language. I saw Mor Karbasi performing on television one morning, singing a ballad and using a language that was at once extremely familiar and, in certain phrases, completely different, using the kind of melodies I recognized from flamenco music. The subject matter can be similar to flamenco, too: unrequited love, marriage, death, even songs about kings and queens that date back to medieval Spain. My favorite song of Karbasi's, "Asentada en mi ventana," tells the story of a young woman sitting at a window despairing because her lover is marrying someone else. He sends her bonbonicos to eat, presumably sweets that were given out as favors by newlyweds, and she sings about how bitterly she ate them because he was another woman's bridegroom.

Listening to Mariangela's musical research, you can hear the dark, moody Phrygian mode used so often in Spain alongside Turkish and Italian opera melodies, encapsulating the journey of Thessaloniki's Jews through Europe. "As time passes, the music becomes more simple," she said, which is apparently an indication of it becoming more and more influenced by Greek traditional music. In researching one song, she found no sheet music for it in Greece, but did find music for almost identical lyrics in the Sephardic tradition of Bosnia and Herzegovina. As the city's Jews were sent to Auschwitz, these songs of heartache and loss traveled with them.

Ninety-four percent of Thessaloniki's Jewish population were murdered in the Holocaust.[3] Just twelve hundred Greek Jews live in the city today, compared with approximately fifty thousand living there in the late 1930s. It is one of the many reasons why today's Ladino-speaking population predominantly resides in countries like Israel and the United States, to where speakers fled for the umpteenth time in their history to find refuge following the Second World War. The precise number of speakers is not known, but estimates range from sixty thousand to two hundred thousand, which probably encapsulates a wide range of linguistic abilities. Ladino is described as moribund, or nearly extinct, as it is no longer spoken as a mother tongue even in the countries with a higher saturation of speakers. In Israel, which is believed to have the highest concentration of speakers, most young people will grow up speaking Hebrew and English instead.

One could argue that this decline was always to be the fate of Ladino in the twentieth century. With the rise of early modern nation-states, Thessaloniki's Jews had increasingly already been speaking Greek. A leading Jewish journalist wrote in 1939[4] that "assimilation to Hellenism" had been so successful in Salonika following Greek independence that "even when we speak Judesmo, one still sees we are Hellenes. Judeo-Spanish, which once overflowed with Turkish words . . . today shows clear signs of Greek influence." Thessaloniki had only been annexed to Greece in 1912; from that point, Jewish children were taught Greek at school for the very first time, and this rapidly changed their linguistic worlds. In another newspaper, a reader asked for pages to be printed in Greek, because "as things are going, in time readers of Judeo-Spanish will be rare, since the younger people are reading Greek newspapers more, and in the schools Judeo-Spanish is no longer studied."

Mariangela witnessed it in her research, too; in studying the songs of the Holocaust, she discovered a significant repertoire of Greek as well as Ladino songs. None of these had been investigated before; historians and musicologists knew about Yiddish songs and orchestral music at the death camps, but very little about the musical production of Greek Jews. As she gathered material, she realized that the songs that were written in the ghettos of Thessaloniki were in Ladino, while the songs in Auschwitz had largely switched to Greek, perhaps motivated by the melting pot of countries they found themselves in. As people were away from their city, their lyrics, Mariangela has found, sang of patrida, the Greek word for fatherland, of Thessaloniki and the Greek flag. The Jews of Thessaloniki had long been Salonikan, but it is clear from some of the last songs many sung and wrote that they were becoming Greek and Jewish, not one or the other.

But if this trend had persisted, without the cataclysmic German invasion, the sheer volume of Ladino speakers still identifying as Jewish in Salonika might have acted as a protective shield, ensuring that the next generation still had many elders from whom to hear the language. Language revival and reclamation efforts would have had more heritage speakers to work with, more material and an entire necropolis to study; Jacky wouldn't be one of the only speakers left. Crucially, more speakers of Jacky's father's generation would have survived into the era of modern technology, where so much more could have been recorded and saved from elders to preserve the distinctly Salonikan variety of Ladino.

The Nazi occupation, Greek collaboration, and the Holocaust led to the mass murder of Ladino speakers, but also to the destruction of vital books, graves, and artifacts, along with a legacy of generational trauma that meant that the number of speakers could never recover in Salonika. That Mariangela is the first who has tried to uncover this lost Sephardic musical heritage is perhaps indicative of a lack of wider national support, and she suggested that it hasn't been the easiest journey convincing researchers in Greece that these songs were worthy of academic inquiry. "I always wondered why people don't pay attention, because people don't care about the music. They don't think it's significant. They want to focus on other things. But there is a time for everything."

There is *especially* time for music, a key tool for language reclamation. In South Africa, a house genre called Kwaito has been found to promote South African identity through the use of non-English local languages,[5] just as a Welsh pop revival has been found to have strengthened young people's connection to Welsh culture. In the Tiwi Islands of Australia, archival recordings of long-deceased singers have been revived by performances from the community's elders to engage children in their language, which has just over two thousand speakers, and with the oral tradition that has carried it for so long.[6] Speakers of Basque and of Scottish Gaelic, both endangered languages, have used song in ingenious ways to revive them; one vocal group from the Basque diaspora in California performs songs that preserve noka, a traditional form of address used toward women in whom one could confide. In Nova Scotia, "transcription frolics" gathering groups of speakers have been organized to crowdsource the documenting of Gaelic song lyrics in a vast database.[7] Two of the revivalists involved in these projects have argued that the pleasure of music is an overlooked solution to language decline, in a field dominated by serious discussions of sociolinguistics and education. They point out that, as well as making us human, "music and musicking are also just plain fun—and as such, we suggest, amenable to teaching the languages they use, whether or not language learning is the goal of musicking or not."

I got to capture some Sephardic musicking myself when I headed to the top floor of the Thessaloniki Jewish community's headquarters to watch a choir rehearsal. The Jewish choir, made up of men and women my parents' age, were preparing for a performance later that day in honor of Sukkot, the festival commemorating God's protection of the Hebrew people when they were freed from bondage in Egypt. They were going to sing a Ladino song, "Adio kerida." "Goodbye, beloved" it means, and its origins are lost to time, although the first line sounds eerily similar to the first sung bar of Verdi's "Addio del passato."

According to Mariangela, an urban legend recalls Verdi hearing the song from a Jewish neighbor rather than Jews taking it from an opera, but it is unlikely we will ever know in which direction the music went. One of the singers, Hannah, who is also the general secretary of the Jewish community of Thessaloniki, told me, "I know a little, not enough" of Ladino; her English was excellent, and that's what we spoke. "You know enough to sing it?" I asked her. "I know enough to sing," she replied proudly. "I'm learning. I'm always learning." I thought about the songs I sang for Nonna; how I have lots to learn, too.

Singing in Ladino "is a very emotional experience," Hannah said. "My father said, if somebody spoke it, they can communicate with all the people and all the languages in Europe."

I asked her whether she connected with her religion when she sang in this choir, as well as with the language. "To be Jewish is not only to be religious," she answered. "It's many things. It's a way of life. How you live. What you eat. How you speak. It is all the life. And the songs—we have the songs."

Like my treasured "Asentada en mi ventana," the singer of "Adio kerida" laments how her lover has made them feel. *No kero la vida / me l'amargates tu*—I don't want to live, you embittered me. Perhaps that is what the original composer was writing about—a love gone sour. But later singers turned to "Adio kerida" to commemorate the Holocaust and to the nihilism and pain of losing a loved one. And now it appears to be acquiring new meaning, not only among Salonika's Jews but as an anthem for the global Sephardic community, across the former Ottoman Empire, the Americas, and elsewhere. I have found films made from Cuba to Sarajevo in the last twenty years, which have been titled *Adio kerida*, each one about a different Sephardic community, but all with the same story—their language and their traditional ways of life are fast disappearing. Even now, six hundred years after they were expelled from Spain, Sephardic Jews are finding new meaning in their centuries-old story of a people long exiled and long persecuted; where descendants are mourning the loss of a blazing zenith of Jewish identity in the Mediterranean.

■ ■ ■

"After your generation in Thessaloniki, do you think Judeo-Espanyol will disappear?" I asked Jacky, back in his flat.

"Yes," he said. I waited, wondering if he was going to elaborate. But he didn't; he was definitive.

"And how does that make you feel?" I asked.

"A little bit sorry," he said, thinking. "But I can't do anything about that. I proposed to the Jewish department at the university that I am ready to educate a young person to continue the job we started, but . . ." He tapered off.

It was clearly challenging getting support for this in Thessaloniki; projects here have often been funded by international, Jewish-led organizations. However, support might also come from another government—the Spanish one. A decade ago they offered a path to citizenship to anyone who could trace Sephardic Jewish ancestry, pass a Spanish (not Ladino) test, and do a citizenship exam (and, of course, have the personal funds to pay for the application, which involved a trip to Spain). The call for prospective citizens lasted from 2015 till around 2019, and this year the government has reported that about 75,000 descendants have obtained Spanish citizenship, out of an estimated 3:5 million Sephardic people worldwide. Before it was approved, the justice minister Rafael Catala said: "This law says much about who we were in the past and who we are today and what we want to be in the future: an open, diverse and tolerant Spain."[8] The Spanish government also helped set up an academy for Ladino in Israel, which is funded by the Israeli government, and promised to assist elsewhere with their language academy, the Instituto de Cervantes.

In practice, it sounds as if this hasn't completely come to fruition yet. I had read in the press about a much-vaunted Judeo-Spanish language program that was supposed to be introduced here by the instituto, but when I inquired about it, all these years after it was first promoted, they were only offering Spanish classes. Por el momento no impartimos clases de judeo-español aunque está también entre nuestros objetivos, I was told—they aren't teaching Judeo-Spanish, although it is one of their goals.

While the execution might be patchy so far, the mere fact that the Spanish government should feel that they, and not only Jewish communities, are responsible for Ladino's survival, speaks to a rarely offered form of linguistic repentance that other countries could learn from. A few years ago, the linguist Ghil'ad Zuckermann called for the creation of a Native Tongue Title in Australia, where he has conducted a great deal of fieldwork and has assisted in language reclamation for indigenous communities. Native Titles there help restore property rights to Aboriginal groups that have been dispossessed; Zuckermann proposes a linguistic compensation scheme that mimics it, the Native Tongue Titles. Unlike existing grant schemes that are competitive and may be rescinded by hostile governments, a broader, national compensation scheme could bring them the "explicit legal protection" they are entitled to. A 2017 study found that language-related projects attracted only a small amount of funding in Australia compared with the wider pool available from federal and state Aboriginal affairs departments; assuming that offering grants instead of laws will save languages is naive at best and linguistically fatal at worst. Both grants and laws would, I'm sure, be a huge boost for many languages around the world.

In the meantime, however, some Spaniards are trying to reclaim Ladino as a language for Spain. In 2014, when the linguist Carlos Yebra López was on a work visit to Israel, he was invited to a concert and heard Yasmin Levy sing—you've guessed it—"Adio kerida." He asked where she'd learned Spanish, because her adios had no *s* and her querida had a *k*. He was shocked by his own naivety when he learned this was Ladino, a language that began in Spain, and that he, a Spaniard, had never heard of it. He has since dedicated years of his life learning the language, to interviewing speakers, and building a digital archive called Ladino 21, with more than 383 interviews and informative videos on the language. "I consider Judeo-Spanish as part of my story, as part of the story of the Iberian peninsula," he told me. He said that people within and outside Spain see it as only a Catholic country. "Learning and teaching Judeo-Spanish for me is reclaiming the diversity of my own heritage, of my linguistic heritage."

Fortunately for budding learners in Thessaloniki, Jacky Benmayor has also been teaching Ladino; without the missing course from the Spanish government, it's the only way to learn Ladino in the whole city. He has taught it for four years at Aristotle University, the same university that was built over the Jewish burial grounds. It is mainly Greek students without Jewish heritage who appear to take it. "They want to learn it because it's something that has been hidden from them," Jacky explained. He isn't sure how many have taken his classes, particularly as "you start with twenty-seven and finish with seven." It sounds suspiciously like my Arabic class at university, which began with around forty and ended with less than half that number. Jacky thinks at least twenty have studied it diligently in the time he has taught. He has accomplished all this as a retired businessman, and I somehow suspect he's not going to slow down over the next few years. He stood up from his sofa and walked over to his computer, slowly and with a thick, chesty cough that accompanied my entire interview with him. "Let me show you," he said. "I have the first lesson for beginners tomorrow." He opened up a resource that he uses, although he complained about it; it started with teaching *hi, how are you*. "We don't use it!" he said. "I like things that are more interesting." He showed me some poems, heavy with nostalgia and written by a Salonikan poet who now lives in Israel, which he prefers to teach.

Jacky's father, Leon, was the only member of his entire family to survive the Holocaust, and Jacky credits him and his return to Salonika with his Ladino fluency. Leon was buried with a tombstone engraved in Hebrew, Ladino, and Greek, and even a lyric from an Italian song I know well: "Non ti scordar di me": "Don't forget me." Leon loved to sing it. Popular Italian songs clearly traveled easily to Thessaloniki, and in Mariangela's Holocaust collection I found another familiar face: "Mamma, son tanto felice," an Italian song about returning to your mother after a long period of separation. A song doesn't have to be in Ladino for Sephardic Jews to look after it as if it were their own. As guardians of one of the most kaleidoscopic lingua francas of the Mediterranean, their heritage has preserved many others.

Though Jacky is not a singer, his name came up again when I was talking to Mariangela. "I always go to him before I publish something," she told me. She explained that a lot of people perform a Ladino repertoire with a Spanish accent and pronunciation rather than an authentic Ladino one. "He teaches me how to pronounce it properly." It helps to have "that verification—that what we produce comes from the community."

Jacky hadn't mentioned his work with Mariangela when I interviewed him, and it occurred to me that he has probably advised and educated countless researchers over the years. He doesn't boast about it, and I wondered how much of his assistance has gone unrecorded. Happily, there are active revival efforts around the world for Ladino in general, but the idiosyncrasies of the Salonikan variety are far more vulnerable. Whoever it is that gets involved now—be it Greece, Spain, or Israel—all they can hope to do is recover a fragment of a language that nobody previously cared to protect. Salonikan Ladino will survive in song form in the city's Jewish spaces, but when Jacky eventually passes, it is not only a language variety that will disappear, but a library—somewhere to study, to consult, and to leave enriched by scholarship. I think a person can be a living library, as much as a place can. This city, which has already lost so much, is set to lose much more.

THE STORY OF KARUK

> **uknîi:** "a story from the time of creation is about to
> be recited"[1]

When Maymi was pregnant with her first child, she had a dream that would alter the course of her life forever. "It sounds wishy-washy," she said, "but in the dream I was talking to my niece. She was nonverbal at the time, and I was holding a baby, and I said to her: 'Xurish is going to start speaking before you. You need to start talking.'"

When Maymi woke up to her belly and still-unborn child, she wondered: What does xurish mean? This was a decade ago, when some of the elders of her tribe were still alive, so she went to her friend's grandmother to ask. "The child must be hungry for acorns," the elder explained. "Xurish means acorn meat."

Few words get more Karuk than xurish; the *kh* at the start and the *ish* that suffixes so much of its vocabulary. It sounds like the noise the Klamath River is making below Maymi and me, sitting high above its forceful flow, on a cliff edge overlooking the dense redwood forest of Northern California. It's ironic that the English word "acorn" is one of the few that has been taken as a loan word in Karuk because the tribe has at least ten words for the many types and uses of acorn that the Karuk values. A generic, catchall term for *any* kind of acorn didn't exist in Karuk—until the white settlers came.

Maymi ate the acorn meat. By the time her son was born, named

Xurish, her knowledge of Karuk had been transformed. Now she has three children, and as we speak her middle son Dennis is making a thorough inspection of the scenery around us, gathering oak galls and obsidian till his pockets bulge. Each new item of flora he notices is named, once in English and then often in Karuk, too, as if each were an aide-mémoire to the other.

It is a very different life from the one that Maymi could have had. She remembers when she was at university, trying to get an education that would lift her above the poverty line she had lived under her entire childhood; she would have panic attacks when she found out that yet another elder in her community had died. "I thought: 'The language is going to die. It's going to die in our generation.'"

Now, more than ten years later, almost all of Maymi's young family speak Karuk. But in the rest of this vast forest spreading out beneath our feet, there are barely twelve adult speakers left.

■ ■ ■

It is often the case that a people who've lost their language have also lost their land, and there's possibly no better place to tell this story than here where the West Coast meets the Pacific Northwest. California is the most linguistically diverse area in North America, and was even more so just two centuries ago. Twenty known language families have been estimated in the state, mothering between eighty and ninety different individual languages, of which over half are now fully dormant. For perspective, there are currently twenty-four official languages in the European Union, and just three main language families (Slavic, Germanic, and Romance) across the whole continent. Some of California's linguistic richness is down to geography—a coastline, dense forests veined with rivers and creeks, mountains. Another related reason is that it took the English-speaking colonizers of North America a very long time to head all the way over to the west of the continent as the early United States was being formed. In California, Spanish colonizers only went as far north as Santa Barbara.

In the 1800s there were about three thousand speakers of Karuk. The tribe is one of California's largest, and their ancestral lands stretch over 1,600 square miles along the Klamath River. The swoop of the valleys and the web of rivers prevent easy navigation, making it fertile ground for language diversity. This is how language worked before the foundation of modern nation-states, especially in highly biodiverse parts of the world; one region housed many languages, and everyone would have possessed a certain level of multilingualism or at least mutual intelligibility. In Northern California, you would speak Karuk in Karuk territory, and the minute you crossed into another tribe's home you'd speak their language. That's why a language with "only" three thousand speakers was capable of lasting so long. Your language signified your identity, and someone else's language signified theirs. Simple enough for people whose way of life had gone largely unchanged for centuries.

Karuk territory today is hours away from the nearest city. To find Maymi, I drove with Ollie, a local reporter, high into the thick woodland of Humboldt County, where stately redwoods and tan oaks stood generations old. I had been staying in Arcata, a small town on the coast where the nearby forests are heavily promoted as camping and hiking destinations. But there wasn't a hiker in sight. We passed through the Hoopa Tribe Reservation, belonging to one of the only California Native American tribes who were not forced to move off their original lands. A lack of signage, unusual in big, brash America, made the roads look strangely anonymous—you couldn't tell what any building was for—and we passed in silence. In a couple of hours we arrived at an outpost by the Salmon River, the only place to get any internet in Karuk territory, and while we sat with the windows open, waiting for a message from Maymi, we were eyed quietly by passing locals. I'd have been watching me, too, if I lived somewhere with a history like Humboldt County's.

When Maymi found us, she took us to Katimiîn, a historic village that was the center of the world in Karuk spirituality. The scent of cedarwood spiced the air as she led me to a seat on a log next to an enormous earth-charred pit circled with wood. It was a brush dance pit that was in the process of being rebuilt, she explained, which was once used to help heal children. But the cedarwood they need to rebuild it is hard to come by. "Cedarwood is endangered now. We build our houses from it because it can't get black mold. But the trucks here have brought in a disease that kills it. It took the tribe ten years to get enough wood to do this," she said, gesturing at the logs around us. Trucks had indeed been the only other traffic we met on the road, trucks I hadn't even thought twice about. It had not occurred to me that the foreign bacteria that they transport could be harmful to the wildlife here—not unlike other foreigners who turned up here a few centuries ago.

Look on Google Maps and you'll find nothing to tell you you're at Katimiîn. All the names around here descend from European languages: Somes Bar, Orleans, Butler Creek. Until recently, Katimiîn was part of the 95 percent of Karuk Indigenous territory that was under federal management. Under President Biden in January 2023, a new piece of legislation was introduced called the Katimiîn and Ameekyáaraam Sacred Lands Act; 1,200 acres were transferred back to the tribe including this sacred site. In the middle of it is Sugar Loaf, a chunky red peak that stood before us, at the confluence of the Klamath and Salmon Rivers. "It's called á›uuyich, it means Little Big Mountain," Maymi tells me. But it's the cutesy Sugar Loaf that's marked in US history and legislation as a named feature in the newly restored Karuk lands.

These lands have a long history of being named—and claimed—by others. Humboldt Bay was named after Baron Alexander von Humboldt, the Prussian geographer who traveled around the Americas throughout the 1800s (ironically, he never once set foot in California). It was an expedition inspired by Humboldt's persona as a "second Columbus" that earned the bay the name in 1850, "discovered" by gold rush explorers who had little interest in what the people who already lived there called it. Hostilities began almost immediately between the settlers, who were busy founding towns, and the Native Americans, who had been living there since before the birth of Christ. Between 1840 and 1870,[2] the Native American population of California fell from two hundred thousand to about twelve thousand due to displacement, disease, and violence. Their rivers were panned for gold, and their land was sold and built on, creating new homes and a new, dominant, white community. One particularly violent takeover still remembered in Northern California was the 1860 Wiyot Massacre: Wiyot land had been bought by a settler, and three days later, white ranchers encircled and killed a hundred members of the tribe.[3] The island had been Wiyot land for centuries, and was acknowledged as the center of their world. The island wasn't returned to the Wiyot tribe until 2019, more than fifty years after the last native speaker of Wiyot, Della Prince, had died.

It's thanks to decades of indigenous resistance and the civil rights movement that, in 1975, Congress passed the Indian Self-Determination and Education Assistance Act. This reversed a policy that allowed settlers to force Native Americans off their reservations or sell their land, and provided funds and recognition to Native American tribes. Four years later, the Karuk were finally recognized federally as a tribe for the first time, despite being one of the biggest in California. That didn't mean everybody suddenly got their land back. The United States Forest Service relinquished Katimiîn a laggardly forty-five years after they achieved federal recognition, and much of their land still remains in federal hands.

With the loss of their people and their land, the Karuk also lost their language. Generations of children from the region's tribes were forced to attend Native American residential schools, first established by missionaries, where children were forced to adopt a Christian, European mindset. Children were punished for speaking their native language, and they were made to feel so ashamed of it that they didn't pass their language on to their own children. Tove Skutnabb-Kangas called this "subtractive language education." Rather than simply adding English, the education system instead imposed it as the dominant language and took away what remained of the child's native tongue. This enforced reeducation occurred in schools all over the world in the nineteenth and early twentieth centuries. It happened with other colonial languages, too; in French schools, a symbole, a kind of slate, was hung around children's necks to humiliate them if they spoke another language. One, recorded as late as 1949, read je parle Breton—I speak Breton.

Though some children were able to avoid entering schools that enacted similarly harsh punishments in the US—usually through going into hiding when the authorities came looking for them—the National Native American Boarding School Healing Coalition[4] estimated that in 1926, 83 percent of native school-age children were attending such schools. As *High Country News*[5] wrote in 2019, the US essentially allocated $2.81 billion (adjusted for inflation) to destroy native languages between 1877 and 1918. Compare this with the $180 million that the government has apportioned for language revitalization since 2005 and you quickly see how the scales are weighted against indigenous communities.

Maymi felt it important to show me the degradation of land nearby, as acute a loss to her as her language. Where settlers saw a loaf-shaped mountain, Maymi sees a catastrophe. During my visit, she points out the wreckage of a landslide, after an unsuccessful attempt at building a dam on the river—a river that's already been hurt by dams elsewhere along its course, built by electric power companies. In 2022, the US Federal Energy Regulatory Commission announced it would decommission four dams on the Klamath River, to save its fish, in the largest dam removal in US history. But federal efforts to correct their own mistakes are coming too late in some cases. In 2023, the Klamath Salmon Festival, held by the Yurok tribe that lives downstream, will not be serving salmon: The fish population is so low from the over-damming they won't touch it. As well as endangering their core food supply, the violence of the damming has also attacked how the Karuk build a sense of masculinity.[6] Removing the historic role Karuk men have held as fishermen providing for their communities, not only at festival time but at all times, has meant that they have had to renegotiate, against their will, what being a Karuk man actually means, in a world where there is no fish to provide.

The forests are suffering along with the rivers. For thousands of years the Karuk carried out prescribed, intentional burning in the woodlands, which maintained growth on forest floors and protected areas in the long term from wildfires. But when the territory was claimed by the US federal government, this ritual burning was banned. The forest floor overgrew and now wildfires decimate the land every summer. It has been a battle to persuade the US Forest Service to concede its position, and even now their hand has been forced by the changing climate. These days the Karuk are allowed to conduct planned fires as long as they have a federally qualified, tribal-born boss present and apply in advance to the service for their approval. It shouldn't escape our notice that the restoration of both land and language rights relies on applications and approvals, bureaucracy and funds that ultimately lie beyond the Karuk's reach.

By the time Maymi was a teenager, a decade or so ago, there were few native speakers of Karuk left. "The main words we knew would be for ceremonies, body parts, pif, which means fart," she said, smiling. "I think a lot of us didn't even know the words we were using *were* Karuk, we thought they were slang. When someone at elementary school said 'epiphany' we'd laugh, and they'd ask, 'Why is that funny?' and I'd say 'How is that not funny? E-*pif*-any?'"

When Maymi left school she wanted to find a job where she could walk in "both worlds," as she described it to me: to live both as a member of the Karuk and as any average American, wanting to do well in the world. She found herself drawn to one Karuk couple in particular who had bridged that gap: Julian Lang and Lyn, his wife.

. . .

I had never met Julian before, but I had met an otter statue he had painted, which stood in the doorway of the only store in the area. Twenty minutes or so into my conversation with Maymi in Katimiîn, he arrived to join us there. He had three lines of tattoo scoring each cheek and wore his long black hair tied in a ponytail. Maymi's youngest child's mouth widened into a grin; Julian was obviously somebody he had seen a lot of. I wasn't surprised. Julian and Maymi have spent at least five hundred hours together.

Julian is a Karuk elder now, but back in 1992—already well over a decade into his work as a scholar and an artist—he had an idea. There were one hundred speakers of Karuk left then, and if each one took on a younger member of the tribe they'd be able to create one hundred more speakers and the language would survive another generation. Leanne Hinton, who today is one of the world's leading experts in language revitalization, was the first to hear Julian's idea, and she thought it such a good one that she brought it up at a language-loss conference. The Master-Apprentice Language Learning Program was born, in which fluent speakers would be partnered with new learners and they would have to spend a minimum of ten hours together a week. The program has ten guidelines:

1. Don't speak English.
2. If you don't understand what's going on, use nonverbal communication instead.
3. Teach in full sentences, not word lists.
4. Learn language that's used in everyday life.
5. Learn and do traditional activities together.

6. Focus on listening and speaking—not reading and writing.
7. Learn and teach through activity, like cooking together.
8. Use audio and video recordings to add to your language learning.
9. The apprentice has to be a self-starter, actively learning.
10. Have patience with each other, and sensitivity to each other's needs.

At a glance, it reads like an immersion program, a cornerstone of language learning since time immemorial. But there is one important difference: Participants get paid. It's more like a stipend than a salary, but that small amount of cash, matching the US minimum wage at $15, is enough to make a crucial difference to participants' ability to fulfill the time commitment. In California, individuals apply via the Advocates for Indigenous California Language Survival (AICLS) organization, which delivers the funding that has has mainly come from a charitable body, the Lannan Foundation. Now tribes in Australia, Mexico, Brazil, and Canada are also rolling out master-apprentice programs, too.

Julian currently has four apprentices on the go; he managed to persuade the AICLS to continue funding him and Maymi twice after their first program together as "she kept having kids," he said. Maymi had first approached him to ask for good phrases to use as baby talk for her first child; he responded with some ideas and then suggested that she should become his apprentice. "My son's ten now," she said, then joked, "That's how long I've been his language slave."

Anybody who has ever tried language immersion can relate to it; we do it for the good of our brains, but it's *hard*. The work was worth it, though. Maymi is now considered conversationally fluent and is part of something called the family language program, meaning that she is being funded to get her family to the same level as her. And true to her mission of wanting to break generational cycles, she has become a bilingual, clinical social worker using Karuk expressions with the young people in her care.

Karuk "has a different worldview," she explained. "It forces you to be slower, it has context, you can't speak quickly. It has these tonal, long vowels. If you don't say it in a slow way, like water flowing, you'll say the wrong things." She mainly works with native teenagers, and one of the positive affirmations she uses in Karuk shows the language's complexity; the English equivalent of "I am smart" in Karuk directly translates as "I am thinking that I know that I am able to do a lot of things."

Another feature of Karuk is that it doesn't differentiate humans from plants or from animals, as English does. "We don't have words like beef and carcass and body. It's all meat." As a social worker, Maymi uses Karuk expressions with her clients and finds that the Karuk understanding of the world can be helpful: "It feels like you're less alone in the world. I can't just live. What about the river? What about the salmon? It's a more holistic way of thinking—it leads to social justice."

So Karuk is now spoken in the family and in the workplace, too. It's worth remembering that language works as a potent identity marker—I am speaking *this* language because I am *this* kind of person, which means holding *this* value or behaving in *that* way. This sense of affirmation has a clear positive impact across our lives. What Maymi has practiced locally has been supported by international research: Indigenous language use improves the health of indigenous communities,[7] particularly their mental health. In Canada, there are strong associations between Indigenous language use and lower suicide rates, a remarkable statistic for anybody, but a transformative one for indigenous people. In the US, suicide is double the rate among indigenous as it is for non-indigenous people. A common language, definitive for a shared experience, is what keeps people feeling connected. Rob a people of their language, and you're effectively withdrawing a public health intervention.

Maymi didn't use the term herself, but both she and Julian would qualify as language activists; their work advocating for Karuk is anchored in a desire to see a changed world *beyond* language. Language activism goes beyond the idea of simply gaining fluency in a language; it's about standing up for it. It's about resisting inequality.

While we were talking, Dennis walked up to us to show us his obsidian. "What can you make with that?" I asked him. "Knife!' he declared immediately. "For púufich." Julian and Maymi translated for me: deer. Then he darted off again, into the poison oak terrain, and we followed him cautiously, deeper into the forest. Dennis was doing something called translanguaging—using all the languages in his mental portfolio to communicate and dropping Karuk words naturally into English sentences. This is what multilingual people naturally do, and even more so when specific words trigger associations between multiple languages. Every single one of us is capable of a different translanguaging experience, like the surzhyk speakers of Ukraine or my mum and nonna when they dart around between three languages. But Maymi's family really are unique in the smorgasbord of Karuk and English they can deploy, something they can share with Julian and only a few others in the entire world. Here in the land freshly restored to their custodians, and in Dennis's mind and mouth, the púufich were regaining a name they've always had.

■ ■ ■

My exposure to Karuk hadn't given me an entirely different worldview yet, but I was eager to tell Julian the two words I had learned— one type of acorn and a fart. He joked that I was semifluent, and after a while walking as a group, Julian and I sat down on a fallen tree trunk. A mosquito danced around my face and he abruptly thumbed it square into my forehead when it landed there to dine. I felt very quickly that Julian had an ability to make you feel at ease, with a rounded timbre in his voice that gave patience and pause to his English as much as his Karuk. He slipped seamlessly into the language, frequently telling a full story that would last several minutes in Karuk before giving me an abridged English translation. He gestured to the former village ground where we sat. "This is Katimiîn. Before flooding came and wiped out a lot of land, this extended way out to the village of Ishirok. These were some of the biggest villages in our ancestral history. Everybody local knew the name. But all the street signs are in English."

Julian grew up in a home filled with women. His grandmother was born in 1900. This family memory of an indigenous land still undisturbed by white settlers meant that he heard Karuk throughout his childhood. As a young adult he committed to becoming fluent, visiting elders who could help him to keep speaking the language after his grandmother passed. Then, hungry for even more knowledge, he started visiting university archives; fortunately, the linguistics departments of California universities were born when many of these languages were still alive with speakers, unlike the East Coast of the US where the native languages had long been wiped out. Karuk, as a result, is one of the best documented languages of the area because a University of California, Berkeley, linguist, William Bright, took it on as the first project of the Survey of California and Other Indian Languages in the 1950s, now known as the California Language Archive.

UC Berkeley looks like a mini-city of august temples surrounded by a nature reserve; as I walked through the campus on my way to see the archive for myself, I felt dwarfed by it. Near the archive's door is a noticeboard with a history of the department, including a letter from the university's president in 1950, Robert G. Sproul, refusing to fund a linguistics department. I like that it is displayed here; they are rightfully proud of their history of innovation, which necessitates an appetite for troublemaking. A long letter had been written in response to Sproul, supported by eleven academics, who listed a number of reasons for setting up the department. Unsurprisingly, it points out that "other universities already have these departments." They added that American Indian languages faced endangerment, and could go understudied if action wasn't taken quickly.

But the letter forgot to mention one crucial detail: the communities or tribes themselves who spoke such languages. Blunders like this have been extensively criticized. The current director of the archive, Professor Andrew Garrett, told me: "When linguists started paying attention to endangerment as a phenomenon, the emphasis was always the loss to science. We scientists will lose information about language. Though that orientation continues, there's much more emphasis on the human and cultural rights of indigenous people. It's not that we as scientists will lose information, they as people are losing heritage."

As you might expect, books cover the walls of the archive office, and there is a temperature-controlled room for the most precious materials. Back in the seventies, Julian would have had to physically visit archives like this one himself. Now, a decent amount has been digitized and is accessible online, though Andrew says that with more funding they would be able to digitize more and ensure the department was always fully staffed.

The archive's manager, Zachary O'Hagan, stepped in to show me around. He was newly returned from a trip to Peru supporting indigenous languages in the Amazon. To start with, Zachary pulls out a notebook full of transcriptions made by William Bright, who studied Karuk and interviewed speakers in such detail that he was made an honorary member of the tribe. They were careful, meticulous sentences in pencil recording Karuk stories, without translation. For someone who already spoke Karuk, it could be read with ease. For researchers, it provided a corpus of study to help research many different elements of language: sentence structure, tenses, vocabulary. "We have hundreds of boxes like this," Zachary said, pulling out a small box full of cards, each with a different word on it. According to him, they're some of the most valuable resources in the archive.

The cards aren't digitized: The paper is too thin to be fed through a machine, so the process can't be automated and would take a long time anyway. Languages with only these kinds of resources remain inaccessible to anybody who can't regularly visit the archive. Fortunately, Karuk has an online dictionary and text corpus named by—surprise, surprise—Julian Lang: *Ararahih'urípih* ("Karuk language net"). William Bright's written notes in this archive have been uploaded to it, and Lang built it out alongside linguist Susan Gehr, who is of Karuk heritage. I typed in acorn to see what would come up. Ninety results appeared, including:

áatiship / aatíshipriy- to raise up with a pack basket full of (acorns or the like) on one's back

ákith- to handle or move (a soft mass, such as acorn dough)

chanáksaay- bread made with green acorns

iyvax- to remove shells from acorns

xánpuut- acorn of the maul oak

xánthiip- black oak or its acorn

xuntápan- acorn, esp. that of the tan oak

vûuksaha / vûuksahi- have a work contest (as in shelling acorns).

It was a delight to see all these expressions appearing almost magically on a web page, something that would have been totally impossible in the era when Julian and the university's linguists would have been poring over physical resources, a process that often must have taken months at a time. Sitting on our fallen tree, I asked Julian about his experience raiding archives. He said he saw the work of very different kinds of linguists, some focused on the science, others on the communities. "Our recordings and our linguists were very sensitive and saw something beyond the linguistic, scientific study of language," he said. "They really saw the culture."

When I told him I had learned that acorn was a loan word, he explained that there is a story behind all the different acorns; that they were all young maidens at one time, wearing caps distinctive from one another like the seeds that lay scattered on the forest floor. He told a little of it in Karuk, and it was mellifluous, rising and falling like an endless poem.

After a while, Julian said that he needed to leave to begin preparing for a flower dance. "Do you want to come and see where we hold it?" he asked.

· · ·

In their own language, the Hoopa tribe are na:tinixwe (pronounced NAA-tin-ish-weh)—the people of the place where the trails return. While the Karuk speak a language that is an isolate, meaning no other language like it has ever been found on any linguistic family tree, Hoopa is a Dené language, one of more than fifty in an area that spans more than four million square kilometers between the Pacific Northwest and the southern United States. The Karuk, who live upriver, share close cultural ties with them, if not a language family—and they also share the same linguistic fate. There are fewer than a hundred speakers left.

Before driving into the forest to meet Maymi and Julian, I had had brunch with Muriel Ammon and her father, Danny, who are first- and second-generation Master-Apprentice Program partners; Danny had been an apprentice once himself, and was now a master to his daughter. He hadn't started learning Hoopa until college; his grandmother was fluent, but she was part of the generation that went to the Indian boarding schools and died before Danny learned about her language. "She didn't teach any of her seven boys to speak

Hoopa, and probably ninety-five percent of the Indian kids who went to that school did the same thing," he told me.

So rather than learning from his grandmother, he did the Master-Apprentice Program and was matched with a fluent elder called Calvin Carpenter. They made a 320-hour commitment for six months, which they repeated three times over, an astonishing time investment for anyone to make, never mind on top of work. Calvin used to come into Danny's office every day to chat to him. Danny remembers Calvin telling him about "the belt line" at his boarding school during his childhood. If teachers caught pupils speaking Hoopa, they'd be lined up and whacked. Calvin, despite such treatment, had not let go of his mother tongue.

Now, Danny is passing it on to his daughter, and together they have done two rounds of the Master-Apprentice Program, a year and a half each time. When the first round started, it coincided with the COVID pandemic, and they stayed on the Trinity River, the great tributary of the Klamath River where the Hoopa are from— no TV, no internet. "We were so used to speaking in English, it was hard to get started," Danny admitted. But they found activities to do that gently raised Muriel's ability to speak Hoopa—playing Monopoly, cooking breakfast. Aside from this, Muriel told me that the only other main chance she has had to speak their language was at coming-of-age ceremonies for women: the flower dances.

These rites of passage were common for many tribes in this area but had been stopped during colonization. Not only were they not considered Christian or European, but they would draw young women to the attention of the settlers and then become targets of sexual violence. Muriel, who is in her twenties now, was the first in her family in years to experience a flower dance, and she's seen women in other families who have had them become community leaders since. "At these dances there are the ceremonial leaders who will use [the Hoopa] language for prayer, songs that our families have passed down to us." Thanks to the songs and prayers, "more people are speaking Hoopa at the ceremonies. I'm able to pray in Hoopa language, that's something I couldn't do before."

For her own ceremony, Muriel remembers seven days of singing, seclusion, running, and crafting through the woodland. She remembers singing a song unique to her and wearing a deerskin dress her family made for her. She also remembers lots of fasting; all she could eat was acorn soup and acorn water. But her most distinct memory was standing in the center of the pit as her community sang and chanted around her, and feeling that this was the most tangible expression of love she had ever felt. "People always ask, how did this change you? Well, I know very intensely what it feels like to be loved." It occurred to me that the rites of passage in my own culture—first kisses, eighteenth birthdays, virginity "loss"—aren't about being loved, they're more about Doing Stuff Grown-Ups Do. Do I know intensely what it is to be loved by a *group*? Have I ever felt such love from an entire community?

Danny remembered thinking that everything he was doing was for Muriel—helping to build the house, setting about new trails in the forest. "What I didn't realize was that everybody that came to it was touched. It wasn't just for Muriel. It was for the whole community."

The Master-Apprentice Program in Northern California hasn't just restored languages to the people who were losing them. It has revitalized ceremonies that unite the community, including one that empowers girls to become *Hoopa* women, *Karuk* women. Linguists and scientists may have been concerned about the loss to scientific knowledge that comes with language loss, but to most people— heritage speakers with no scientific background—it's about something more fundamental and more visceral. It's so we don't forget who we are.

The price of not forgetting who we are is currently $15 an hour, thanks to American philanthropy, the same rate you might be paid for non-skilled labor. I do not think Julian or Maymi are unskilled;

nor do I think $15 an hour fully rewards language activists like them for what they are setting out to do. Imagine if more of the Californian cultural elite threw their weight and wealth behind these efforts or the US government devoted more resources. How many more communities like the Karuk and the Hoopa could be enabled, if they so wished, to reclaim their language alongside their land?

■ ■ ■

The midges and poison oak were threatening to become completely unavoidable, and Ollie was watching my every move as if I was an errant toddler. It was a good time to get going. As I chirpily got into his car, he thrust hand sanitizer in my hands and told me to wash all my clothes the minute I got back to my hotel room. Julian and Maymi had been welcoming, the local flora and fauna less so. Outside the car windows the sun began to sink in the west.

We trailed after Julian's car, passing more solemn legions of redwood until they turned into undergrowth, trailers, and tents. When we got out of the cars, we found a Karuk man sitting and drinking beer by an open fire. "There's a fucking bear!" he declared, telling Julian that he could have sworn he saw one in the woods. "There's no bear," Julian assured him. Something about it being the wrong time of day or year. Any sign of a road had already disappeared by this point; we set off on a footpath deeper into the forest, closer to the river. As we continued walking, Julian told us all to mind a turd, narrowed his eyes to inspect it, and turned to me apologetically: "Okay, there probably is a bear."

The trees eventually bowed to reveal a clearing, with a large, open circle distinct from the small brush pit I'd seen earlier, surrounded by small mounds of rocks that had been piled on top of each other. They were somehow both ordered and disordered, each their own miscellaneous hilltops but all roughly the same size, evenly plotted around us. I counted thirteen of them; each one represented a woman who has completed her flower dance. Julian's grandmother had told him these rock piles used to be dotted around everywhere.

Just like Muriel, Danny, and the Hoopa, Julian and his wife, Lyn, have revived the flower dance ceremony for the Karuk tribe. Decades ago, Lyn had begged Julian to try to reestablish the tradition for their daughter. "We were in love," Julian told me. "We were talking about it. I thought—whatever you want, honey." He set about researching it, because the last person in the family who had had one was his great-grandmother's older sister, so no one living could remember it. Inevitably, he had to put hearsay and the testimony left behind by colonial historians together. Bit by bit, Julian and Lyn brought together the songs and practices that they could trace. Now Julian has overseen many flower dances, and it was time for him to get the ground and the hut ready for another one, for another young woman. I couldn't stay—these ceremonies are closed practices to outsiders—and was honored that I had been allowed to see this much. I imagined a nameless young woman blindfolded, as I was told she would spend most of the days-long ceremony. On the final night, her father will remove the blindfold, and she will see her community again not as a girl, but as a woman. When they leave, there'll be another pile of rough stones; small, patient mounds waiting for further company.

Thirteen rock piles stand today, alongside a Karuk language that, if the Master-Apprentice Program continues, may also stand a little longer. There are many countries I could have visited to demonstrate how colonialism kills languages. But few nations hold a grip on the popular cultural imagination like the United States; none have the same weight, power, and control across research and technology. The land of the free was once an incubator of abundant language diversity. Now, 78 percent of people in the US speak English—and only English—at home. In a single generation, from the nineteenth to the twentieth century, linguicide's broad scythe cut through the country's abundant words and worlds. It is only with great effort that some of that damage can be repaired. Under an administration that has seen the country lurch to the right, and has even sought to restore colonial names to indigenous territories and places, the life of such languages seems to rely as ever on the communities that still remember, and respect, what these disappearing words used to mean.

We stayed awhile at the ceremonial site, soaking it in, before leaving Julian and Lyn to their preparations. When I arrived back at my hotel, a Facebook message from Julian was waiting for me. "Good to have met you," it read. "As my great-grandmother used to say: 'I wish you could see what I saw.'"

THE STORY OF KURDISH

> **gurgazē:** when the sun shines through rain, which,
> in the Kurdish culture, is believed to be a time during
> which wolves give birth[1]

have always thought the word *earthquake* in English has an eerie poetry to it, perhaps because we only really use "quake" in idioms associated with terror, like *quaking in fear.* It is not the same in some of the other languages I speak; in Italian and Spanish, there's the more neutral word terremoto, from the Latin "moving earth," terrae motus. The Kurdish approach feels closer to the English; erdhej contains the verb hejîn, which can also be used to describe the trembling of an anxious heart. But there are other words, too. One is zelzeleh, زەلزەلە, which I recognize from Arabic and which feels almost onomatopoeic—as if you're wobbling as you're saying it. Bumalarza is the other, like the English boom, as if the very noise, rather than the earth, is shaking around you.

The 7:8 magnitude earthquake that ripped through Turkey and Syria in 2023 was a dark reminder that some events defy vocabulary. Does "quake" really do enough to describe tons of tectonic plates grinding against each other like blunted gears; the deformation of rocks in the earth's crust; the bodies that were thrown, flattened, buried? In Turkey alone, forty-one thousand people died. One and a half million were displaced. And since it happened in Turkey's southeast and Syria's north, many of those affected were Kurds, who have lived in this region for thousands of years. In the immediate aftermath, while families were clawing their loved ones out of the rubble, Turkey's foreign communications center posted on Twitter that they would be providing translation support in all earthquake zones to help people. Turkish, Arabic, Persian, English, Russian, German, and Pashto made the cut; Kurdish was conspicuously absent from the list, even though fifteen million Kurds form the largest ethnic and linguistic minority in the country.

Two days later, it no longer appeared to matter what language people were communicating in as President Erdoğan shut down Twitter entirely for twelve hours. By that point, the Turkish state had detained more than ninety people who had criticized the government's response to the unfolding emergency. At a moment when people were desperately trying to find information—and share it, in a language that they actually spoke—the government prioritized curbing "untrue claims, slander, insults and posts with fraudulent purposes," as they told Reuters. In the following months, Raman Salah, a master's student and translator with Respond Crisis Translation, heard many stories of linguistic discrimination. "There were a lot of elderly people crying out for help in their dialects but no one could understand or communicate with them even if there were so many NGOs to get them rescued," one resident told him. "Kurdish" actually accounts for a broad continuum of at least four dialects; a Zazakî speaker, which is a fairly small dialect compared to the others, told him, "There were many women afraid to speak in Kurdish to save their life. They were thinking they might not get rescued if they spoke Kurdish." Many others were reluctant to speak to Raman—which is unsurprising in a country that imprisons tens of journalists a year for "anti-state" behavior.

Part of the problem when the earthquake struck was that not all Kurdish speakers have a second language,[2] and many of them used to the Arabic alphabet might struggle to read the Latin script in which Kurmanji, the Kurdish variety spoken in Turkey and Syria, is written. Translators Without Borders recommended "communication in Arabic, Turkish and Kurdish Kurmanji at a minimum to ensure information and support reaches as many people as possible." Amnesty International also urged Syria and Turkey to provide resources in local languages, and to remember human rights in their crisis responses; in Syria the Assad regime had blocked at least one hundred vital aid convoys from entering Kurdish neighborhoods. "Survivors of humanitarian disasters have a right to timely, relevant, accessible and accurate information in a language they understand, without discrimination,"[3] they wrote. "Provision of such information can prevent further loss of life."

Without detailed surveys or well-funded research from which to draw data, oral testimonies like those that Raman collected reveal what can happen when a language isn't just ignored, but suppressed. When he isn't attempting to track linguicide, he is getting on with the realities of most Kurdish translation requests he receives: asylum applications. In the UK, most asylum requests received from Turkish and Iraqi citizens are from Kurds. The photograph that rocked the world in 2015 of a two-year-old boy, gray and lifeless on a Turkish shore, was of a Syrian Kurdish child. Most of us learned he was called Aylan from the media, Aylan Kurdi—but even this was a Turkification of his name. He was called Alan—"flag bearer"—and his surname was Shenu. Kurdi was, again, a moniker spread by the press in Turkey, apparently using his heritage as his signifier rather than his family name. Alan's parents had spent years moving around Syria as the country's civil war appeared to follow them city by city. They ended up in Kobane, but when it became a battleground between Syrian forces and the Islamic State, they left for Turkey. They were stateless before they had even left, as Syria's 1962 census stripped more than one hundred thousand Kurds of citizenship; in Turkey, their nationlessness trapped them in refugee limbo, unable to go elsewhere or settle permanently due to their status. People smugglers had promised them Europe, but the Mediterranean Sea showed no mercy for Alan, his brother, or his mother.

It is believed that at least a million Kurds live in diaspora now, and that more than thirty million live in their historic homeland, between Turkey, Syria, Iraq, and Iran. They are an ethnic minority in each nation. Unbelievably, they haven't suffered one linguicide, but four, and yet their language still survives.

■ ■ ■

The first stateless nation to be named as such came surprisingly late in history, and its identity may surprise you. In 1983, Jacques Leruez, a leading authority on British politics in France, published a book called *L'Écosse, une nation sans état* (Scotland: a nation without a state), referring to Scotland's peculiar identity as a nation in its own right, yet without sovereignty because it's a part of Britain. What qualifies as a stateless nation? Do Catalans form one? Uighurs? The Welsh? The phrase has come to mean something more than a people who don't qualify for anything above regional autonomy; it evokes dispersal, disenfranchisement, and, nowadays, war. Since the 1990s, an explosion of nationalist movements and battles for self-determination has propelled the word into common usage, but there is one plight it has come to epitomize in particular.

The Kurds form one of the world's largest stateless nations. They are split between four Middle Eastern countries, each with their own laws, their own problems, and their own distinctive histories of killing languages. For Tove Skutnabb-Kangas, the linguist who helped define linguicide, the experience of Kurdish speakers in the Turkish part of modern Kurdistan was "the most blatant example of linguicide this century." According to her and her coauthor, politician Sertaç Bucak,[4] Turkey gained this unenviable honor "with more brutal means, and more overtly, than any other country in the world to actively kill a language." Turkey's persecution of Kurdish is enshrined within its constitution and legal system; globally, no other language in the world has been as actively criminalized as Kurdish within the last century.

There has always been a region of Kurdistan, if not always a state. This region today is in some places completely occupied by a nation-state and in others semiautonomous. There is no autonomy for Kurds in Turkey and Iran; in Syria, there is the de facto autonomous region in Rojava, which at the time of writing is now contending with the fall of the Assad regime; and in Iraq, the constitution recognizes the Kurdistan Region in its northern territory. Kurdistan's name with its Asian *-stan* ending indicates what kind of language the Kurdish speak. Kurdish belongs to a mighty language group called the Indo-Iranian languages, with more than three hundred tongues darting from the eastern edges of Europe through the Caucasus, Anatolia, Levant, Iran, and even all the way to the Maldives. Kurdistan means place or land of the Kurds, just as Afghanistan is the land of the Afghans.

I'll refer to Kurdistan in this chapter as the region, and the homeland it is perceived to be, by Kurdish speakers. The Kurdish "language" they speak may in fact be understood as several languages; the two main dialects, Sorani and Kurmanji, diverge enough from each other to be mutually unintelligible, and they're also written in completely different scripts (Arabic- and Latin-based, respectively), following the writing systems used by non-Kurdish languages around them. Smaller dialects like Gorani, Zazaki, and Badini also join this sweeping continuum of a language that is spoken across an area that is bigger than Germany, as well as a diaspora that extends across Europe and the US.

The region of Kurdistan has been split for centuries. First recorded as a province in the twelfth century, in 1639 Kurdistan was subdivided between the Ottoman and Persian empires, but both of them had shrunk to monarchies or republics by the early twentieth century. When the Ottoman Empire fell following the First World

War, many Kurds hoped that their long-awaited state, no longer under the yoke of any empire, would materialize. Instead, the British and the French stepped in, eager to divvy up the Ottoman carcass and govern the many different ethnic groups who were allegedly "peoples not yet able to stand by themselves under the strenuous conditions of the modern world," as the newly formed League of Nations put it. European powers made deals on who had a mandate where, drawing borders to clarify what was British and what was French. In the Treaty of Sèvres, which was signed in 1920, Kurdistan appeared for the first time in an international treaty, a first form of international recognition for their political rights. Records held at the British Library show how Kurdistan would have been bordered; in one map drawn up after the war, it nestles between Persia, Armenia, and a big patch simply deemed "Arab Countries."[5] This independent Kurdish state would have lost land to the east, as the British recognized Persia's sovereignty (and, more important, their own sphere of influence) under *another* treaty, the Anglo-Persian Agreement, which they wished to protect. Kurdish lands in Syria and Armenia were similarly ignored. So, even if the Treaty of Sèvres had been properly ratified, it still wouldn't have united all the Kurdish regions into one independent state, and such a state would still have been run by British colonial powers.

But even the little of Kurdistan that the Kurds had been awarded was lost three years later when a different treaty was upheld instead of the one signed in Sèvres; this new treaty met the conditions of Turkish nationalists who did not want to sacrifice territory they saw as theirs. By the mid-1920s, the Treaty of Lausanne had divided Kurdistan between the Turkish republic, the French Mandate of Syria, and the British Mandate of Mesopotamia and Persia. It was now up to these new nation-states to decide how to treat a Kurdish minority—one that had just been denied self-determination and weren't best pleased about it. The century of turmoil we have witnessed since has proven how catastrophic these colonial decisions were, and their legacy opened the Kurdish language to linguicide from four different directions. All of them have left the language, and its people, to fend for themselves in different ways. But two countries have been especially murderous, and it is their actions that I will be focusing on.

Farangis Ghaderi, a lecturer at the University of Exeter, met up with me on a sunny day in April, in the common room of the university's Institute of Arab and Islamic Studies. She is the director of the Centre for Kurdish Studies, a department that was set up in 2006 and remains the only one of its kind in the UK and one of only two in Europe. The few Kurdish departments that exist in the Middle East are often policed; Ghaderi was once asked to lead a literature course at a new Kurdish department in her native Iran—except the reading list was mysteriously missing the vast majority of influential Kurdish texts she wanted to teach. Most Kurdish literature is, predictably, politicized, with writers yearning for nationhood and recognition. Ghaderi would have loved to have studied Kurdish literature at university herself, but back then it wasn't allowed at all. Her parents, both illiterate for much of their lives, spoke to her in Sorani Kurdish, the language variety spoken in Iraq and Iran. Her father slowly taught himself how to read and write Farsi (Persian's endonym) and Kurdish, and shared his own poems with her. But the Kurdish books he kept were out of bounds. For Ghaderi, who was excelling in Persian literature at school, they were irresistible. "He discouraged me from even touching them," she said. "He was worried they would get me into trouble."

Reluctantly, Ghaderi's father taught her what little he had learned of the Sorani Kurdish writing system, which uses a modified script she would have largely been familiar with from Farsi. She went on to study English literature, before finally returning to the Kurdish canon for her PhD. She tells me that you can now study Kurdish in private schools in Iran, and that you can even do a bachelor's degree in it, which she is excited about. Every year, with the green shoots of cultural activism and protest movements breaking through, her family sends more videos of celebrations where everyone is in traditional dress, proudly displaying their identities. In one clip, Ghaderi saw a woman wearing the same traditional headdress that her mother had stopped wearing years ago over criticism from her community that it marked her out as "different." It is true that there is some progress around language rights in Iran, but it remains under intense state surveillance. A Kurdish press exists, but it is not free; young people can learn Kurdish, but it's often been online or informal. Speakers are courted as a potential voting bloc, but a police presence still controls the areas they live in. If Kurds want to register their children with Kurdish names at birth, they may find the name rejected for not being on the "approved" list.

It has been eight years since Ghaderi last went home. There is no way she would have been able to conduct her research into Kurdish politics and literature had she tried to pursue her PhD in Iran. "Because of my work," she said, "I cannot go back."

Ghaderi's work isn't controversial—at least, it wouldn't be in the UK. But in Iran, where Kurdish identities are politicized and marginalized, Kurdish studies cannot escape scrutiny and surveillance. Ethnic minorities across Iran face systematic discrimination and violence; many of them, including the Kurds but also the Baluch and Azerbaijani Turks, are Sunni Muslims in a majority Shi'a nation, and the state likes to argue that activism from minorities equates to threats to national security. So when the small flashes of rebellion that Ghaderi had seen in her family's videos burst into open defiance after the 2022 killing of Jîna Amini, known globally as Mahsa, persecution against the Kurds was inflamed once again. Amini had died in the hospital under suspicious circumstances following her detainment by Iran's modesty police for allegedly miswearing a hijab. Ghaderi wrote about how one of the songs sung at Amini's funeral, "Be Tenya Cêy Mehêllin" (Don't Leave Them Alone), was taken from a poem that had been written decades earlier in Iraq, when Saddam

Hussein's brutal regime killed and injured thousands of Kurds in a large-scale chemical attack. The same anthems of resistance and sadness return whenever the Kurds need them: "Bless their [thirsty] throats with the Sunrise, and their wounds with roses," the lyrics plead. "Cover them with songs, and the woodland's green."[6] Jîna means "giving life" and Amini's grave bears the inscription: "Dearest Jîna, you shall not die, your name will be a symbol."[7]

The world knew her as Mahsa because of Iran's suppression of Kurdish names. Just as many Kurds do, Mahsa went by two names, an Iran-approved name in civil administration and another at home. It is why the phrase "Jin, Jîyan, Azadî" flew around the world with such force during the 2022 protest movements. Meaning Woman, Life, Freedom, this slogan was first coined by the Women's Protection Units of the PKK, the militant political group recognized as a terrorist organization by Turkey and the wider Western world, though many contest this: Their women-only units are the same formidable all-women units that famously defended Kurdish areas against ISIS. But it found new vitality in its echo of Jîna's name. Very little foreign coverage recognized that this phrase came from the PKK or that Mahsa's name was in fact Jîna. Ghaderi sees this as yet another erasing of Kurdish identity, in which the Kurdish language has been sidelined in Iran for the sake of national unity.

Even though minority languages are recognized in Iran's constitution, a child in the country is legally guaranteed the right to be educated only in Persian and no other language. Kurdish language teachers have been imprisoned in Iran for teaching children, individuals such as the educator Zara Mohammadi, whose cultural association helped bring language and literature classes to Kurdish villages for free. She was jailed in 2019 for ten years for the crime of "forming a group against national security" before eventually being released after completing a year of her sentence. Ghaderi's father was not wrong to worry about his daughter.

The effect of this policing is that Iran has somehow banned a language without imposing an actual language ban. In the 1930s, amid a rise of nationalism and modernization in the country, a language academy was established to mandate "proper" Persian, and its founder, Mohammad Ali Foroughi, did not believe a ban on other languages necessary because he didn't think non-Persian languages were literary enough to contend with Persian, whose literature would "homogenize Iranians." "Enforce speaking in Persian," he once recommended. "Fortunately, Turkish and Kurdish are not literary languages, and our minorities lack the literary and educational ingredient and will be easily assimilated into Persian language and literature."[8]

Fortunately, Ghaderi's father's book collection had already long shown her that this was not the case. In fact, Exeter has an entire archive of Kurdish books, newspapers, and pamphlets that attest to active publishing throughout the nineteenth and twentieth centuries. Even if those documents didn't exist, though, a language without a literary tradition is no less valuable. Oral storytelling is highly prized for Kurds who call their remarkable art form dengbêjî—"voice telling." A bit like a bard, a dengbêj is capable of committing vast numbers of words to memory. These narratives are full of stories of forbidden love and threatened honor, set in the mountains of Kurdistan. There are some stock characters who feature in them, like an old man who appears near water. He brings good fortune, as does Shahmaran, a creature who is half-woman, half-snake. Despite the wisdom she shares with humankind, Shahmaran is repeatedly betrayed by humans. Within the dengbêjî, tenses blur, and the reciter becomes the protagonist, mixing the present with the past to bring the listener into the story. A dengbêj needs to be skillful, modulating their voice and gestures to make you believe they are a lover, a villain, a hero. Dismissing storytelling traditions like this as inferior is a convenient tactic for policymakers who have pursued assimilationist agendas to absorb all who are not ethnically Persian—the Kurds, the Balochis, and countless other identities—into the Iranian state.

It is also convenient to silence the voices of dengbêjs, when, in the absence of the ability to write freely or indeed the right to become literate in the first place, they are sometimes the only source of events that occurred in Kurdish history. Trained like Julian trains Maymi today in Karuk (see previous chapter), it is a master-apprentice art form, and true as well as fictional stories are passed down. In 2011, the dengbêj Gazin borrowed from old kilams—spontaneous, melismatic expressions, drawn out in a long lament—to create a new story relaying recent earthquakes that had occurred in Van, in Turkey.[9] In it, she sings of how her life was interrupted one day: "When I turned toward Erdîş and Wan and all its villages / Oh God, a verdict again, the verdict of earthquakes, mother, these are bad times." Reports circulated shortly after the earthquakes happened of letters with nationalist slogans and parcels full of rocks allegedly sent as aid by the Turkish government, and these events are repeated in Gazin's new kilam, where she reads out one such letter: "This is what the Kurds deserve."

■　■　■

In contrast to Iran's sly linguicide, Turkey opted for unabashed violence, both legislative and physical. Once the republic was established in 1923, the next few decades saw Kurdish banned in public spaces and in publishing, along with sweeping Turkification of place names, transforming the landscape on paper. A map of changed place names in Turkey looks like a gradient, deepening in red the farther east you go. An estimated four thousand Kurdish place names have been changed since the 1910s. The only other ethnicity with more place name changes in Turkey is Greek. The difference, of course, is the Greeks have long left or were killed in Anatolia after the First World War; around a fifth of Turkey's population today remains Kurdish. Just like Mahsa, most renamed towns and villages have one name in Turkish and another for the Kurds who remember, and repeat, them.

For many, this isn't just about recalling a name that once meant something to a family; it's also about preserving a historic record of abuse. Search for Tunceli on Google Maps and that is the only name you will see the area carry, and yet all the signs in Tunceli refer to it instead as Dersim. On a visit to the area, anthropology student Niko Shmitz said that his Turkish friends told him not to call the area Dersim because this was the name "sympathizers" (i.e., Kurds) who attacked the Turkish state used.[10] Shmitz's hosts in Dersim, on the other hand, told him not to call it Tunceli because *that* name was forced on the area in the 1930s when ethnic minorities, including the Kurds, were forcibly resettled around the country to try to assimilate them. Local Kurds who tried to reject the move rebelled and were then killed by the state in the tens of thousands. Shmitz's Turkish friend said calling the place Dersim could be seen as disrespectful to the achievements of Mustafa Kemal Atatürk, the father of the Turkish republic. It prompted Shmitz to wonder "why people care so much about a name being disrespectful for Atatürk, who doesn't care anymore, but so little about it being disrespectful for thousands of people living there."

Turkey's linguistic enforcement beats even the French language police for eccentricity; incredibly, for eighty-five years Turkey banned the letters q, w, and x in official contexts because they appeared in the Kurdish and not the Turkish alphabet. In 1983, Turkey passed law 2932 to ban Kurdish in both private and public life; by that point, Kurdish had become such a bogeyman that it wasn't even referenced in the law, which instead stipulated: "It is forbidden to express, promote or publish thoughts in any language apart from the primary official language of states recognized by the Turkish State."[11] Not long afterward, when the Kurdistan Workers' Party—the PKK—launched an insurgency against Turkey in 1984, Kurdish solidified in the eyes of the state as a language not only of a dangerous minority but of separatist terrorists. It did not matter that there had also been Kurdish parties that sought peaceful, democratic solutions for "the Kurdish question"; they would be shut down, too, just like their language.

Attitudes have relaxed slightly since the 1990s, mainly because of international pressure and Turkey's attempts to appease and even join the EU. As a result, Turkey has been forced to rescind some of its most linguicidal policies such as banning the speaking of Kurdish in public, and to allow private Kurdish lessons for the first time in the history of the republic. But other obstacles remain entrenched in Turkish society. The tweet during the earthquake, willfully pretending that a Kurdish region did not require Kurdish translation, exposed the ridiculous lengths the state will still go to for a Turkish-only world. In a 1999 Human Rights Watch report, Şefik Beyaz, the head of an organization called the Kurdish Institute in Turkey, said: "The authorities will not allow us to have a sign that says Kurdish Institute or to register as such, but when the police call they say, 'Is this the Kurdish Institute?'"

The institute was founded in 1992 and offered language courses as well as publishing a literary magazine. In 2016, it was shut down by the authorities along with several other NGOs following a failed coup against Erdoğan, even though the rebellion hadn't been started by Kurds, and in fact the PKK had told people to stay away from it. But anyone critical of Erdoğan's government, violent or peaceful, was punished in a two-year-long state of emergency; any excuse will do, it seems, if there is an opportunity to prize the language away from its people. Gradually, some NGOs have been able to reopen and activists have practiced semi-clandestinely since, walking a tightrope of promoting Kurdish culture without being seen to promote Kurdish separatism. Their attempts to teach Kurdish continue to be blighted by ongoing security tensions on all Turkey's Middle Eastern borders with Kurds, as well as tight state control by Erdoğan's government. The status of Kurdish in Turkey is still very much in jeopardy.

The inability to educate children in Kurdish or to publicly discuss language rights without being accused of being a national security concern has been cataclysmic for the transmission of the language in Turkey. Parents are often too scared to request Kurdish lessons for their children,[12] and decades of persecution also mean that there aren't enough teachers to respond to the demand. "The level of violence against the Kurdish language in Turkey is astonishing," Ghaderi said. A friend of hers who lives in a Turkish village told her that her son was sent back home for asking his cousin for a pencil sharpener in Kurdish. "Now he has to wait an entire year to start school again," she said to me.

In September 2019, a survey of language proficiency among six hundred young Kurds aged eighteen to thirty[13] across four different Kurdish provinces found that only 18 percent of them could speak, read, or write in Kurdish. Twenty-six percent could speak but not write it, and the rest of the group could not speak Kurdish fluently, couldn't understand it fully, or did not know it at all. Despite this uneven and diminishing language ability, their will for Kurdish to survive was clear—86 percent of them wanted their children to learn Kurdish. The Kurdish Studies Center released similar results in 2020 after interviewing nearly fifteen hundred Kurds around the whole of Turkey; they found that just 30 percent of them spoke Kurdish to an advanced level, and 31 percent at an intermediate level.[14] Those who reported a very strong Kurdish identity were more likely to speak Kurdish well, suggesting—unsurprisingly—that those who had experienced more Turkish assimilation were far more likely to be monolingual Turkish speakers.

Ghaderi is disturbed by the long-term impact this crisis will have on young people's ability to engage with Kurdish literature in Turkey. The idea clearly troubles her despite the success of her post here in Exeter, and the other progress that is gently being made across Kurdish studies, both in the West as well as the small inroads being made in Kurdish autonomous regions. Even though she taught herself how to write in Kurdish, it still takes her much longer to write academically in Kurdish than in English because of those crucial years of literacy that she missed out on as a child.

You might at this point be thinking that surely all these laws violate human rights. Of course they do—but, like Russia's linguicide in Ukraine, this is a state that doesn't seem to have much of a problem violating human rights in all areas. Quelling protest movements, imprisoning journalists, and killing supposed anti-state actors seem par for the course. Turkey has been condemned for human rights violations against the Kurds by the ECHR as well as organizations like Amnesty International and Human Rights Watch, but beyond that, Turkey has not faced any kind of international penalty for linguicide, nor for many other abuses. Without meaningful enforcement, international human rights organizations like the UN are ultimately powerless to affect what member states actually do. Linguistic rights, which are usually tightly connected with minority, cultural, or educational rights, are detailed within many human rights instruments including the Universal Declaration of Human Rights, and yet there is no institution dedicated to monitoring them; that's why you have people like Ukraine's Taras Kremin logging abuses so that they can be considered within other rights violations. Other human rights treaties do have monitors; there are committees set up to observe everything from racial and gender discrimination to the rights of children and migrant workers. There are treaties that protect against discrimination based on race and sex, but it is very rare to see "language" in that list. Democratic countries are guilty of ignoring attempts to alter this: The European Charter for Regional or Minority Languages, which was adopted in 1992 to protect and promote vulnerable languages, has not been ratified by France or Italy, two countries with historic and extensive records of linguicide.

While Kurdish has been suppressed in Iran and openly eradicated in Turkey, it is a slightly different story in Iraq and Syria, where there is now some semblance of autonomy for Kurdish speakers, who are speaking, teaching, and publishing in Kurdish. In Iraq, it's because the constitution has granted Kurds rights since 2005; in Syria, it's because the Kurds successfully seized it, commanding de facto autonomy of Rojava—"the West" in Kurdish—since 2012, when the Assad regime withdrew from Kurdish-majority areas during the Syrian civil war. Despite Iraqi and Syrian persecution of Kurds throughout the decades, children have been able to learn Kurdish in schools for some time in these regions and broader minority rights are also protected. In Iraq, Kurdish is an official language, and in the Kurdish Region of Iraq (KRI) it is used in all domains; in Rojava, children have been going to Kurdish schools following the Arab Spring and the seizure of traditionally Kurdish lands.

Unsurprisingly, these have also become regions where many other language rights are protected, too; both the KRI and Rojava protect the rights of families to teach children in their mother tongue, whatever it is, meaning it is a more accommodating place than others in the Middle East to speak and preserve languages like Assyrian and Turkmen. Iraq's example shows that linguistic rights can be returned; Syria's example shows that they can be seized anyway amid state fragility and war. Kurdish is still not totally safe in Rojava and Iraq either; full autonomy would be the ultimate solution to Kurdish linguicide. The long shadows of Arabic and English loom over Kurdish and threaten to dominate it if it is not empowered across all areas of life.

So, without the ability to self-govern, effective human rights instruments, and in many places with rapidly diminishing numbers of speakers, Kurdish faces a second century of existential damage. Turkish Kurds in particular risk losing entire generations of speakers, who are too afraid—for legitimate reasons—to pass it on. As human rights defenders continue fighting for their language and identity, researchers like Ghaderi are now trying to focus on another domain. It doesn't rely on an international court, nor even on the ability to speak Kurdish. It's a way of spreading language that unites us all: telling good stories.

■ ■ ■

Kareem Abdulrahman had never really thought before about how long Kurdish sentences are. In his former job, as a journalist for the BBC's specialist media monitoring service, he would take two sentences in Kurdish and sometimes translate them into four or five in English. The sentence structure wasn't nearly as important as the facts he was trying to convey, almost always detailing war and conflict from Kurdish media, which he would then faithfully transpose into English. Such news stories had followed him his entire life, which began in the late seventies in Sulaymaniyah, in Iraq. He was born soon after the Second Iraqi-Kurdish War, which the Kurds had lost. The autonomous region in Iraq was still decades away; Kareem was twelve years old when the Ba'athist government under Saddam Hussein chemically bombed the Kurdish town of Halabja, killing five thousand civilians in their fight against Iranian-backed Kurdish militias.

BBC Monitoring doesn't really serve the public; those who subscribe to it tend to be NGOs or governments, which are trying to track local conversations from afar. But Kareem always tried to keep his eyes open for stories that weren't just about turmoil. In 2008, he reported on a Kurdish author, Bakhtiar Ali, whose latest book was performing extremely well in Kurdistan. Once he filed the piece to his editor, he wondered: *Could I review this book, too?*

By this point, Kareem had become something of an expert in Ali's work, in the way journalists often do when they're given a new commission (a feeling I know well). He pitched a review to the *Times Literary Supplement*, which had a section for novels that weren't written in English. He was floored when he got his copy and saw that the review had been featured as the cover of the magazine. An agent swiftly got in touch and asked him if he knew about any professional Kurdish translators so that the book could be published in English. That's when Kareem realized there weren't any literary translators, and just as the book review had seemingly fallen into his lap, so, too, did the chance to become the translator for the world's first Kurdish novel to be published in English. It came out in 2016.

When he tried applying the same practice to his BBC translations, slicing up Kurdish's elongated phrasing, he checked himself; Did he have the right, he wondered, to turn Ali's two sentences into four? "The writer is using language to both convey content and also style. I had a very good editing workshop; one of the best tips I've had was to think about whether the writer is using longer sentences to convey something or not. Is it a literary device? Is it Bakthiar's style? Or does almost everybody in the language do it? If it's the latter, you change it; if it is the former, then you think twice."

Some of the sentences have stayed the same deliberately because they reveal something invaluable about Kurdish cultural expression. "May their grave be filled with light," an expression that is offered when a deceased person is mentioned, was a Kurdish phrase that Kareem originally attempted to try to find an English interpretation for, before realizing it held greater value when translated literally. Translating is full of anxiety, he said, that you eventually make peace with. He is inspired by the translator Daniel Hahn, who says that *Hamlet* has been adapted by hundreds of directors, all with the same dialogue and yet no two productions are alike. And nor, apparently, are Kareem's own translations. "I am sure if you give me back the book, I would do it differently," he said.

In Kareem's view, the Kurds have been so busy surviving that the development of professional literary translation out of Kurdish has been stunted. He didn't even have an authoritative Kurdish-English dictionary to rely on; many exist, but none, in his view, are definitive enough to use with 100 percent reliability. He relies heavily on his own multilingualism. Combining his knowledge of English, Arabic,

Farsi, and Kurdish, along with help from Google Images searches, he managed to locate the words for types of boats, or mountains, or flowers that don't grow in the West; the kind of highly specific words that bring fiction to life and that rarely appear in daily conversation. But even when they find ways around the lack of Kurdish resources, Kareem and the translators who will come after him have other obvious barriers: the ongoing suppression of Kurdish creatives in Iran and Turkey, as well as the overwhelming dominance of the Anglosphere. Writing in Kurdish is literally a matter of home or exile, freedom or prison, and even life or death.

Many of the great Kurdish poets and writers have faced detention or been killed. Musa Anter was assassinated in 1992, believed to have been killed by Turkish state intelligence. Sherko Bekas lived in exile in Sweden till the fall of the Ba'ath regime because his work was banned under Saddam Hussein. Writing in exile has become so much of a norm that a researcher called Ozlem Galip[15] compared one hundred novels written in Kurmanji in an attempt to discover how Kurdistan was construed in Kurdish literature from afar. Almost all of them emphasized the importance of welatparêz, love of the homeland, a word in which I recognize Arabic's footprint of wilayat, or state, which Kurdish borrowed during the Ottoman period. Loving that homeland is not simply about affection; it is all that love demands of us. Loyalty. Sacrifice. Struggle. Several classic Kurdish novels take betrayal against the homeland as pivotal and destructive plot points, where such traitors are condemned as a caş, a donkey foal. Calling someone a donkey in the Middle East is a lot worse than calling someone a donkey where I live in England, and in Kurdish in particular it means someone who collaborates with occupying powers. Galip also found traitors described as a snake and a partridge—mar and kew. The snake is much maligned in many global cultures, but the partridge here makes the list because it's believed to be disloyal to its own species, a bird that, if captured, helps hunters lure other birds. An oral, poetic culture before it was ever a literary one, Kurdish is redolent with proverbs full of small, emphatic meanings like this. One of the best known is Ji çiyan pê ve tu heval nînin, or هیچ دۆستێک له جگه چیاکان —, "no friends but the mountains." It is meant to signify the Kurdish sense of abandonment by all the countries that have ignored the people's cries for statehood, leaving them only their landscape.

With so many writers in exile, representation and translation in the West can bring awareness of what the Kurds have battled to wider, global audiences. Bakthiar Ali, unsurprisingly, lives in Germany, where he can write freely and where there is a rich culture of book festivals. "All major cities have a house of literature," Kareem said with awe, and Bakthiar's events can be attended by up to three thousand or four thousand people. Yet there is still a great imbalance in translation literature, where English is the dominant source country for translations and where Anglophone markets in turn have a poor record of translating into English. So appalling is the Anglophone ratio of translated publishing that the University of Rochester ran a project called "Three Percent," highlighting the chronic underrepresentation of foreign literature in English markets. Add on to this the fact that Kareem is normally expected to translate samples and write synopses for works he is translating before he is offered a contract, and you begin to understand why it took so long for a Kurdish novel to be translated into English. That agent who contacted him after the *TLS* review ended up rejecting Kareem's proposal; twenty rejection letters later he finally got a lucky break with someone else.

Translation is a powerful weapon against linguicide: Amplifying non-English-speaking writers would not only do a lot of good for Kurdish, but for all languages that are vulnerable to endangerment and devaluation. Translation can be, as the scholar Martha García González has described, "a mechanism to promote the language itself";[16] it can, of course, also be a means of subordination. For instance, translating a Kurdish work into Turkish can reduce the readership of it in its original language, something Farangis says has happened with the work of renowned Kurdish author Mehmed Uzun.[17] But either way, translating minority languages into globally dominant ones also gives them a wider presence and value. Beyond the text itself, Kareem's awe describing German book festivals shows the additional prestige a book can lead to, for its authors and for the community they come from.

Now, Kareem is practically a full-time literary translator, who has access to training and networks that help him better his craft. When we met he was looking forward to a shared residency with Bakhtiar Ali at Stanford University, where they would go on to hold a conference about expanding the still young discipline of Kurdish studies beyond literature. While he is optimistic about the progress that is being made, he is nervous about the culture that is still being lost every year, as the number of speakers declines, much of which has never made it to a book or the printed word and remains in the minds of aging speakers. This anxiety is so prevalent for Kurdish language activists that there is a growing movement of folklore collectors seeking out stories to preserve, a practice that has grown in popularity in Turkey and Iran over the past decade and which Ghaderi and her colleague Joanna Bocheńska have published research on. The recording of Zazaki folklore in particular appeared to intensify after 2009, prompted by a UNESCO report on language endangerment. One folklore collector Farangis and Bocheńska interviewed, Loqman Nadirpûr, said that Kurdish has similar stories to those like Cinderella and Snow White, but within their own tradition, and yet their children are consuming them via Disney instead. "We have more interesting stories in Kurdish that if they are made into movies or animations, they would be much more fascinating than the likes of Harry Potter," he told them.

Mem and Zin is the most famous Kurdish epic, written by Kurdish writer Ahmad Khani in the 1600s, which has been passed down the ages in oral prose and poetry as well as its original text. In the epic, fairies—pari—learn one day that a young boy and a girl exist who are more beautiful than anyone else on earth. They live far apart, heirs to rival cities, and so one of the fairies transports the girl, Zin, to Mem's bedroom, where they both wake up in a haze. Before they know it, they wake up again, in their own bedrooms, but each with a ring on their finger that they have exchanged with the other. They had fallen in love in what had felt like a dream. A series of obstacles is set up between the two lovers until Bako, a jealous sorcerer, eventually poisons Mem. Zin dies a week later of a broken heart and is buried with Mem, but so rabid is Bako's green-eyed monster that he breaks apart the roots of the rosebush that has been planted above them to set the lovers apart, separating them even after death.

All these stories have been passed on orally or, to use the Kurdish expression, sîne be sîne—from chest to chest. Kareem thinks a lot of the repetition in the texts he translates from Kurdish to English is a vestige of this oral tradition, in which repetition would have made lines easier to remember. This repetition is also present within words themselves, where sounds echo each other. As one folklore collector put it: "There are dozens of sounds to describe water: when it falls on stones it is xuşxexuş, if it falls from above it is şireşir, when it boils it is bilebil, when it drops it is çipeçip, and when a man is entering water it is çelpeçelp." This evocative Kurdish folklore deserves to be protected as cultural heritage; in a world of linguicide, and governments that ignore human rights, perhaps an organization like UNESCO could award the Kurds the recognition they have long waited for, if not for their state then at least for their language and the rich world it contains.

"When people hear 'Kurd,'" Kareem told me, "they think of war, bombardments, Erdoğan, Saddam. This is true to some extent, but there is more to us. We have a culture, we have a literature, we have the same problems. Our hearts get broken. We have fathers who were not there for their children." The violence and trauma are "part of history—we can't deny that. But the worries are what everyone else is worried about. Can I have a home? A job? A relationship? A lot of these are best expressed in fiction." For him, translation is about creating a bridge; something you can relate to, whether you are Kurdish or not. It reflects the human condition, across our differences. This is why stories like *Mem and Zin* last, despite the best efforts of governments and warmongers to erase them: they tell us something true about ourselves.

The Kurdish language has been failed by governments in both the East and the West. As speakers respond to this as best they can—in survival, in protest, in poetry and prose—the least that many in the West could do would be to support Kurdish revival efforts, to defend their language rights, and to amplify Kurdish literature and works as avidly as it does Arabic and Persian efforts. It would be much harder to invalidate Kurdish if the wider world recognized its value. But as well as protecting Kurdish, such recognition would better connect us to its speakers. To honor Kareem's words, I will, as an unqualified translator but a dutiful journalist, report the last thing that he told me in our interview verbatim. He says it far better than I can—and in his fourth language:

To create that bridge with other cultures, that's the image I like to think about when I think of translation. On the one hand, with the rise of right-wing politics, there is this idea that the other is dangerous, unfamiliar, not like us. But I think one of the great things that literature does is—you think they are human. They are like me. I would like to think it would contribute to a world where we are not terrified of the other. We are not othering the other. When you see films and songs and novels from a different culture—even when you go back a thousand years—it's like they're talking about today.

THE STORY OF KICHWA

> **llakichina:** to make someone feel sorrow

We were walking up the gentle incline of the shoulder of a god. By my side was six-year-old Coya, darting between her parents' and her grandmother's llamas, who were more than twice Coya's size. Her two long braids bounced as she moved, and she squealed when one of the llamas swerved in her direction, looking for a new patch of grass to chomp. The sun was setting over the valley where Coya lived, and where, in an eternal embrace, Taita Imbabura and Mama Cotacachi lie side by side.

Taita (father) Imbabura, and his wife, Mama Cotacachi, are deities who are two volcanoes in the western Andes. Taita is inactive, whereas Mama is only lying dormant. Whenever one mountain acquires a snowy peak, it is said that one god has visited the other. Their slopes, however, testify to a notoriously fractious relationship; a large boulder on Imbabura's shoulder is said to have been thrown there once by Cotacachi in a fit of rage, when she was aiming for his head. She in turn has a cleft on one side, said to be her lost heart after one of Imbabura's dalliances with another mountain.

Happily, the couple I was staying with seemed to have a far healthier relationship. Luis and Martha have two daughters, Amy and Coya, the latter the more extrovert of the pair. Coya had a permanent cheeky smile and a natural curiosity for the world. "What are those spots?" she asked me one day.

"These are freckles," I said. "A lot of people have them in my country. I get more when it's sunny."

"Eres rubia!" she replied, astounded, as if I was from another planet, and then ran off, singing to herself. I had learned rubia meant blond in my Spanish lessons at school; *perhaps it also means "fair,"* I thought, until her dad laughed and said: "Coya, what are you talking about?" She asked lots of questions like this, excited to analyze the stranger staying at her parents' house. I told Luis that she would make a good journalist one day, although, with a name like hers, she may be destined for finer things—Coya is Kichwa for "queen." Women during the Inca Empire, which first occupied and colonized the Ecuadorian highlands the Túquerres family live in, were often given this name if they were married to or descended from the Inca ruler.

The Túquerres home felt like a small paradise to me, where I was greeted by two enthusiastic dogs and clusters of spear-like red flowers I had never seen before. Their living room gleamed with photographs of Amy and Coya and the medals and certificates they have won at school. The Túquerres live next door to Luis's parents, although in Cotacachi "next door" can mean a ten-minute walk across a huge field or through vegetable patches that are more like botanical gardens. Avocados and papayas hung pendulously from the trees, flanked by long rows of squashes and marrows. Tubers are everywhere in Ecuador, as they should be, because it was here in the Andes that the potato was born. In fact, Quechua—a language family that spans the west of Latin America—helped give us our English word "potato," which is a mix of Quechua papa and Taino batata. In Ecuador, I didn't hear anyone say patata once. Potatoes are papas, cholas, chauchas. Llama, too, is a Quechua word. Kichwa is what the language is called in Ecuador, where it enjoys its own idiosyncrasies, as well as being the country's largest indigenous language.

After we had been walking awhile, veering left into a wide field, a minuscule woman appeared in the distance, using a long branch as a walking stick. Coya clasped her hands together as if in prayer and rushed to her. "Una bendición!" she chirped at her abuela. She was requesting a blessing in Spanish. The woman smiled, whispering a prayer as she gave the sign of the cross over Coya's little face. I introduced myself in Spanish, and she nodded back at me politely. Coya's grandmother probably understands a great deal, if not all, of Spanish, but she can't speak much of it.

I thought back to when I was six. There aren't any llamas in Holloway, but in Nonna's garden I remember the ladybugs I would find on her fuchsias and how I would let them crawl into the palms of my hands. When I used to stay the night, we would pray together before going to bed, and just as Coya and her grandmother prayed in Spanish, Nonna and I prayed in English. Coya and I both have the privilege of grandmothers who offer their love in the language easiest for us to understand. But both of these facts—Coya and her abuela's shared faith, their lack of a shared language—reveal a great deal about what has happened here in Ecuador. I didn't hear Amy or Coya utter any Kichwa during my stay with them, although their parents speak it fluently. Luis, who seemed to be in his late thirties or early forties, told me he also didn't learn how to speak Kichwa until he was twelve years old.

"How did you speak to your parents?" I asked him once. He shrugged, as if he hadn't thought much about it before. "We managed," he said. Across the kitchen table, he deployed soft admonishments in Kichwa with lightning speed to Coya, who'd been talking with her mouth full or scraping her chair on the floor. She grinned back at him, and then at me, and giggled, and I'd smile back conspiratorially while Luis rolled his eyes. It's true: some things don't need to be translated to be understood.

I loved spending time with Coya, but it was actually her mother whom I had traveled more than nine thousand kilometers to meet.

Martha has worked in education in her province for years, and has been a prominent language activist in her Kichwa-speaking community.

Kichwa has been spoken here in the Andes for about five hundred years, and across Ecuador as a whole there are twelve other indigenous languages recognized by the state, all of them particular to their region. This language abundance is what we'd expect from one of the planet's seventeen megadiverse countries, host to a long coastline and part of the Amazon as well as a few dozen volcanoes. Human societies have flourished here since the area was first inhabited over ten thousand years ago. Trade networks and chiefdoms developed, and sophisticated raised-field farming began to climb through this tectonic landscape until the Peruvian Incas arrived from over the Andes and established their own civilization. Their conquest gave Ecuador its first—but not its last—known lingua franca: Quechua.

Runasimi, as its own speakers would call it—meaning "the people's language"—looks less like a language family tree and more like a forest. Ethnologue records more than forty varieties of Quechua, which is unsurprising given there was no single standard version of it under the Incas, who ruled over the largest state in the world in the 1400s. Today, Quechua's continua of dialects can be found in Argentina, Bolivia, Chile, Colombia, Ecuador, and its original homeland of Peru. These "many Quechuas" are not necessarily mutually intelligible, and in each land Quechua touched, it made contact with dozens of other indigenous languages, evolving here and there to produce localized varieties like Kichwa; within Ecuador, there are also, technically, many Kichwas. Quechua varieties are all agglutinating languages, meaning words are built up of roots to which suffixes are added, as in Japanese or Swahili. We do it a little in English, too, gluing words together to make an entirely new one, like sleeplessness, where we've taken the word sleep and added -less and -ness to create an entirely different meaning. Imagine us doing this for almost every single word in our language and you can get a sense of how Quechua behaves.

The three-generation cycle—a Kichwa monolingual grandmother, bilingual mother, and Spanish monolingual child—is repeated across Ecuador today. According to recent estimates, while seventy thousand people in Imbabura describe themselves as Kichwa, just twenty-three thousand of them can speak it, with the rest of the population shifting toward monolingual Spanish, the language of the colonizers who conquered the Incas. To be indigenous is rare—they make up just 7 to 8 percent of the population—and to speak one of the country's thirteen or so indigenous languages rarer still among younger generations. Spanish is a lingua franca between diverse indigenous peoples and those who identify as mestizo (mixed heritage), and increasingly Spanish is substituting indigenous language diversity. The number of native or fluent speakers of Kichwa across Ecuador has plummeted in the last few decades; between 1994 and 2014, regions across the country have experienced a loss of between 10 to 30 percent.[1] I found Martha's name in an article[2] about activists revitalizing Kichwa in Imbabura. "Martha Túquerres, one of the activists, says that they will make a map of pregnant women and midwives in the Andean zone. The objective is to make them aware of the importance of maintaining a link with the maternal language during pregnancy," it read.

I was intrigued; this wasn't a language revitalization method I had come across before. There are plenty of language programs out there that address young children, like kindergartens or alphabet books, but far fewer that seem to target children before they're even out of the womb. When I contacted Martha to arrange an interview and asked her where I could stay locally, she sent me a link to her own house where she regularly hosts tourists. I would learn that lots of people in her community do several jobs, smartly finding opportunities here and there to make a living. Such people do not stay monolingual for very long.

Martha's first language is Kichwa, but she is fully bilingual with Spanish and spent time studying at the university in Costa Rica before returning to Ecuador, first to work in the capital Quito for the Ministry of Farming and finally back home to Cotacachi. When I met her, she was a district director in the Education Ministry, and on a visit to her office one day I got to observe quietly as employees endlessly popped in and out of the door, asking Martha this or getting her approval for that. She was always impeccably dressed, as were her daughters whom she and Luis fastidiously tugged, hoisted, and plaited every day for school. Every morning, Martha, Amy, and Coya would all emerge from their front door with a white blouse adorned with embroidery: their cinched woven belts, called chumbis; two layers of woolen skirts, called anakos; and, for Martha, a fachalina, a sash that she tied on her right shoulder to designate her status as a married woman. Her walca—a necklace with gold beads—had many rings to it. The beads' size are supposed to increase with the knowledge that a Kichwa woman accumulates; I wasn't clear about exactly what the different beads signified, but I was certain that she knew her stuff.

Once her office had quieted down, she wanted to show me a book so that I could see written Kichwa. It was a bilingual copy of the Ecuadorian constitution; Kichwa itself has only been an official "intercultural" language in the country since 2008, when the Ecuadorian constitution adopted sweeping reforms. Along with a much-needed expansion of indigenous rights in Ecuador that granted people land rights, self-determination, and the power to use their own justice systems, the constitution became the first in the world to grant personhood to nature. Even the Spanish section used Kichwa terminology; Mother Earth is mentioned first as Pacha Mama, and when it establishes what it calls "a new form of public coexistence," it announces it will achieve sumak kawsay—the good way of living. Sumak kawsay is a Kichwa idea that we might now describe as anti-capitalist—a communal, collective way of life, a communion of people and planet, that was popularized during Ecuador's indigenous rights movement. The opposite of sumak kawsay is llaki kawsay, individualized disenchantment that overvalues the material world.[3] *Bad* living.

It sounds like there has been a lot of bad living in Ecuador over the centuries. The Incas had not been in Ecuadorean territory for very long when Francisco Pizarro, the Spanish conquistador eager for the kind of gold that his peers had just plundered from the Aztecs, led a successful ambush of the Incan ruler Atahualpa in Cajamarca, Peru, in 1532. Though powerful, the Incas had made themselves vulnerable to external threat with a raging civil war, and the Spanish saw their opportunity. Following Atahualpa's execution, Pizarro took Atahualpa's ten-year-old consort Cuxirimay Ocllo as his concubine, and six years later he had two sons by her. Cuxirimay ended up outliving him and marrying another Spaniard, Juan Díez de Betanzos, who learned Quechua and interviewed Cuxirimay along with other Incas about their life and history, leaving us with one of the best records of the Spanish conquest of the Inca civilization—*Narrative of the Incas*. Only eighteen chapters of it were known about until the 1980s, when a further sixty-four were discovered in Spain. In its prologue we see how severe the language barriers were between indigenous people and the Spanish conquistadors; Betanzos complained that he encountered many inaccuracies in his contemporaries' reports on the locals because the Spanish had been less interested in fact-finding and more interested in "subduing and acquiring the land."

Kichwa, an oral language, was given a Latin alphabet by its colonizers. The first person to attempt to document Kichwa was possibly not Kichwa at all; he was a Jesuit missionary whose surname suggests he was descended from Spaniards who had left Alcocer, a town in Spain's south. In his own book on Kichwa, Hernando de Alcocer explains that preaching in "the language of the Inca" delivered great fruit and benefit, although he also prayed that "the price of the blood and redemption of Jesus Christ is not wasted on these miserable Indians." His book wasn't only a grammar but a guide for priests who wanted to evangelize effectively; he points out that while many understood Kichwa, very few were capable "of dedicating themselves to the humble ministry of confessing, teaching and preaching to these destitute people." Imagine this being one of the first books on your people's language. Missionaries learned Kichwa quickly, co-opting the Inca Empire's language so they could evangelize more swiftly and seamlessly elide into its power structures. Then there was change; by the seventeenth and eighteenth centuries, under the rule of the Spanish Bourbon dynasty, a more rounded switch to Spanish began, with policies banning indigenous languages in schools and public life creeping in as the Crown hoped to quell rebellion.

Martha's constitution is a sign of greatly changed times—but she wasn't showing me it to discuss the transformation of Ecuadorean political thought. She wanted to explain how hard it was for her to read it. "Writing in Kichwa is very complicated," Martha said, reading out a line of Kichwa. "Now, I'm practicing more and more, the fluency is coming when I read. But it's taken me four or five years." She bent back the spine of the book and pointed at a word. "The writing says this is Kariwami. But *we* say it khariwami. Khari is man, wari is woman." The change in sound is enough to confuse a fluent speaker like Martha; it would be like someone writing "thog" instead of "dog." She kept reading, hunting down another word to confuse her, which didn't take long. "Here, it's written Kushiyeringa— *kushiyatanchi* is what it should be. It's faster for us to say it this way. It means how to be happy. Well-being."

She flicked through the book to the Spanish version of the constitution. "I wouldn't read the Kichwa here. It's a lot faster reading the Spanish. And so resources for us are often better when they are audiovisual—not reading."

Like Kurdish, Kichwa was an unwritten language for the vast

majority of its existence, and during Martha's own lifetime its spelling has been changed at least three times. Many words Martha knows are also not included in Unified Kichwa, the standardized form of the language in which the constitution is written. While Martha still finds it challenging selecting the "right" Kichwa word, or spelling it, that isn't actually her biggest problem.

A day earlier she had to chair a meeting where parents requested that the school spend less time teaching Kichwa and that teachers should make room for something more "valuable." Martha expects this view also comes from their own experience as children. "They possibly got bullied for speaking Kichwa at school," she said. "Even in the workplace. And if they don't think it's needed for work, they don't see the interest in it." She paused and reminisced for a moment. "In my own home, my parents didn't see a value in speaking Kichwa."

Martha is effectively seeing history repeat itself, except this is a linguicide that now seems to be coming from within as well as outside the community. Kichwa has spent more time being value*less* than valua*ble* in Ecuador. The difference now is that it isn't a distant Spanish king declaring that all his subjects should speak Spanish—it is often Kichwa people themselves who declare it useless or who admonish others for using it publicly.

One Peruvian linguist calls this social pressure to reject an indigenous language asfixia linguistica—linguistic asphyxiation. The traditional Kichwa words are being denied oxygen. In Occitan, there is a similar word for the cumulative effects of being made to reject the mother tongue: vergonha. Occitan speakers know this fate well; France once had many languages, split between the langues d'oil of the north and langues d'oc of the south, so called because oil and oc were close to how these languages said "yes" in medieval France. But, as Charles de Gaulle is said to have once put it, "How is it possible to govern a country with two hundred and forty-six cheeses?" The quote might be apocryphal, but the attitude is entirely evidenced by the French state, which has been hostile to pretty much any other indigenous language; French has been the sole language of public life ever since the French Revolution. Vergonha is a powerful word, and likely understandable for any Romance language speaker; in French it's vergogne and Italian vergogna. I translated it into its Spanish equivalent for Martha, vergüenza, and I translate it into English for you now: shame.

The irony is that Ecuador is progressive when it comes to multiethnic identities, actively promoting them, just as the constitution demonstrated. But fifty years of language revitalization isn't much in the face of five hundred years of wider ethnic suppression. Bilingual education programs were introduced at the end of the twentieth century, finally giving indigenous communities a chance to learn in their own languages as well as in Spanish. But research in the nineties in Martha's Cotacachi revealed that Spanish-speaking elementary-school teachers and principals who opposed bilingual education were still telling their pupils that Kichwa was "backward," that it had no grammar and an inadequate lexicon.

Prejudices about the Kichwa language—and, indeed, any language—are not rooted in linguistics or science; they are the product of years of discrimination. There are, ironically, plenty of moments where Kichwa's lexicon or grammar is wider than the Spanish equivalent, although the point remains that Kichwa would still not be any less valuable even if it did have a narrower lexicon. In Spanish and English, I am restricted to saying I have a hermano or a hermana, a brother or a sister; in Kichwa, I'd have a turi and a ñaña, while a man would have a wawki and a pani, as their words for brother and sister depend on the gender of the person referring to them. A Kichwa speaker can add suffixes that signify whether they received the information they are saying firsthand or secondhand; whether they're reporting it, quoting it, or inferring it are all signified by different markers. Near the Amazon, if you add -mari at the end of a word, it means you're talking about a topic that is familiar both to yourself and whomever you are speaking to, for example, the party you both attended last weekend. Many people in the world of news or public health could only dream of members of the public being so engaged in the evidence behind the statements they made.

Even if Kichwa didn't have any of those features, it still wouldn't be any less valuable. Yet the shame persists. Linguists who have spent time in Kichwa schools have found that such linguistic shame has frustrated their efforts to ascertain how many young people do speak it. Nicholas Limerick found that when he spoke in Kichwa at indigenous schools, students told him that they didn't know how to speak it, and would point to someone else who they thought could. The person who had been pointed at would then also say that they couldn't speak it, and would be accused by the others of lying, saying the student must be embarrassed or ashamed. It's as if the shame is passed around; no one wants to claim it or acknowledge what it means.

■ ■ ■

Twenty minutes south from Cotacachi is a city called Otavalo, with a picturesque public square lined with palm trees. On the Sunday I arrived I found a brass band playing there, and lots of locals had come to sit and watch, eating jellies and ponches, a white foam drink with a great splodge of red syrup on top. Like Cotacachi, Otavalo was nothing like urban Quito, a comparative melting pot of Ecuadorean and other Latin American identities where indigenous and rural life felt absent. In Otavalo, trucks were heaving with freshly harvested vegetables, and around town there was a meeting of worlds, where hoodies and jeans could be accompanied by formal black hats, ponchos, and coral jewelry, and where everyone had long, shining black hair, often braided or tied up. One elderly woman, who I saw leaving Mass, was almost entirely in traditional dress except she wore no shoes. As she walked, I saw another woman of about the same age shake her head at the sight, in soft despair. Thirty percent of Ecuador's population continue to live below the poverty line, and Ecuador's indigenous communities are vastly overrepresented in this figure.

A living museum, established in 2011, reminds visitors of the lasting impact of Spanish colonization. When I arrived at the Otavalango Museum, it seemed empty and I wondered whether the opening times online were inaccurate. The large white building that is now a little dilapidated was once a hacienda, a large estate farmed by indigenous people, usually in a system of forced labor. It was opened in the mid-1800s when Ecuador was not yet a country of its own but part of Gran Colombia. It doesn't exist anymore, but it was a massive state that included lots of northern South America and Central America that was consolidated when the Spanish Empire was ousted. Long rows of iron windows betray one of the building's former uses as something called an obraje, which locked indigenous people into exploitative labor just as in the haciendas, except they'd be stuck inside, spinning, weaving, and cleaning wool. I was about to turn back when a big black dog ran out, barking, and behind him Sary appeared. Sary was a little taller than me, with a gray sweatshirt, a coral necklace around his neck, and the same black hat I had seen on the men in the square. He belongs to one of the twenty Kichwa families who have become the first indigenous owners of this building. He greeted me and invited me into the first large building; despite the many tourists I had seen buying ponchos in Otavalo, it looked as if I was their only visitor that day.

"The first owner of this factory had two laws," Sary explained, gesturing to the now empty concrete floor and the high vaulted ceiling supported by slim wooden beams. "One: work twenty hours, rest for four. And two: don't call indigenous people indigenous people—call them beasts of burden."

This first owner was José Féliz de Valdivieso, the first president of Ecuador. Over the next two centuries, owners of the hacienda-cum-factory came and went, some more benevolent than others. Unlike plantations in the US, where the majority of labor came from enslaved Africans, in the highlands of the Andes Spanish colonizers instead used debt peonage to build their labor forces. This work was normally done on land that had been seized from indigenous communities, who then had no option but to rely on such forced employment to provide them with work and food. It had begun years before this Otavalo obraje began its work, and would continue into living memory. Sary's grandmother began working there when she was only eight years old. She told Sary stories about grim punishments for late starts; one former boss is said to have put cigarettes in workers' mouths and ordered them to walk one hundred meters before trying to shoot the cigarettes from their mouths, a story that reminded me of the terror the Omani Sultan Said bin Taimur inflicted upon his own workers. Former laborers of the obraje today remember bosses throwing objects at their heads as they worked on, the blood running down their faces. They recall a drunken brother of a patrón once shooting an employee, who ran away bleeding, and who never returned. "These stories are passed voice to voice," Sary told me. This is not necessarily because Kichwa is primarily a spoken language, but because it was too dangerous to write them down, in Kichwa or in Spanish, its speakers fearing repercussion from their masters. Perhaps it was also because, sometimes, the stories were just too sad.

The stories and the language survived this forced labor, but many of the people did not. In 2021, researchers used Peru's electoral roll to analyze surnames from the areas where forced labor known as mita took place.[4] This was an Inca practice of tax labor that was appropriated by the Spanish state and used to force a seventh of a district's adult male population to work in mines every year. They were able to establish that this forced labor, introduced in 1573, decimated the native-born male population in mita districts, and that there are far more indigenous surnames today in Peru that have survived from non-mita areas.

That these local families abused by colonial powers banded together and bought the Otavalo hacienda is a remarkable act of resistance, one that is given new meaning every day as it puts on events for the local community or offers tours to reckon with the horrors of the past. Sary told me that it was his grandparents' and parents' fight for workers' rights that has enabled him to protect his future; the first thing they did when they found fair remuneration was to invest it in their children's education. "I'm an engineer, my brother is a lawyer. My wife is studying so she can become an accountant," he said. They are university graduates, just two generations after their grandparents escaped child labor—and they are also proud Kichwa speakers. If he and his wife have children, he will teach them Kichwa; but what the data is showing, and what Martha sees in her classrooms, is that there are fewer and fewer would-be parents like Sary. Anecdotally, and in perplexing contradiction, this language shift seems to coexist with many people in Kichwa communities being very proud of their identity. It was totally normal to see people wearing indigenous clothing while I was in Otavalo, for example. It reminded me of my own experience back in London, where diasporic Italians had stopped speaking Italian but still felt very Italian. In cities like Otavalo with large indigenous populations it seems that there was less shame, if not about their language ability, then about their wider ethnic identity.

The other side of shame is hope, and pride; hope that children will have a better life than their parents or grandparents did. Back in the eighties, a study that interviewed Kichwa speakers in Otavalo found that parents wanted their children to be monolingual Spanish speakers because they feared bilingual education would deny them access to social mobility, an opinion most strongly held by the rural poor.[5] The linguist Kendall Kinn, who did fieldwork in two Andean communities in the nineties, found that younger, economically secure community members were often those who were more likely to value Kichwa and to support its revitalization. I'm not surprised. Of course people have more time to think about their language's survival when they have access to education, and freedom from worrying about money, food, and clothes. Shame may be a language killer, but so is miseria, and the longing for a better life.

While there appears to be considerable support for bilingualism today in Ecuador, it's not necessarily a bilingualism that prioritizes indigenous languages. Researchers in Ecuadorean schools found a rigid hierarchy around bilingualism, with people perceived to be "elite bilinguals"[6]—those who spoke Spanish with a language like English or French set above minoritized bilinguals, who spoke an indigenous language. Spanish's place was unquestioned; English, indigenous pupils said, was their key to competing with mestizo peers and keeping up with globalization. No one would wish to deny them that, but does Kichwa have to come at the expense of Spanish and English? Even in a country with a remarkably decolonized political system, it is uncomfortably obvious that the colonial languages, their five-hundred-year-old-prestige, and the access and privilege they award their speakers, still triumph over a language that reminds people of home, of hardship, and, like the hacienda, of the past.

■ ■ ■

When shame has permeated a language, it can't be revitalized without first being revalued. Speakers need to feel as if a language is important again and, most crucially, important enough to pass on to their children. These language reclamation efforts started late into Kichwa's linguicide; it was in the final decades of the twentieth century when anti-colonial and labor movements, growing across the continent, began to consolidate in Ecuador. Amid their country's new status as an oil economy and agrarian reforms that once again threatened to benefit elites, indigenous groups mobilized to fight against land grabs. Education and literacy were major aims of these resistance efforts, and in the 1970s and 1980s language activists and educators began decolonizing the alphabet. Letters that are redundant in Kichwa pronunciation were removed, like *b* and *f*, while sounds like sh and ts, so characteristic of spoken Kichwa, were added.[7] By 1998, a third wave of changes came in; *q* and *c* were nixed altogether and were replaced by the *k* that now fills so much of written Kichwa today, including its own name. Kichwa was left with nineteen letters, and a new, "shallow" orthography, which sounds like a bad thing, but is counterintuitively excellent for a population wishing to rapidly become literate in a language. It essentially means words are more likely to follow similar and clearer patterns—unlike a language like English, for example, that is full of arbitrary rules that confound children and those with special educational needs.

Along with this alphabet change came another, even more dramatic intervention: the introduction of a standard Kichwa language. There were many Kichwas spoken between the jungles of the Amazon and the snowcapped mountains of the Andes—and many activists and academics decided that handing them all just one Kichwa to speak would somehow synchronize and unite indigenous communities.[8] But to try to turn many Kichwas into just *one* Kichwa was a gargantuan task. In theory, it might make sense to create a language standard, in the hope that it would build a seismic wave of Kichwa speakers that would robustly counter the negative and racist attitudes of the time. There was only one problem: When you pick one kind of Kichwa, you leave out all of the others. Linguists have since said that Kichwa standardization managed to create a standardized Kichwa that, in its written form, failed to capture most of the sounds that speakers actually produce.[9] Throughout my time in Ecuador I met many Amazonian Kichwa speakers who complained about how Unified Kichwa prioritizes an Andean Kichwa, which they don't speak. For a great deal of Kichwa speakers, Unified Kichwa does not unify them; it leaves them feeling like their Kichwa wasn't prestigious enough to be chosen as the standard and so wasn't worthy of being taught in schools or used in official public life.

It is true that Unified Kichwa more heavily represents highlands dialects, but, as we have seen, even Martha's Kichwa diverges significantly from Unified Kichwa, to the point that it has taken her years of study to familiarize herself with it. The standard was not simply created as a guide for communities to use; it created one that speakers would forever be tested on. Now, exams that are set to test language aptitude will judge speakers by their ability to read and write in Unified Kichwa, as opposed to the variety of Kichwa they grew up with. Luis, Martha's husband, failed the language test Ecuadoreans must take if they want to take certain jobs connected to the government. He is a fluent Kichwa speaker, but because he isn't a fluent *Unified* Kichwa speaker, or writer, he didn't pass. He has no plans to retake it, and I don't blame him; how can a system like this work if it ends up suppressing Kichwa speakers all over again?

Similarly, establishing bilingual education across Ecuador has not magically solved their language crisis. It was the first bilingual education model to be introduced in the whole of Latin America in 1988, in areas with high indigenous populations, and it promised children access to lessons not only in Spanish but in their community's language. In the early 2000s, the numbers seemed good; there were ninety-five thousand enrolled in 2007, and nearly one hundred and fifty thousand in 2015. But a 2009 UNESCO report found that students at bilingual schools were performing considerably worse across the board. This has nothing to do with the Kichwa language and everything to do with the fact that such schools are more likely to be in rural areas where there are only one or two teachers and sometimes no internet connection.[10] Teachers at bilingual schools make up the majority of Ecuadorean teachers who don't have a university degree, meaning many of them lack professional teacher training. Bilingual education doesn't work in isolation if teachers can't access better training opportunities to deliver it and if the economic conditions of indigenous communities are not improved.

Martha put her Kichwa constitution down and turned to her computer, a huge, wheezing PC. She opened up a survey that community organizers had been working on developing. It was designed for residents in Cotacachi and asked questions like *Who taught you Kichwa? Who can write and speak it in your family? In which spaces do you speak Kichwa? With whom do you speak the most in Kichwa?*

"We want to know what the reality is; who speaks Kichwa most in the family? And at what ages?" she asked. "Because something is going on in our families—and with this, we'll be able to develop strategies."

Martha is right to gather detail that goes beyond government census data, which, like most censuses, simply asks people what languages they speak and leaves it there. In Cotacachi, the most recent census in 2010 revealed that only 25 percent of the population speaks Kichwa despite 50 percent of its population identifying as indigenous. Eighty-six percent of the population speaks Spanish, which means we can make an educated guess about how many of those speaker numbers are monolingual Kichwa elders (probably most of them) and how many individuals are bilingual between the two languages (probably most younger speakers of Kichwa). But deeper questions can shed far more light on *where* the language is being lost. A study by linguists of nearly four thousand speakers across the country in 2016[11] found that while 70 percent of Kichwa-speaking adults were speaking to their parents in Kichwa, that rate immediately dropped to 50 percent when they were speaking to a brother or sister. By the time they were speaking to their partner, just over 40 percent were speaking in Kichwa, and with their children only around 25 percent were speaking Kichwa. Martha suspects that her survey will show the same results: that it is parent-to-child where the language is disappearing most rapidly. Intriguingly, the rates of speaking Kichwa to a mother or a sister are ever so slightly higher than speaking to a father or son; this is probably because of patriarchal norms that are not remotely unique to Ecuador, in which women are more likely to spend more time at home and are less likely to be literate, leaving them more likely to be monolingual.

This is why Martha believes that Kichwa women are central to the language's survival. "Trusting women with greater empathy and power here is going to make the process more successful," she told me. It's not that they don't have faith in the men, but, rather, that the women traditionally play so many roles—"mothers, advisers, doctors in every sense"—and are the ones handling communication within the home. As a result, they have the capacity to create real change.

A number of institutions, including UNESCO, would agree with Martha that women have a key part to play in language revitalization. The task force behind the International Decade of Indigenous Languages calls for "the need to create favorable conditions for gender equality and women's empowerment through preserving, revitalizing, and promoting Indigenous languages," arguing that women are "custodians of cultural wisdom" who "carry the responsibility of transmitting not only words but traditions, rituals, values, and the very essence of their people. Through their voices, stories come to life."[12] I was reminded of how Malwina Gudowska (see "Emigrate") had talked about Polish and this simultaneous privilege and burden that women carry as tradition holders and language transmitters in families. But it is clearly something that Martha believes, and endorses, too. She explained that women's organizations here tackle what may be perceived as women's issues, like gender violence, but also defense of water quality, land rights, and even the conservation of seeds. International funding organizations are acutely aware that women's groups like these are capable of distributing resources to where it will be used well because they are already probably in charge of addressing a community's many needs.

Martha and her fellow community organizers hope that the

Kichwa survey will help provide them with hard data to win more funding and direct it to where it's most needed. For now, they're doing everything they can to engage pregnant women in their community to speak their native Kichwa not only to their children but to their pregnant bellies. "We need to speak to them like they are already outside of the womb," one traditional midwife, or partera, told Martha's team. It was the project that I had learned about when I'd first discovered Martha's work in that news article.

These beliefs are grounded in what we know about babies' language acquisition. Babies not only prefer their mother's voice immediately after birth, but also appear to prefer their native language. Melody and pitch can be heard through amniotic fluid and the uterine wall, and every language in the world has its unique acoustic "print" that a fetus hears called a prosodic pattern. Just three days out of the womb, babies cry in different languages; a study from 2009 comparing thirty French newborns and thirty German newborns found that pitch and intensity varied on the basis of the child's nationality, mimicking the melodic qualities of each language; the German babies reached their maximum pitch and intensity at 0:45 seconds, whereas French cries took longer to crescendo, at 0:6 seconds. In 2024, new research revealed that newborn babies of bilingual mothers respond differently to sound stimulus than babies of monolingual mothers; they are sensitive to a wider range of speech, whereas monolingual babies selectively tune into one, familiar language.[13] The scientist Judit Gervain described this prenatal learning as "bootstrapping"[14] the acquisition of grammar and lexicon, something that is useful for any language a child learns, never mind an endangered one.

Parteras are vital in a country where 86 percent of public hospitals are located in urban areas. "We didn't grow up speaking Spanish," one says in a video Martha's team made, gently pushing and massaging the side of her patient's swollen stomach as the father, in his white shirt and black poncho, sits nearby watching. "The father must speak to the child in Kichwa from the moment it is in the womb. The mother must raise the baby speaking Kichwa, and when the baby is born, you both must say: 'My child! How good it is you have come to this life! Protect me, care for me, and when I am old you in return will care for me and swaddle me.'"

Martha agreed. "Kichwa needs to be loved and heard from the moment the woman is pregnant," she said. As she explained, many of the local midwives only spoke Kichwa, and so they're using that language when they examine the mother: "They say beautiful words." Two of her colleagues cried at the recollection, overcome by the knowledge "that there is someone else concerned about the well-being of the child, that there is this connection . . . it will help us to understand that it's not only a language, it's part of our culture and can strengthen us and motivate us not to lose it."

Martha's research with pregnant women is, for her, an attempt to understand where language transmission breaks down within the generations. So far, the second generation is looking like a "problem" group, one she admits being a member of. "Without realizing my children and I are speaking mainly in Spanish. If I don't make more of an effort, they will only be able to listen to Kichwa. And when they have their own children, it will be lost completely." Even Martha, who has worked hard to reduce shame and valorize Kichwa in her work, has not been impervious to the wider devaluation of Kichwa in her community.

Martha's innovative project with pregnant women and her passion for her work have stayed with me for a long time; it made me think, for the first time, about how a language can only be treated with love and value when its speakers are treated that way, too. Studies or experiments that have looked into language revitalization with children often focus on educational programs, just like the ones the Ecuadorean state introduced decades ago to transform the literacy of everyone in the country, no matter what ethnic group they came from. Language nests, originating in New Zealand, are another famous example of such projects; Māori language revivalists created kōhanga reo in the 1980s where very young children were immersed in preschools with elders who were fluent in the language and would interact with them only in Māori. In many cases, these children ended up becoming more fluent than their parents, who have become a "missed" generation of language acquisition. They had been inspired by the work of Samoans before them, who had introduced their own language nests in diaspora in New Zealand; what was distinctive about the Māoris' efforts was that they were establishing such nests in their own indigenous lands and not as migrants. By 1996, there were one hundred seventy-six Pacific island language nests, meaning 38 percent of all Pacific island children attending preschool institutions were enrolled in nests.[15] Countries around the world with long-suffering minority languages have adopted the language nest model, and there could even be one where you live. If not, you have almost certainly witnessed the results of them; Hana-Rāwhiti Maipi-Clarke, New Zealand's youngest MP at the time of writing who is famous for performing the haka in parliament and demanding indigenous rights in her homeland, speaks fluent Māori. She was able to attend a language nest and enjoy the expansion of Māori language rights, partly thanks to a policy that her own great-aunt helped to introduce decades ago when she presented a petition to parliament with thirty thousand signatures asking them to prioritize saving Te Reo Māori.

In Ecuador, the word for baby talk is huahuayachishpa;[16] say it quietly and you will conjure the soft words of the midwife I watched in Martha's videos, like a spell. Unsurprisingly, huahuayachishpa heavily uses the Kichwa diminutive -gu-, just as how in English we might say "little" a lot to describe a child, and it replaces harder syllables with easier ones. When baby talk has been studied elsewhere—sadly focusing primarily on English and European languages—linguists have found that we are all broadly similar when it comes to talking to infants.[17] We use a higher pitch, our words carry greater melody, and we speak more slowly. It is be-lieved that this makes it easier for babies to understand us,[18] their brain activity shooting up and their brain waves literally syncing up with the rhythms of their parents' speech. As babies become children, we start to speak a little lower and more quickly, but the musicality remains. We still exaggerate our vowel sounds, espe-cially in English. Without thinking about it, our language mirrors our children's development, helping them acquire language as if it's within our muscle memory. It is an innate, ancient awareness we have developed to ease our children into speaking like us, and becoming one of us.

But huahuayachishpa is also about something else. It's not only how you speak to a child—it's also what you choose to say. It is as much about making a child laugh, or consoling them, as it is the prosody of your speech. As Martha said, it's about love. Families eager to teach their children Kichwa have more than five hundred years of oppression and linguicide to contend with, the long roots of misinformation and shame still impacting learners today. They do not have five hundred years to revive it. With each new birth of a Kichwa child, Martha has correctly identified that there are two op-portunities that come with it. One is to raise a Kichwa-speaking child and another is a final chance to reach the child's mother, and help them both experience a language that not only gives love, but deserves it in return.

THE STORY OF HEBREW

> הסברה **(hasbara):** "explaining," a term coined by
> Nahum Sokolow to describe the mass communications
> of modern-day Israel[1]

In the middle of London there is an eight-hundred-year-old scroll that really shouldn't be there. Pull apart the two wooden rollers that join it, known as its Etz Chaim, trees of life, and you can see great holes in the cow-skin parchment, held together by stretched sinew, as silver as a spider's web. Historians can tell the scroll's age by the Hebrew script it bears, a particular means of writing that only existed for a short period of time centuries ago in Prague's Jewish community. It would have taken twenty cows' worth of skin to make it, which would have amounted to at least a year's supply of the animal—but that is what a Torah is worth to the people it serves.

Behind me, in a building in Kensington that also houses Westminster Synagogue, were reams and reams of other scrolls, some plainer, some more ornate. Over the years, more than fifteen hundred Czech Jewish scrolls have passed through here since they were salvaged from a museum decades ago. The Nazis had once rounded them all up, just as they had done to the communities that had created and relied upon them. The scrolls are all that remain, a forgotten Nazi deposit that, fortunately, never made it to whatever destruction they were intended for.

Each one that has been rescued and preserved in the Memorial Scrolls Trust Museum represents one of our last remaining links to Czech Jewish life before the Holocaust, to eighteenth- and nineteenth-century Bohemia and Moravia. Prague was nicknamed "Jerusalem upon Vltava" for its reputation as a center of Talmudic learning. Some of the scrolls were bound in precious sashes called wimpels, the swaddling clothes of a Jewish child that is then cleaned and decorated with the child's name and blessings. They are testaments not only to the care with which these scrolls were treated, but the close ties between a believer and their sacred text, brought together with cloth and thread at their birth, their bar mitzvah, and here, long after death. They show us what people believed and read; but what they do not show us is what people *spoke*.

Jewish communities in places like what is now Czechia were polyglot: They spoke Yiddish (the West Germanic tongue of the Ashkenazi Jewish community, which literally means "Jewish" in the language itself), as well as Czech, German, Hungarian—the list goes on. As we learned with Ladino in Thessaloniki (see "Expel"), where speakers grew more and more bilingual with Greek, Jewish people were increasingly bilingual in Yiddish as well as a language of a European nation-state throughout the 1800s and 1900s. Both Yiddish and Ladino were written in Hebrew script, and between girls and boys, literacy in the Hebrew language itself would have varied from basic prayer-book comprehension to complex religious studies. Crucially, Hebrew was nobody's mother tongue and had not been since ancient times. In the Prague of the early 1900s, Hebrew was heard only in religious settings like the synagogue, where Jewish worshippers would come to pray and see the Torah scroll taken out of its ark and read by a baal korei, a master reader, skilled in Hebrew pronunciation and cantillation.

Members of the congregation would be called up for an aliyah, "going up," to recite blessings between the baal korei's chants. So precious is the text that the scroll cannot be touched with human hands, and so a yad, a long silver stylus with a pointed hand carved at the end, is trailed along the script instead to guide the reader. Torah scrolls must be handwritten and take around a year to write; the scribe, or sofer, knows that it must have no more or less than exactly 304,805 letters. Just one mistake renders the entire scroll invalid, and while scribes are allowed to make corrections as they go, sometimes having to slice at their fresh ink with razor blades, if a mistake is found later in the middle of a public reading then the entire Torah scroll is immediately cast aside and sent for repairs while a special replacement copy is brought out.

This is why many of the scrolls now housed in the museum have had to be restored; any ink that has faded from the page with the passage of time has rendered the document inadmissible for public readings. I once went to the house of one of the scrolls' indefatigable restorers, Mordechai Pinchas, and I can remember how full of tomes and sheets of paper it was, piled everywhere, just as you would expect from a scribe and scholar. "Every letter I write in this Torah is a victory against Hitler," he said plainly, armed with his white feather quill. But before he begins writing he always first takes out a small scrap of paper and writes the world amalek on it—"the bad guys" of the Torah, he said. The sons of the villainous Amalek were recurrent enemies of the Israelites in the Hebrew Bible until their tribe was eventually defeated during the exodus from Egypt. "God said 'Blot out the name of amalek from under the heavens,'" Mordechai explained. "So before a scribe writes, he writes the word amalek, and then crosses it out with three lines." He showed me the envelope that held his amalek scraps, ready to burn later. "Sadly, Amalek is still around. All anti-Semites out there from Hitler onward. And we're seeing quite a lot of them today. They're Amalek and Amalek has never gone away. It's our job to make sure that they do."

But while the Torah has remained the same since ancient times, other elements of Jewish life, and identity, have not. Back in Prague, a legend has it that the cornerstones of the Altneuschul, the Old-New

Synagogue, come from the ruins of the Second Temple, the great Jewish place of worship in Jerusalem that was razed first by the Babylonians and then the Romans. Some say Jewish exiles carried the temple stones to Prague all the way from Judea; others say angels salvaged them from the ashes. Yet all these stories agree on the promise with which the stone was brought, the religious condition known in Hebrew as al-tnai: that once the Temple of Jerusalem was restored, the stones must be returned. A Third Temple has never been rebuilt, but something else has. The Jews of Eastern Europe could never have imagined that it was not a physical stone that would one day be brought back to their perceived homeland, but something else that was just as foundational: the language that their people had not spoken outside of prayer in almost two thousand years.

■ ■ ■

Hebrew is astonishing living proof that linguicide can be resisted. It is frequently said of Hebrew that it is the only language in history that has ever been successfully raised from the dead. This wasn't only an extraordinary linguistic project, but a political one; there would be no modern Hebrew without Zionism. Even today, language is continuously politicized and weaponized by conservative Israeli politicians. One lawmaker in 2016 tried to claim that Palestinians don't have a right to their land because "there is no P in Arabic." When Waleed Taha, an Israeli Arab politician, delivered a speech in Arabic in the Knesset in 2022, a number of Israeli Jewish politicians reacted with horror. Gesturing to both Taha- and the Arabic-speaking deputy speaker, David Amsalem shouted, "[You want] baklava and coffee? Do you have no shame? Look to the low point we have reached. Two Arabs are talking among themselves, making fun of us." In a video he posted afterward, another politician, Itamar Ben-Gvir, labeled Waleed Taha a "terrorist": Arabic technically has a special status in Israel, and is allowed to be spoken in the Knesset, but for contemporary Israel's most intense ideologues, Hebrew should be the only language in Israel, with Arabic and its speakers silenced. A century ago, this was a country where locals, migrants, and settlers spoke at least ten different languages. The same cannot be said today.

While Hebrew is the only language that can claim linguistic resurrection on the scale it enjoys, this title remains a half-truth, conveniently ignoring how much the language had continued to evolve since ancient times. It remained very much alive for the scholars who worked in it. But it is certainly true that Hebrew disappeared as a *vernacular* language among ordinary people following its final thrust in southern Judea in the third century CE before its speakers switched the language they used for daily life to Aramaic, having assigned Hebrew to religious worship. The great lingua franca Aramaic had already been displacing Hebrew for so many years that linguists believe Jesus, a Jew from Nazareth, spoke Aramaic as his everyday language. But while Hebrew disappeared from daily life, it gained a new life elsewhere as a language of liturgy and then literature, particularly for men who studied Hebrew in Jewish schools, or yeshivot. One of the main protagonists credited for Hebrew's revival, Eliezer Ben-Yehuda, was only able to bring spoken Hebrew back to life because of the religious, literary, and philosophical contributions to Hebrew that had been made in the centuries that preceded him. And even though there has been a continuous Jewish presence in the land of Palestine since antiquity, it would take a well-traveled Russian Jew to bring Hebrew back to vernacular life there.

How Ben-Yehuda achieved this resurrection remains contentious and debated today. Whatever you think of the origins of this language that today is spoken by around five million native speakers, it is undeniable that not one of them would exist had its texts not been documented, preserved, and valued centuries after its last native speaker died in ancient Judea. It is a sublime linguistic irony that the reason Hebrew could be revived is one of the same reasons it was killed off in the first place—when its speakers decided it should be used for spiritual purposes, rather than everyday speech, they ended up fossilizing it for their descendants. Thousands of years ago, Hebrew switched status from a vernacular language to lashon hakodesh, the Holy Tongue. It would go through several other names and stages to get to what is spoken in contemporary Israel by native speakers today, which many call Modern Hebrew, to distinguish it.

To tell Hebrew's story—from its fading away to its blazing return millennia later—is to discover what religion and sacred status can do to a language, both killing and preserving it. Other kinds of linguicide we've covered in this book have accompanied genocide, stolen lands, and the rise of the modern nation-state; the unique linguicide Hebrew experienced left it pretty lively for a supposedly "dead" language, ending its spoken existence but giving it an alternative vitality on parchment and paper.

Hebrew is not alone in this; a lot of sacred languages are also, technically, dead ones. For example, Hindi is not the language of Hindu prayer; that is Sanskrit, an ancient language of the Indian subcontinent in which epics like the Mahābhārata and the Rāmāyaṇa were written along with the Vedas, the faith's seminal scriptures. In western Christianity, debates have rumbled for hundreds of years whether masses should be delivered in a population's local language or Latin, which unlike Hinduism and Sanskrit wasn't even connected to any of the languages of the New or Old Testament were first written in. The New Testament was written in Greek long before it was translated into Latin. Then, when the early Church took hold from the empire's capital in Rome, Latin took on what would become a millennia-long role as the language of Christendom. By the time the Roman Empire collapsed and diverse nation-states sprang up across Europe with their own distinctive languages, Latin began to signify not just the way the literate and the faithful wrote or spoke, but a value system and heritage to preserve.

Languages help religions last. One way of ensuring a belief system will outlive you is to write it down. Some of the earliest writing systems that have been discovered, such as Egyptian, Mayan, and Runic scripts, all seemed to be used to memorize ritual performances.[2] The professor of religion studies Brian P. Bennett wrote that a sacred language is made so by being mythologized, specialized, and studied rather than acquired naturally. It also requires a community, not just an individual, to perceive its special status. For Bennett, a language wasn't sacred just because a god had been said to speak it; the act of mortal dedication to studying it and using it in religious ceremonies was just as important.

It's also worth pointing out that a sacred language can be perceived as important or special without many believers having a clue about what is actually being said. As Protestants pushed for vernacular preaching in the Middle Ages, Catholics defended Latin regardless of whether or not worshippers understood it. In both their lifetimes, Latin and Sanskrit were once broad lingua francas that united the literate in an age long before nation-states, language standardization, and secularization—but it doesn't matter that they aren't lingua francas anymore. They remind us of a time when scholarship meant knowing your sciences *and* your religion, and the language that went with it.

While this book has broadly charted our cultural amnesia around languages that weren't written down, sacred languages like Latin and Sanskrit show us a very different way that a "dead" language may, in fact, live on as long as the religion they're associated with lives on with them. It is why I sing in Latin every Sunday, at the Italian Catholic Mass in London at St. Peter's Church in Clerkenwell. The Gloria, Credo, Sanctus, Benedictus, and Agnus Dei punctuate every eucharistic ritual. That we might not understand every word is almost part of the appeal, with a hymn of praise drifting through us and endowing unknown properties as if it were an incantation.

Much as Latin didn't start off sounding like Harry Potter spells, Hebrew didn't start off sounding Talmudic. It was as far back as the tenth century BCE when royal scribes first documented the courts of the ancient kingdoms of Israel and Judea in the spoken language of their time. Hebrew varieties remained a national language there until the siege and fall of Jerusalem in 587 BCE, the first time the Temple of Jerusalem was destroyed and when Judeans were forced to live as exiles in Babylon. In writing and in speech, Hebrew morphed from being the language of a nation to that of a diaspora, where identities were tied to ethnicity as much as faith. The anxiety of keeping their faith in exile is captured in the famous "rivers of Babylon" lines in the Book of Psalms, where Babylonian captors told the Jews to sing a song from Zion. "How can we sing the songs of Yahweh / while in a foreign land?" they responded.

Centuries later, during the Roman period, the Dead Sea Scrolls—ancient biblical texts only rediscovered in the twentieth century—were composed almost entirely in Hebrew despite the Greek and Aramaic that were flourishing around Jewish scholars at the time. The ancient descendants of Judea continued to build the canon of Jewish work in its original language; even two thousand years ago, the writers of the Hebrew language were already demonstrating how fiercely they could protect it. But in so doing they were trapping Hebrew in amber. Whether in their homeland or in exile, Hebrew now had a special purpose: to maintain the religious practices and identity of a people.

Jan Joosten, professor of Hebrew at the University of Oxford, has spoken about the changes that Hebrew experienced during this period. Words that had once been general started to become specialized,[3] just as Brian P. Bennett has observed about the traits of a sacred language; for instance, Torah once meant simply teaching or direction, like making sure your child had good table manners, but in later years began to refer to the first five books of the Hebrew Bible. Mincha, which used to mean "gift," became "offering" or "sacrifice." Tamid, which meant "always," started to designate the daily offering in the Temple of Jerusalem. As these words began to refer to specific details of the Jewish faith, loan words from Aramaic filtered into their quotidian register. This was Hebrew's sacralization. These ancient Jews "considered scripture their home country, and its language their native idiom," Joosten said in 2017. "They didn't speak the language of a land, they spoke the language of a book."

This is the "Shield of Faith" that a select few languages can thank for their survival today. Syriac, Coptic, and Ge'ez, all Near East or Afro-Asiatic, also enjoy ongoing use in liturgy across Christian traditions to varying degrees, and the Amish in the United States speak a German variety they have preserved, known as Pennsylvania Dutch. Without its ties to religion, the linguist Nicholas Ostler says, Hebrew would have faced the same obsolescence as its sister language Phoenician. For a language to truly bolster its shield of faith, Ostler argues, "it must be significantly different from that of the population that surrounds it." It is certainly the case with Hebrew that scholars and rabbis carried it with them to new countries and communities where Jews were minoritized. This biblical Hebrew—despite offering fewer than ten thousand words—became the foundation of a language that would go on to be used for thousands of years.

As Hebrew became sacred, Mishnaic Hebrew—the language of the Talmud, the source of Jewish law—also became known as Leshon Hazal, "Tongue of the Sages." Mishnah comes from the Hebrew verb root to repeat, and refers to the oral teachings of Judaism that were repeated and taught from teacher to student. But Mishnaic Hebrew was not restricted to ancient writings or to rabbis; it was a transitional language from antiquity to the medieval period that was used by scholars and poets, too. Distinctive Jewish identities like Sephardic and Ashkenazi blossomed with their own traditions and Judeo-vernaculars that would become Ladino and Yiddish while Hebrew remained the language of literacy. From the Golden Age of Spain, where Jews had become major contributors to public and artistic life during a period of tolerance under Islamic rule, and across the wider Mediterranean, everything from medicine to son-nets found life in Hebrew in the works of European Jews. Between new coinages and transliterations from other languages, the hypo-thetical Hebrew dictionary plumped up an extra twenty-six thou-sand words despite no one actually *speaking* them to each other.

It is hard to perceive of such a language as being "dead" when new words were being actively invented. The Vatican today contin-ues to create Latin neologisms with its Pontifical Academy for Latin; this does not make it a living language. A page on its website[4] lists everything from refugee camp and flirting—campus exceptorius and amor levis—to gin and snob—pótio iunípera and homo affecta-tus. Coining new words and writing them down somewhere does not necessarily mean they all take off. And particularly for the medieval Ashkenazim of central and eastern Europe, Hebrew's sacred status still placed it on a pedestal as a language to only use seriously and with reference to God.

Still, by the mid-nineteenth century, Hebrew was a long way from becoming anybody's mother tongue again. Young European Jews were becoming fluent not in Hebrew or even their local Jewish lan-guage, but in newly standardized languages like German. The lin-guist Lewis Glinert describes new generations of German Jews in the nineteenth and twentieth centuries as becoming "functionally monolingual," which was "as much a part of becoming modern as better-known phenomena like secularism, urbanization, mass poli-tics, communication and literacy."

Hebrew had not gone through the nineteenth and twentieth cen-turies unchanged, either. It was still very much a language of the printed page; of works of religion and philosophy but, increasingly, of periodicals and contemporary literature, too. A language that had been a way of transmitting history, dogma, and doctrine was now turning its face to the future. One young man—eyes dazzled by the dream of a promised land—decided it was time for a new nation to have its old language back.

■ ■ ■

Baby Ben-Zion wasn't sleeping, and his mother, Devora, had not been getting much sleep either. It had been a little over a year since she had first moved to Jerusalem with her new husband, Eliezer, leaving her hometown in what was then part of the Russian Empire for an overcrowded city riddled with disease. Desperate and far from home, she quietly sang her baby a Russian lullaby.

She had known Eliezer since they were teenagers, when her father had first charged her with teaching the languages of modern Europe—French, German, and Russian. A young, precocious Jewish boy, he was four years her junior and had been kicked out of his yeshiva. But her father had seen something in him, and she did, too, so much so that their eventual engagement withstood his tuberculosis diagnosis, his determination to live in Jerusalem, and, perhaps most life-altering of all, his condition that they would never speak in Yiddish again. Despite Devora's own multilingualism, Eliezer had asked her to promise to lead a married life in a language she didn't speak a word of. It was in the same language in which Theodor Herzl, the journalist and father of Zionism, protested that Jews couldn't even buy a railway ticket—Hebrew.

In the Old Testament, Zion was one of the two hills of ancient Jerusalem, and the seat of King David's royal capital. In the nineteenth century, as eastern European Jews fled the pogroms of the Russian Empire, the fated return to these ancient biblical lands where Jews would no longer be a persecuted minority became an ever more attractive idea. It was not the only place being considered for a new Jewish homeland. Herzl famously once asked: "Shall we choose Palestine or Argentine?" In 1903, the British colonial secretary even offered the Zionist Congress five thousand square miles in Kenya. But Palestine, which had been under Ottoman rule for more than three hundred years by the end of the nineteenth century, was the only acceptable option for people like Eliezer who were effectively proto-Zionists. The Ottomans, wary of nationalist move-ments upsetting their power monopoly, set about containing such Jewish migration, although enforcement was not even, and did not stop ambitious young men like Eliezer.

Eliezer wanted to father the first Hebrew-speaking family in nearly two millennia and so Devora's Hebrew lessons began on a boat to Jaffa in 1881, joining the thousands of Jews who had begun to migrate to the Holy Land. In his memoirs he recounts a moment when the ship passed through two mountain cliffs and he declared, "How beautiful this place is!" (!יפה המקום הזה).

Devora, who was a fast learner, echoed him: "Truly, this place is beautiful" (.באמת, יפה זה המקום).

Their conversations, probably mainly in Yiddish, gradually be-came more and more Hebrew. By the time she gave birth to her first child, named Ben-Zion, son of Zion, Eliezer expected her to follow suit and speak only in Hebrew to him. According to his later autobi-ography, Ben-Zion was kept in another room if foreign guests were invited over and felt he was even kept from "the chirping of the birds and the neighing of horses, the braying of donkeys and the flutter-ing of butterflies, because even they are, after all, foreign languages, at any rate not Hebrew."

Supposedly he had still not said a single word by his third birth-day. One day, as Eliezer was coming home, he could overhear the lilt of a Russian lullaby Devora must have learned as a child. He flew indoors in a fit of rage, and Ben-Zion, either excited to see his father return or fearful of what he was about to do to his mother, cried out, "Abba." The Hebrew word for father became the first word sum-moned from a native speaker in eighteen centuries.

Eliezer had not always been Ben-Yehuda, a "son of Judah." He was born Eliezer Yitzhak Perlman, the child of a Hasidic Jewish couple in Luzhki, a Lithuanian town within the Russian Empire. At 4 percent of the Russian Empire's population in 1881,[5] the Jewish community had become one of the largest in the world, but increasing anti-Semitic sentiment had pushed them to the Pale of Settlement, a vast territory that today includes all of Belarus and Moldova and parts of Ukraine, Lithuania, and Poland. It was the only place in the entire empire where Jews were allowed to live, with very few exceptions, and as a result the young Eliezer probably woke up, went to school, and came back home without ever needing to speak a non-Jewish language. At home he spoke Yiddish, and at the yeshiva he would have studied Hebrew and Aramaic texts—hence why it was Devora who later exposed him to the European languages that had otherwise evaded him. In a different time, Eliezer Yitzhak Perlman might have become a rabbi.

But around him, everything was changing. Borders were about to be rewritten; Luzhki is now in Belarus. In Eastern Europe, a great period known as the Haskalah had been well under way for nearly one hundred years at that point—the Jewish Enlightenment in which secular writing and publishing in Hebrew shaped a new, modern, and assimilated Jewish identity within the Western world. Hebrew was not only the language of rabbinic opinions, medieval treatises, and prose—it was becoming a language of modern journalism, spreading the thoughts and aspirations of Jews who were increasingly calling for a nation of their own.

One day, one of Eliezer's teachers, Rabbi Yossi Bloyker, showed him a stash of secular literature in Hebrew, including the Hebrew translation of *Robinson Crusoe* that had been produced by a Jewish teacher in Vilnius. He had had to coin new Hebrew terms, from outside the world of the Talmud and the Torah, for the story to make sense, like Crusoe's telescope—קְנֵה הָרְאִי—and his compass—מַרְאֶה־פְּאַת־הצפון. "He began to tell me, little by little, that there are books written beautifully and poetically in the holy language," Eliezer remembered. But he barely got a chance to get past a few pages of *Robinson Crusoe* before the head of the yeshiva entered and confiscated the book.[6]

Such works were heretical to orthodox Jews who saw Hebrew as a sacred language, not one to be exploited and especially not for secular writing. Disagreements over how Hebrew should be used followed Eliezer his entire life. For Zionists who were coming from all over Europe looking for a language that could unite their movement and establish a Jewish nation in Palestine, Hebrew was not necessarily the obvious choice. There were at least six languages they could have chosen, between the languages of nation-states and Jewish languages like Yiddish and Ladino. German was actually once the most popular option, especially as it was considered a language of science and secular thought, and many of the founding fathers of Zionism were secular themselves. Ultraconservative Hasidic Jews, given their sacrosanct views of Hebrew, used Yiddish in daily life instead. The controversy around secularizing Hebrew even got Eliezer excommunicated from the Orthodox Jewish community in Jerusalem at one point, who forbade its members from reading his works.

Following his arrival in Palestine, Eliezer Ben-Yehuda was one of the very few to argue that Hebrew should not only be a Jewish nation's written but also the spoken language. Few following the Haskalah would challenge that Hebrew could be a language of literature, even newspapers—but a language of everyday chitchat? Unlike many other young Jews in Europe, Ben-Yehuda had seen that it was possible. The tuberculosis diagnosis that could have ended his life instead brought him to Algeria to convalesce in the sun; there, he met Jews whose only shared language with him was a tentative Hebrew. He heard their Sephardic pronunciation and fell in love with it. A year before he left for Palestine, he wrote an article in the Hebrew-language newspaper *Ha-Magid* that Hebrew's revival was contingent on it becoming a spoken language again. "And how can that work other than by making Hebrew the instructional medium of our schools? Not in Europe, nor in any of the lands of our exile, while we are an insignificant minority and no amount of teaching effort is going to succeed, but in our land, the land of Israel."

His project began with his family, starting on that fateful boat trip to Jaffa. His wife, Devora, died at just thirty-six from tuberculosis and three of their children were lost to diphtheria. Devora's sister Paula moved to Jerusalem, married him, and changed her name to the Hebrew Hemda, becoming his second bride and acolyte. "My father had mainly enemies, not friends, for doing what he did," his daughter Dola recalled in a BBC documentary about Hebrew's revival. "For restricting, for ordering people to speak Hebrew." Their childhood was a lonely one. "We were not allowed to go to places where Hebrew was not spoken. In fact, we were sort of excommunicated by all people who arranged parties because they knew that we were not allowed to be in places where Hebrew was not spoken. People used to laugh at us in the street because they didn't understand what we spoke."

But among the earliest Zionist villages, Ben-Yehuda's idea of immersion-based Hebrew learning caught on. Within a decade, the first Hebrew kindergarten and primary school had opened in Palestine. Ideological divisions between Ashkenazim, Sephardim, and Mizrahi Jews, who were separated by their distinct languages, could be bridged by Hebrew. Then, years later—as Europe went to war, the Ottoman Empire collapsed, and the Bolsheviks seized power in Russia—there was enough Hebrew spoken for the British to recognize Hebrew, Arabic, and English as the official languages of Mandatory Palestine. This was the same country they had just endorsed as a "national homeland for the Jewish people" in the 1917 Balfour Declaration. Language and nation, as they have done so many times in this book, were about to advance hand in hand again.

Setting up schools, however, wasn't enough for Ben-Yehuda or his Zionist colleagues. They needed new words—and new attitudes—to push Hebrew to the top of the pecking order.

■ ■ ■

Ben-Zion and his siblings might have been the first new native speakers of Hebrew, but they weren't the only ones for long. By the time of the Second Aliyah in 1904, where about forty thousand Jews came to build agricultural settlements, Russian Jews arriving in Palestine had already been preparing in Hebrew-speaking clubs back home, and in 1907 the Zionist Congress announced that Hebrew was "the language of Zionism." Ben-Yehuda had helped pull off an impossible linguistic feat, raising a language back from the dead. But was it really the same language they had spoken in ancient Judea?

As "Hebrew" began to blossom among its new native speakers, it became clear that it desperately needed expanding; it lacked words to describe a world that had moved on since biblical and medieval times. A few years into his life in Jerusalem, Ben-Yehuda began to publish *HaZvi*, or *The Gazelle*, a Hebrew-language newspaper for Palestine's increasing Jewish population. To report on the modern world, Hebrew would need more words, but that didn't necessarily mean that they had to be *new*.

One example was the word for gun, which first existed in Hebrew as a phrase clunkily meaning "firing tube." "This phrase is so foreign to the Hebrew ear, like a bastard in its form and shape," Ben-Yehuda wrote in his newspaper in 1896. "Every time we come to use it our soul is disgusted by it. And we do not know what to do with it and how to use it in plural, and how to conjugate it." Instead, he looked at etymologies in other languages—the French fusil, the German Flinte—which all harked back to the first pistols, which were fired with flint ignition. Biblical Hebrew may not have had a word for gun, but it did have a word for flint: ekdakh.[7]

Another word he needed was reporter. In the beginning, the Hebrew word for reporter was sofer—the exact same word used to describe the scribes of the Torah. Over the centuries, sofer became a catchall term for anyone who wrote as a profession, a capaciousness that might have worked while Hebrew was a language of scholars but no longer helpful for the future of mass information. In an article in 1883, Ben-Yehuda mentioned katavim[8] for the first time. Drawn from the k-t-v root meaning to write, its better meaning was "writers." The very medium he was writing in needed a new name, too—a newspaper was then clumsily named מכתב עתי (michtav iti)—a "letter in time." Here, he looked for inspiration from German's *Zeitung*, literally "to do with the time(s)." Hebrew also had a word for time—עֵת (et)—and so he added the suffix ־וֹן on to it, just like Germans had once added ung to Zeit, producing עיתון (*iton*).

Ben-Yehuda's neologizing, drawing from his knowledge of other European languages, means that some of Modern Hebrew is crafted not from biblical "authentic" Hebrew but from influences far farther west. It has also led some to question whether the language Ben-Yehuda and his contemporaries refashioned can rightly be called "Hebrew" at all. Ghil'ad Zuckermann, who we briefly met in "Expel," is an Israeli linguist whose pioneering work founded a field called revivalistics, studying spoken language reclamation—bringing a language back from obscurity—and revitalization—energizing a language that might be slipping from speakers' grasp. He has now spent more than a decade in Australia, where he helps Aboriginal peoples revive their languages following the lessons of Israel's Hebrew revival. At least, that's what most of the world calls this language; Zuckermann calls it Israeli.

"I categorize Israeli under the family of revival languages," he told me over a video call from Adelaide. Not Semitic, like Hebrew, or Germanic, like Yiddish; a new family that also counts the varieties of languages like today's spoken Hawaii'an and Barngarla, one of the Aboriginal languages he is helping to revive. He argues that they don't have single parents like ordinary languages—English is Germanic, French is Romance. Today's Hebrew, for Zuckermann, has two parents, not one.

It's undeniable that the vast majority of the lexicon of what Zuckermann calls Israeli is Hebrew; there were at least thirty thousand words to work with from millennia of Jewish writing by the time revivalists got hold of it. This is especially true of basic words. The ancient Judeans may not have had telephones, but they did have homes, relatives, feelings, and countless other nouns that are still in use today. How words are formed from their root letters and how verbs are conjugated is equally still similar, because these were the foundational stones that built the language at its very beginning and were always less likely to change. But what about how Hebrew sounds?

In the first century of Zionism, the main mother tongue that an olim, an immigrant to Israel, would have brought with them was Yiddish. Their sound bank influenced Hebrew so much that the characteristic Semitic 'ayin, a voiced consonant made by squeezing air through your pharynx, has been diminished to a slight glottal stop, if used at all, because the new Hebrew speakers couldn't get their mouths around the consonant. A similar sound to the 'ayin exists in Arabic, and is challenging to learn if you're used to most European languages where it's absent; I probably have a 75 percent success rate every time I attempt it, and I've been trying for over a decade. Calques from Yiddish flood Hebrew, in which an idea from Yiddish has been copied and translated word for word. If you ask "What's up?" in Israel today, you say ma nishma, which actually means what shall we hear?—directly from the Yiddish vos hert zikh, what's heard?[9] And a glorious array of Yiddish loan words fill Hebrew, such as shvits—panache—and shlumper—a slob.[10]

Across word order, meanings, and shapes, Yiddish left an indelible mark on revived Hebrew. So, too, have other languages with which Hebrew has had long-term contact, like the Arabic of Palestine, but, according to Zuckermann, Yiddish is the primary parent alongside Hebrew and the language should recognize its dual heritage. Revival languages, to him, contradict the traditional family tree model of language classification. Biblical Hebrew may have been clearly Semitic, but today's language as it is spoken in Israel belongs in a "revival language" family, along with languages like Neo-Hawaii'an.

Many find the idea that Israeli Hebrew isn't a true or authentic representation of the "original" Hebrew language abhorrent. Zuckermann told me he's had his lectures boycotted, and even received death threats, from opponents on both political sides. On the right, he was seen as anti-Zionist ("Are you saying we do not speak the language of Isaiah?"), and on the left, he was seen as nationalist ("Why does he call it Israeli? What about Israeli Arabs?").

Zuckermann takes the criticism from both sides as a good sign—like he's getting close to the truth. He feels some sympathy for Eliezer Ben-Yehuda, not as an Israeli hero to worship but, rather, for what he had to put up with. "He worked his ass off," Zuckermann said. "And he was jailed by those who were religious, who denounced him to the police and said he was desecrating the holy tongue." Religiosity, or at least the purist zeal that comes with it, still shapes the language. In its early life, Hebrew's sacred identity set it apart; now, even though it's a theoretically secular language, the religious connotations persist. Zuckermann has observed several religious terms in biblical Hebrew that have been secularized and reapplied to the nation-state. "The Knesset building"—mishkan akneset—uses mishkan, which refers to the inner sanctum where Moses kept the Ark in the wilderness, and Knesset, which in Mishnaic Hebrew originally referred to the Jewish people, or community; it would be as if the word parliament originally meant the people of (Christian) God.

Back in the 1920s, the philosopher and historian Gershom Sholem, a German Jew who had recently migrated to Israel, worried about the secularization of Hebrew, not because it could corrupt a holy language but because it could destroy secular society. "If we—the generation of the transition—resuscitate the language of the ancient books so that it can reveal itself anew to them, must then not the religious violence of the language one day break out against those who speak it?" He argued that Hebrew was "pregnant with catastrophes," and that the return of inherent religious language to the Jews would force everyone, including secular Jews, to practice the faith. "In a language where he is invoked back a thousandfold into our life, God will not stay silent,"[11] as he ominously put it.

By the 1940s, a Hebrew Language Committee had been active for a decade along with a Hebrew-only movement, chipping away at the European and Arabic languages also spoken in what was Mandatory Palestine and which eventually became Israel. New Jewish settlements had been given Hebrew names, like the modern housing estate built next to the ancient Jaffa port city that was eventually named Tel Aviv, after a biblical hill city that was actually originally in Iraq. The British had also begun to restrict Jewish migration during this period, nervous of upsetting Arab Palestinian allies who feared being dispossessed of their land; the British needed Arab support if they were about to have another world war. This world war would, of course, come to be defined by a genocide that decimated millions of Jews in Europe at the exact time they needed an escape route and place of refuge. Jewish groups resisted the immigration limits and a mass migration of European Jews continued. In 1947, the British—war-weary, watching their empire shrink and unable to police the Arab-Jewish tensions that they were wholly responsible for—handed the crisis over to the UN and backed out. The UN decided the solution was a Jewish state, an Arab state, and two mixed cities of Jerusalem and Bethlehem to be ruled by an international committee. Arab communities roundly rejected it and they and the Jewish militias attacked each other. By the time the war ended, Israel controlled all the territory it had been awarded in the UN partition as well as nearly 60 percent of the area proposed for the Arab state. The Nakba—Arabic for "catastrophe"—where Jews killed fifteen thousand Palestinians, began a new refugee crisis, with seventy-five thousand people displaced to Gaza, the West Bank, and countries like Jordan and Lebanon. And where the Jews of Israel had won, so, too, had Hebrew. English was dropped as an official language.

In the 1940s, the early Israeli government declared that "the citizens of a Hebrew state cannot continue to appear in personal and public life with foreign names, which account for 90 percent of the surnames among us. A radical change is required." New Jewish arrivals to Israel usually had their names automatically Hebraized, just as Eliezer Ben-Yehuda had once changed his name voluntarily. A person living in 1940s Israel would find that everyone from their next-door neighbor to the highest government officials suddenly had a new name, and some parts of the state rigorously enforced such shifts, such as the Israel Defense Forces (IDF), which, in fourteen months, managed to change twenty thousand recruits' names. A booklet released to the public made suggestions like turning Rosenberg to Rosen, Abramovich to Ben Avraham. Some names retained the original sounds; others the original meaning. Prime Minister Ben-Gurion was originally Gruen—green—but by the 1910s had become Ben-Gurion, son of the lion cub. Yet others with his surname had pivoted to Yarok, the Hebrew word for green.

In a matter of years, it wasn't only the words people used but the names that they called one another that brought the Old Testament's protagonists—their flint, their scribes, and their teachings—back to the Levant. To the untrained ear, it would be almost as if Hebrew speakers had never left.

■ ■ ■

How much would you pay to learn a language? Anyone who has ever booked a place on a weeks-long course can expect to spend nearly a thousand pounds on it, maybe more. But if you live in London, and you want to learn Hebrew, it's not uncommon to pay £300 to £400, and even as little as £200, for thirty hours of learning—that's just £6 an hour. It's an absolute steal, and could equate to below minimum wage for the teacher if they only have a small class. In reality, they are normally subsidized by another organization, one that is eager for students to leave class not only with improved language skills but with a certain idea about the Israeli nation-state, too.

This is the World Zionist Organization, founded by the very man who wanted German to become Israel's language instead—Theodor Herzl—and they have a budget of more than $1 billion to fund projects around the globe.

Sometimes, learning a language is even free. All Jews who make aliyah are heavily encouraged to attend an *ulpan*, a Hebrew language school for adults from a word used to describe a studio or learning environment. An absorption bucket, a pot of financial assistance, is theirs for the first six months of their move while they dedicate themselves to the ulpan. That is, if you're Jewish; non-Jews are not entitled to this state support, because technically speaking a non-Jew can't be an olim, someone who makes aliyah. You can't return to the Promised Land if you weren't promised it in the first place.

The first ulpan was founded in 1949. Their challenges have changed over time; back then, Zionists were still trying to persuade people to consider Hebrew as a state, and not a sacred, language. But even now, migrants come from all over the world, and many will not have Hebrew as a family language. Ulpanim are needed to educate everyone about life in Israel and to maintain the primacy of Hebrew. You aren't forced to attend one, unless you want a job that requires proficiency in Hebrew, for example with the IDF, but given they're free, many take up the opportunity. Nonetheless, in 2023 about thirty-six hundred immigrants—most of whom had arrived from Russia and Ukraine[12]—were waiting for places in the government's ulpanim.

Unless someone has Israeli family links or has dedicated their life to learning Hebrew far beyond bar mitzvah classes, it's likely that they will need Hebrew lessons. Conscious of this challenge, ulpanim are distinct for their immersion methods, as they rarely offer language lessons only. Lots of the schools run cultural and social programs that can include lessons on everything from Israeli banking to entrepreneurship, crafting, and cooking. They can also vary in quality; all the ex-students I interviewed had different experiences. One did a five-hours-a-day program, Sunday to Thursday, and managed to go from beginner to upper intermediate, although they pointed out that they learned more in the city where they were studying than from the lessons themselves, and they had already taken a Hebrew class at university. Another Israeli did an ulpan that their kibbutz ran for three days a week for six months, and felt like he left being able to read and write at a high-school level, which was better than he had expected. He remembered lots of cultural lessons, including reading exercises about Eliezer Ben-Yehuda and Jewish history classes on the foundation of the state of Israel. A young American woman currently at an ulpan in Tel Aviv told me she has felt that previous ulpanim she has tried out were more focused on reading and writing than speaking and listening, the kinds of skills she felt she really needed to integrate. Her new school focuses on "practical Hebrew," which she has relished. "Very focused on day-to-day usage, expressions and slang," she wrote to me. "It's totally worth it—I'm super happy with them."

Not everyone, however, is content with the programs run by ulpanim. Yaron Abhar Jackson, whose father made aliyah to Israel and lived in an ulpan for six months, thinks ulpanim teach a lot of uncritical Jewish history. He is a political activist, and his description of ulpanim in general was damning. "Both historically and also today, ulpans are a place of assimilation in the Israeli society. Some also would say indoctrination. And the idea is to kind of create a gateway within the Israeli society." That includes learning Hebrew, but also understanding the culture. When his father told him about his experience at an ulpan, where he was forbidden from speaking his native language, Yaron thought it was "violent," and that much of Israeli assimilation demands discarding other identities. Some of the material used in ulpanim also conveniently elides Palestinian history before the foundation of Israel. He references a song the navy put out in the 1960s called "Only in Israel [Rak B'Yisrael]," which praises Israel for having the best oranges and the best people. Yet he asks, "Are oranges Israeli, or of the land here?"

Yaron teaches Hebrew at the appropriately named This Is Not an Ulpan (TINAU), which—subversively, for Israel—is a joint Jewish/Palestinian organization structured as a workers' cooperative, where the school's students can become members. The school also teaches Arabic and "tools for changing, influencing and critically understanding Israeli and Palestinian society," as Yaron's colleague and the school's Hebrew coordinator, Tal Janner-Klausner, added. "That's the fundamental difference—not bringing people into what already is and trying to get them to fit the narrow mold, but to give them tools to smash up the mold. And make lots of different shapes of mold!" And, although TINAU does use the immersion method, they will move to English or Arabic to explain challenging concepts depending on the makeup of the classroom.

In 2018—seventy years after it was made a co-official language with Hebrew in the new nation-state of Israel—Arabic was downgraded to a language with "special status" instead, making Hebrew Israel's sole official language. It was one sign of the growing power of Israel's nationalist right. In practice, Arabic has long played second fiddle, marginal in Israel and prominent only in the occupied territories of Gaza and the West Bank, despite many Arab Jews speaking Arabic as their first language. Many such Jews will now be elderly, their children and grandchildren native Hebrew speakers. Each side of this conflict does not necessarily learn the other's language, and, when they do, it's usually only to boost their intelligence capabilities; Hamas started introducing Hebrew in Gaza schools in a pilot in 2013, and in 2025 Israel made Arabic lessons mandatory for its military.

TINAU's lessons are, it goes without saying, extremely progressive, teaching queer history and using the feminine form of words, rather than masculine, as a default gender agreement in their textbooks. "It's not very popular," Yaron said of their methods. They receive widespread criticism for them, which they say has gotten more extreme since the war in Gaza started in 2023. As a result, the school attracts those who feel excluded from mainstream Israeli society, like LGBT youth and the neurodiverse. Yaron dreams of running courses on Yiddish and Ladino one day, further broadening, in his eyes, what it could mean to be a Hebrew speaker. "We focus quite a lot on slang, and Hebrew that is based on other Jewish languages. There is a lot inherited from languages from the Caucasus, Morocco, Yiddish . . . the heritage from your grandparents is part of Hebrew. It is part of this space."

He is right in that for Hebrew to soar, other Jewish languages like Ladino and Yiddish have had to suffer. Though there are revival efforts in Israel and abroad, both languages are endangered and efforts to preserve Ladino and Yiddish in Israel have come decades too late, after linguicidal policies that prized Hebrew above all else. Early on, Yiddish, the common language of the majority of immigrants, was condemned as being grating, foreign,[13] or effeminate,[14] the language your mother passed to you rather than the patriotic Hebrew of a fatherland; now, Hasidic Jews are Yiddish's last custodians, maintaining it in their isolated Orthodox communities.

Learning and speaking Hebrew today doesn't automatically mean that you are Jewish, but most people learning it today do so because of a Jewish connection or because they are considering resettlement in Israel. It is hard for such a language to be apolitical. Its dominance in Israeli society has been pushed by a prime minister who has an international arrest warrant out on him for war crimes and crimes against humanity committed in Israel's war on Gaza; its revival, still not two hundred years old, happened because Zionists took hold of it. Such a revival has only been possible because of biblical Hebrew's sacralization, a ritual death that allowed it to be salvaged and repurposed for a people's long-idealized return. It has also depended on all of the many other Hebrews, and Jewish languages, that effloresced among Jews in diaspora—but without the zeal of individuals who were happy to occupy land that wasn't theirs, it's likely Hebrew would still be fixed and written rather than a spoken, evolving language. Although Hebrew is often crowned as a unique example of language revitalization, with its ulpanim system imitated in other languages around the world in countries like Wales and Scotland, it cannot be ignored that many of its promoters can be responsible for linguicide themselves. With languages like Yiddish and Ladino, this linguicide is more historic, but with Arabic it is highly active, with little repentance and with a purposeful genocide of Arab identities in Israel and in the Palestinian territories.

Ghil'ad, Yaron, and Tal all mentioned 2025's Israeli Eurovision entry, Yuval Raphael, who was censured by the country's language police—the Hebrew Academy—for getting a word wrong in her song's recording. Raphael had quoted from the Song of Songs, but misspoke the expression for "the rivers," replacing *Une*harot, as it is written in the Bible, with *Ve*neharot, as many young Israelis would naturally say today, dropping ancient Hebrew's "helpful vowel" to simplify the grammar. They made her rerecord it. *Many waters cannot quench love, Nor can rivers drown it* goes the verse's translation in English. Undrowned and unquenched, Hebrew, too, is unrelenting in its survival, resisting a fate that has dispersed and killed many other languages in a similar position. Some would call it divine intervention. I'd call it the very human drive to create, and to destroy.

THE STORY OF DAGBANI

> **o zilin kom nyayisa:** "sweet tongue water," used to describe the carrier of good news or cultivated speech[1]

Many years ago, when Amina was staying with her aunt in Accra, she earned a nickname she had never been given before: Sayinlana, "chief of crying." She was seventeen years old at the time, studying hard for her BECE, the exam Ghanaians need to pass to graduate from high school. As if it wasn't already hard enough to live far away from all her friends for the sake of a better school, Amina had another problem. Her aunt, who had married an African American, loved to cook foreign food, and all they wanted to eat was perfumed rice, as it is often called in Ghana. She couldn't stomach it. "I was called a villager! It was very derogatory. Tinkpanbila!" she said, imitating her aunt. A tinkpanbila is a "village child"; Amina says it can also mean unenlightened or primitive. But Amina wasn't being stubborn; she was just used to a completely different diet, eleven hours north by car in Tamale, the capital of the Northern Region.

There, in a large thatched house, Amina had grown up surrounded by the crops and plants that offered her family their livelihood. The kapok tree in particular provided them with its cotton-like fibers. On some days, Amina remembers watching her grandmother hand-spinning its fluffy, fibrous seed pods into yarn. On others, her grandmother would prepare kantong, drying the kapok seeds under the sun and shaping the paste they made into balls. Her aunts prepared the sort of staple carbohydrates that she loved: dakunkpakpul, a fermented cornmeal dumpling steamed in banana leaves, or a thick, white corn dough, called kaafa. From videos, kaafa looks glutinous and pliant; one chef I watch claims you can smother it on a broken leg, wrap the leg in a bandage, and look forward to it being healed within three days. It's the type of dish your grandmother would make for you if you were sick, just as Nonna used to make me brodo with chicken. In the end, Amina's aunt compromised: Instead of having to eat perfumed rice for the rest of her visit, Amina was allowed fufu, the pounded meal you find all over Accra—but you can't find Amina's grandma's cooking, or the apothecary of flora she foraged from the savannah around her. And you can't find her grandmother's language at any Accra school, either: Dagbani.

Amina has her own formidable stock cupboard today, which she explains to me in great detail as I sit in her show kitchen, watching her cook. In adulthood she has grown even closer to her grandmother's roots, setting up a sustainable food business honoring the crafts she once taught her. Amina prepares a meal with fish, millet, and dawadawa beans, which have a delicious roasted flavor and, when I look them up later, an even cooler spelling in Dagbani: dɔɔ.

When we wash our hands before eating we do so with a soft, aromatic, brown compound that is made from a mix of shea, grown on local trees, and ash from the kapok pods. It is called awabila: Bila means child, although Amina doesn't know where the name comes from; perhaps Awa, a girl's name, made it, for herself or a child. It is known as a gentle, curative soap. Newborn babies are washed in it; in fact, I found a Facebook comment saying it is the first and last soap a person is bathed in. I looked at the toddler strapped to Amina's back, fast asleep, and I thought about her grandmother who is no longer here, and the nearby kapok trees that offer so much beyond the shade that they cast. In mid-December it was already hot, and the dry season had barely begun.

When she thinks about her teenage years, Amina acknowledges that her upbringing gave her a close connection to the land that her peers might have missed out on. Despite this, she started noticing a trend: more and more "continental dishes," as she calls them, creeping into their kitchens, not only in the cosmopolitan centers like Accra but even in family homes like hers in wider Tamale. Wild edibles—just like the ones her grandmother used to collect—have lost their value, seen as second rate to the food you can buy in the shops. "We say in Dagbani Ninvuɣ gbariŋ—you're just going to collect food that you haven't worked hard for. You're a *weakling*." Foraging food didn't make you look resourceful—it made you look cheap, for not buying food in a shop instead.

I had been introduced to Amina by Sadik Shahadu, a Dagbani language activist I was visiting while I was in northern Ghana. I could understand why they got along—he's trying to preserve the Dagbani language and she's trying to preserve Dagbani cuisine. These are, of course, not unconnected. A crop, like a word, is deeply connected to the land it is from. I felt sorry that there were locals here who had fallen out of love with local food and foraging, and I thought about Nonna looking for mushrooms around her family home, a farmhouse called La Serra. I, of course, would have no idea where to look for them if I returned.

Amina isn't the only person who wants to revive interest in indigenous food; go north past Tamale to Kumbungu, about two hundred kilometers south of the border with Burkina Faso, and you can see warehouses with bags of locally grown whole-grain rice waiting for buyers who won't come. In 2010, Ghana spent $450 million importing foreign "polished" rice, because it is often cheaper to buy, as well as being quicker and easier to cook. Yet not only is it less nutritious, it puts fewer Ghanaian cedis (₵) in the hands of farmers.

I met a group of farmers one day with Sadik, three men in their early twenties taking a break from their work in the shade of a large tree. I asked questions, and they would confer as Sadik watched attentively, before translating for me. Sadik was struggling to remember what these different kinds of rice were called, because he used to eat them as a child. "I know there are real names for all these rice varieties. But they're already losing their names," he said. I looked at the red tilled earth and the little puddles of water I saw here and there, fast evaporating. Tomatoes, cabbage, and "garden eggs," a small, white eggplant, all grow here along with the rice; all thirsty crops, in a setting completely different from the damp and misty Po Valley where my nonna was a rice weeder. Compared to the time of their fathers and grandfathers, the farmers agreed as a group that there was a lot less water available for their fields. They are not wrong. There is decreasing annual rainfall here as well as increasingly erratic rainfall patterns.

I wanted to know more about these disappearing rice names, drying earth, and what else the speakers felt like they were losing. The farmers confirmed, via Sadik's translation, that people are leaving the north for the south because of the challenges of continuing to farm here. When they go south "they stop speaking the language. Even the children they have, they aren't teaching them the language."

Dagbani is the third most spoken language in the country and, like most of its relatives in the Niger-Congo language family, is tonal, meaning you can change the meaning of a word by saying it with a rising intonation instead of a lowering one. It is spoken by between one and three million people who identify as the Dagomba, a large ethnic group based in Ghana's north as well as in neighboring Togo. Their celebrated ancestor, Toha-zie, the "Red Hunter," spent years traversing the Sahel and northern Nigeria before finally settling in present-day Dagbon at some point in the fourteenth century. His descendants began a chieftaincy practice that still forms the backbone of Dagomba society today; once selected, chiefs are not crowned but "enskinned," sitting on a throne of animal hides. Dagbani is linguistically unthreatened by lots of measures; it is taught in school to children, and it has many speakers in a region with a growing birth rate. But even that may not be enough to keep the language completely safe. Researchers say this is a climate crisis hotspot, one that increasing numbers of local language speakers could be persuaded to leave in the coming years.

I asked Sadik to tell them that my grandmother also helped farm rice and that I'm sad not to speak her language anymore. "Your mum's side or your dad's?" Sadik asked, and I responded that it was my mum's. Later, Sadik told me that the word for grandmother could also be used for "wife," and that my grandfather was also a "husband." "The other people we can call wives and husbands are our nieces and nephews. They are forms of play—not so serious." I laughed at the idea of Nonna calling my cousin her husband before realizing that, with no grandfathers left or nephews, all I had was one actual husband. Suddenly I felt a little impoverished.

My thoughts returned to the farmers' friends: economic migrants, like Nonna, but perhaps also *climate* migrants. There will be a lot more of them in the years to come.

■ ■ ■

When we talk about the climate crisis taking a language, we often think about the Pacific islands. Rising sea levels there threaten to gulp down atolls, with everything on them—people, flora, fauna—seemingly sinking into their own lagoons. It's rare for a climate-change-induced natural disaster to wipe out a language, but the dispersal afterward can accelerate language shift as people are displaced into camps or towns where residents may speak a completely different language. What linguists are increasingly aware of, though, is the language shift that occurs long before a catastrophic climate event. Anastasia Riehl, a linguist in Canada, has said that "the sea will not suddenly swallow an entire linguistic community in one gulp, dying words left bobbing upon the waves. The speakers will leave their islands before that happens."[2] It is the slow grumble of waiting for the "good year" of farming that people gradually realize isn't going to come again, or the frustration of the floods that keep closing down your business. These are as much a part of the climate crisis's deadening impact on the vivacity of languages as the doomsday weather events that take lives.

When researchers map migration trends in Ghana, they have found the rural areas that are suffering the greatest environmental change on top of poverty, are, predictably, the areas where researchers anticipate the heaviest emigration. When you ask someone why they're leaving home, they're rarely going to cite climate change. Instead, they'll point to more direct challenges, such as not earning enough money rather than climate affecting the opportunities you have to earn money. Scientists investigating climate migration often have to be crafty with the data they link up, like mapping migration trends on top of climate-vulnerable areas and seeing if there are any patterns. Their most recent study, published in 2024, found that the Northern Region where Dagbani and a wide variety of other languages, both big and small in terms of speaker numbers, are found, is an area of significant concern. Increasingly unpredictable rainfall, on top of inadequate climate adaptation methods, means that many will increasingly find it harder and harder to stay there.

Linguists Stella Afi Makafui Yegblemenawo and Mavis Antiri Kodua are investigating what this could mean for Ghana's remarkable linguistic diversity. I met them at their university in Kumasi, a thriving hub in eastern Ghana that was once the capital of the Ashanti Empire. Nearby, the biggest market in West Africa sells seemingly everything you could possibly need: endless varieties of phone cases, dried tilapia, and, intriguingly, pirated Dagbani language books. Stella greeted me from the first floor of the Kwame Nkrumah University of Science and Technology, where she, like Mavis, is a French specialist. French, along with the largest Ghanaian language, Akan, is one of only two languages you can study at the BA level here, suggesting that they are the second languages that hold the most value after English, the official language of Ghana. Both Stella and Mavis were wearing bright wax-print dresses, their blues and oranges bursting with life against the wooden paneling of their dimly lit office.

Stella—like everyone I interviewed in Ghana—spoke so quietly that I had to bring my radio mic closer to her. I wondered whether lots of people in Ghana are softly spoken, or whether lots of people in the UK are rather loud. She told me that, though eighty is the official estimate, Ghana probably has more than a hundred languages if you account for some of the dialects that, perhaps with greater scrutiny, would qualify as languages, too. Stella and Mavis's research confirmed that people were leaving northern Ghana due to increasingly harsh climatic conditions, especially north of Tamale where the country borders Togo and Burkina Faso. Migration to the south meant their languages were threatened by larger language groups.

For the linguists, this is of particular significance as most minority language groups in Ghana are located in the semi-arid savannah of the north, where just four of Ghana's twelve "sponsored" languages may be taught at schools in the area—Dagbani, Dagaare, Gonja, and Kasem. This might sound like good going compared with other countries we've heard about, and so it is—until you realize at least six other nonofficial languages are spoken in the same region and five of them are highly endangered. When they're not taught in schools and are transmitted only orally, Stella plainly told me, they are at risk of dying out completely.

Stella added that large communities moving in droves might have a better chance of maintaining their language, but that increasingly it seemed to be individuals moving internally, lone islands of language who quickly have to shift to a local lingua franca to fit in. For instance, female migrants who leave the north to come to work as kayayei, porters who balance impressive loads of everything from plantains to bottles of water on their heads for hours a day, rapidly pick up Twi, a variety of Akan, so that they can communicate with the clients who procure their services.[3] In central Ghana, migrant speakers of Mampruli, a Gur language from the north that is partially understandable to Dagbani speakers, have grouped together in a rural district in the Ashanti region called the Sekyere Afram Plains, meaning that Mampruli is now rivaling Twi in informal public spaces.[4] Mampruli is becoming a lingua franca for other migrants whose languages aren't as well represented; speakers from the Kussasi, Bimoba, Dagaaba, and Busanga groups, all with their own languages, have started to use Mampruli while other ethnic groups have chosen Twi instead when chatting in places like markets or big gatherings like festivals or funerals. Even the Konkomba, who actually form a majority ethnic group among the migrants, have had their language, Likpakpaln, overtaken by Mampruli and Twi. For working adults, this is probably leading to additive bilingualism, where they possess both their home language and a working knowledge of at least one new language. For their children, however, there is no such guarantee; Ghanaian schools only teach one local language and English.

In what I think is a very wholesome linguistics fact, most migrant workers in the research from central Ghana learned their new languages through friendship, with most of them saying they had learned their friends' language to show solidarity. The others learned their languages through their job or their family; less than 10 percent had had any formal language lessons or schooling. Mampruli is not a government-supported language in Ghana, and so not even Mampruli-speaking children have learned it at school, even though hundreds of thousands of people speak it. Linguists tried and failed to seek recognition for it because Ghana has rigid rules around what can be supported on a government level. A language has to have an established orthography and some kind of literary tradition, despite this being a country where primarily oral languages have thrived.

Mampruli, which is an emerging lingua franca among the migrants of the Sekyere Afram Plains, goes unrecognized by Ghana's Bureau of Languages because the Mampruli people haven't written enough of it down for the bureau's approval. Even though Dagbani is sponsored, with far more speakers, and is taught in schools, Mampruli seems to have the edge in this district along with the widely spoken Asante Twi variety of the Akan language. Children will almost certainly learn Twi in school lessons along with English in this part of Ghana, but not Mampruli, and definitely not the Kusaal or Dagbani language of their grandparents still living in the north. Even the biggest multilingualism supporter—myself included— would concede that children can't learn every language going. But if their family language is completely neglected at school, their chance of speaking it confidently into adulthood will be drastically reduced, especially if their families move when they are very young.

In migrant cities, Stella and Mavis feel there is a further "most corrosive acid" undermining minority languages: naming customs. Names in Ghana can carry powerful symbolic weight. In the Akan ethnic group, children are named after the day of the week on which they were born—Kofi and Afua, for example, would be a child born on a Friday. So if you are, say, a migrant couple who has moved east to Kumasi and you have a baby, you might feel compelled to give them a name that will allow them to fit in with the rest of their peer group. It might be that it doesn't really end up being your choice, but that your neighbors coo "Afua!" when they see your newborn daughter—not because that's her name, but because she was born on a Friday.

"When you are in a host community, you want to feel welcomed. So if your host community says, oh, we are giving you this name so that you feel part of us, a lot of people will accept this," Stella explained. Recently, she had been in a taxi where the driver told her he came from her hometown. She was confused: He'd only given her his name, an Akan one. If he came from her hometown, his surname would have been Ewe. When she asked him why his name was

Akan, he explained that his peers in Kumasi found it "easier to pronounce," so "eventually he decided to adopt it, too." The same thing happened to my nonno; he was called Cirillo and yet he had colleagues call him—nonsensically—Freddie.

For the migrant couples who don't come from the same place—who meet in the cities they move to as they escape the challenges in their rural hometown, which could increasingly be climate-driven—the chances of their children maintaining both of their parents' languages are slim. After all, their parents need to communicate with each other. According to Stella, "where a Fante speaker marries a Bimoba speaker, many simply speak English at home." The same thing happens when they go to school: In Accra, "we have Akans, Ewes . . . so you go to school, and automatically they might speak English because it's a multilingual classroom." It makes sense that children can all communicate with one another in a lingua franca, but is it right that the language is a colonial one? If it should be a Ghanaian one, then which? And should children be denied the right to receive any kind of schooling—even supplementary, if not always primary—in the family language that's actually their first?

What can be done about this? So far, almost no one seems to be thinking about or preparing for this imminent, climate-powered linguistic collapse. Neither researchers nor policymakers are taking concrete action, and there is "no national dialogue," as Stella and Mavis put it, on what this language loss may cost Ghana; no dialogue on what traditional knowledge held by the speakers of such languages may be able to teach communities. Across herbal medicine, childbirth, and farming, countless practices exist that have been found to do everything from improve the nutrient yield of a crop to prevent the overkilling of game, thus ensuring there will always be enough food to go around—and all these practices would have only been communicated through local languages, unlikely to be Ghana's larger lingua francas or English.[5] They argue that speakers need to be supported in maintaining their languages "regardless of where speakers of indigenous languages find themselves." They also observe that planned migration to land that is available and arable, as opposed to individuals moving south into ever-bulging city slums, could allow entire groups to stay together and maintain kinship, traditions, and, fundamentally, their language.

This inaction is shocking and yet not surprising. Stella and Mavis feel that languages in general aren't afforded much importance in Ghana, even sometimes within academia. "Government attention is on science, engineering, STEM [science, technology, engineering, and maths] . . . there is little for the language. But language is also science." At a conference, "everybody was talking about engineering and science," and Mavis said, "But do we forget that whether you're teaching science or math or engineering, you use language to deliver. And so why are we neglecting language? It is something that we are still fighting for."

Linguists in the UK complain about the same thing: declining values placed on languages and the linguistic humanities—historical linguistics, sociolinguistics, and philosophy of language (basically, most of this book). They aren't perceived to meet the skill and technological requirements of the future. Even worse, they're often seen as replaceable by AI, as opposed to as much a part of controlling and harnessing it, as STEM is. But in Ghana, STEM development and innovation isn't a luxury pursuit but a vital game of catch-up, for a continent that was colonized and exploited by the West. Innovation, like digital tools that improve health-care diagnoses in a country that lacks specialist doctors, for example, can concretely improve the lives of all Ghanaians. Ghana is one of the fastest-growing economies in the world, but 24 percent of the population still lives below the poverty line. For better or worse, defending, protecting, or even prioritizing linguistic diversity pales before other more urgent requirements. When the government does promote multilingualism, it's usually to promote literacy in English, the global lingua franca of STEM.

Of course, what Stella and Mavis point out is that languages should be protected specifically to aid the growth and development of Ghana rather than sidelined during it. Local languages are tools with which to express ideas, experiences, and emotions, and in the north they tie people not only to a physical land that they're from but the ancestral distribution of it, "inherited across generations of closely intertwined kinship." Tools and solutions that hold such needs and values at the heart of it will be more successful than one-size-fits-all English-language innovation that fails to account for diversity. Whether it's a small, already endangered language or a larger regional language like Dagbani, all of them provide the kind of cultural resilience that couples with wider development and climate-adaptation goals. Look at Amina and the sustainable business she has developed starting from her grandmother's foraging trips, or at all the farmers who are still managing to survive despite the challenges of their climate because of what they learned from long-dead ancestors. Common languages are what enabled such knowledge exchange. Some of these languages already need protection; if their speakers are increasingly forced to move, they'll *all* need it.

■ ■ ■

On the Bureau of Ghana Languages' website, the head of their Ewe section writes:

> The Bureau of Ghana Languages, the only government department mandated to write and publish books exclusively in the Ghanaian Languages as a way of promoting our indigenous languages is unable to deliver effectively because of understaffing, insufficient funds and logistics.[6]

It impressed me—mainly because I struggle to believe that a civil servant in the UK's Department of Culture, Media and Sport would be able to publish something similar on gov.uk. The writer's commentary has extended into poetry elsewhere; there is a phenomenal video of him, uploaded by Pen International, reciting the poem "Xegbee xe dona"—"a bird speaks its own language"—in Ewe. "A parrot speaks not the language of a crow," the translation goes. "Don't be ashamed of speaking our mother tongue. No one calls someone else's mother theirs."[7]

I did not get to meet him when I contacted the bureau asking for an interview; instead, I spoke to Enoch Adinortey Adibuer, acting director of the bureau and head of the Dangme section. Undisclosed government work meant he was five and a half hours late for our interview, and once I had managed to pin him down he started to joke that he didn't know anything about what I had come to interview him for. Eventually—perhaps dissuaded by the limits of my own sense of humor—he mellowed into something resembling seriousness.

The bureau was created in 1951 by UNESCO, inspired by one core principle: "If you want to make an impact, as far as education is concerned, people must be taught in their native language." UNESCO is correct; research has long found that learners benefit from using their home language in education in early grade years. But for a country with primarily oral traditions, this is a challenge: Without a writing system, you can't write a language textbook. "There were no books in local languages, and often no alphabets; the bureau began first with Ga, then Asanti Twi, Ewe, Dagbani, Nzema, all some of the biggest languages in the country. Researchers then began to build orthographies and writing for other languages."

Where there were no writing systems or literary traditions, linguistic opportunists have often got involved. For Dagbani, a dictionary that is still widely used today only exists because linguists funded by Christian organizations came to Ghana. Christian Bible translators, powered by organizations such as the evangelical nonprofit SIL Global, which is based in Texas, were very active in areas like northern Ghana during the twentieth century, hoping to spread Evangelical Christianity through local languages, either to communities of other Christian denominations or to wholly convert them from faiths like Islam or traditional African belief systems. In 1995, about 98 percent of Dagbani speakers were illiterate, and when this inevitably led to debates about how best to write the language down, it was the Dagbani New Testament Revision Committee making the call, not the bureau.[8]

When the bureau isn't advising on what qualifies as a government-sponsored language, they also have to do the government's translation services and teacher training and produce learning materials. Enoch believes that there are a lot of as yet unread written works in Ghanaian languages that his department has not been able to verify and work with, but that they just don't have the time or money to go through them. At a second office, in Tamale—where Dagbani is spoken, and a lot closer to the smaller languages the linguists are worried could be seriously endangered by climate change—Enoch said they lack the staff to support speakers.

There is clearly not enough money, and the consequences of a poorly paid and staffed bureau seem to multiply beyond abandoned languages. In 2019, local outlets reported that the bureau was in debt to the tune of over GH¢300,000 to printing firms since 2015[9]— over a quarter of a million pounds. Another news story, published that same year, was headlined "Juju Attack at Bureau of Ghana Languages" in which linguists were alleged to have either summoned demons or engaged a voodoo priest to deliver supernatural warnings to the director at the time. They accused that director of allowing translation contracts to be diverted from the bureau to private language companies. The bureau has never published or issued a formal statement addressing these reports.

In light of the hole the bureau seemed to be in, I was skeptical that they would be doing much about the challenge of forced migration due to climate change, but I probed Enoch anyway. The question seemed to confuse him. "Who is forcing them to move?" he replied. I mentioned the increasingly unpredictable rainfall patterns, the failed rice crops, the farming families leaving for a new livelihood down south.

Enoch disagreed. "They are used to the climatic conditions." The real issue, he felt, was a lack of jobs.

This motivated Safiatu, the bureau's accountant, who had been quietly sitting in the corner of the room listening to our conversation, to finally speak up. "For the climate, it wouldn't have significant numbers," she said. She came to Accra to study, and has remained here. She is a Kusaal speaker from the Upper East Region, and she speaks to her children in Kusaal, but they insist on replying in English, as does a nephew she is looking after, even though he spent the first sixteen years of his life back in the region. "It's a big fight in the house," she said, clapping her hands for emphasis. Kusaal has an orthography and books, "but the elders didn't know we had to take the step to write to the bureau to have it approved. It's being studied now."

Enoch and Safiatu agreed that a migrant family may struggle to maintain their language in a new, big city, but they did not see climate change as being a factor in their leaving home. I had a similar skeptical response when I had asked Tony Naden about it; Tony is one of the Christian linguists who has dedicated his life to Ghana's northern languages. He told me he didn't anticipate the total desertification of the north, forcing people to leave and felling their languages in one great climate disaster.

But that's not what I meant; I meant the slow and steady trickle of families like Safiatu's, who in a single generation pivot to one of Ghana's urban lingua francas or just English, the language they have inherited from colonialism but equally the language that will enable many young Ghanaians to participate in the international marketplace. While Safiatu's motivation for studying and living in Accra was purely economical, for an increasing number of people in the north there is now an additional pressure of climate-change-induced weather problems that are making it harder to farm. And so even a great language like Dagbani can be lost in a family, just as emigrants around the world watch their languages disappear, absorbed into the urban mass. For the smaller languages that are losing critical mass in the north, and which aren't recognized by the Ghanaian government, this is all the more deadly; but I was surprised at how seemingly relaxed many in and outside Ghana also seem about bigger languages, too. If young Dagbani speakers don't have a chance to keep it up or pass it on when they move away, it's hard to imagine that they would ever want to move back—and harder still to think about the cultural traditions that might get forgotten along the way.

In another room, the bureau had some books for sale, and I asked if they had something in Dagbani that I could buy to take home with me. They offered a slim Dagbani-English dictionary, which still sits on my bookcase. They pointed out that this was *definitely* a real one; if I went to a big market, like the Kejetia Market in Kumasi, I'd find pirated copies. They were clearly annoyed that profits were going to rogue printers. But I thought about the Dagbani speakers, almost certainly migrants, who for whatever personal reason were choosing to buy one of these books in the great city markets of Kumasi and Accra. Had they moved there with friends? Were they staying with a relative? Were they trying to teach a child? In Kumasi's sprawling market I tried to imagine what else they might be able to read, or find, to remind themselves of home in the city they have moved to—anything to keep their language close against the overwhelming din of English, the happy chatter of their friendship groups, and the perfumed rice boiling away, its starchy steam filling the air.

■ ■ ■

The bureau may have been set up with the best of intentions, but today it struggles to meet the weight of Ghana's great linguistic diversity, and its own rules around how literary a language needs to be are adding to the long list of obstacles that stand between a language and the support it may receive. So, unsurprisingly, some in Ghana are taking the fate of their languages into their own hands.

Just outside Tamale, Sadik drove me to his office, a squat building surrounded by the motorbikes of volunteers who were patiently waiting for us inside. The Harmattan wind was whirring sand and red clay dust into my hair as we walked up the drive, matting it. With its gusts, the Harmattan welcomes in Ghana's dry season and, often, drought. Year after year, Tamale finds itself in a water crisis; children stay home from school or wander off to try to fill their jerry cans. People resort to sachets for cooking and bathing. An hour or so later, when I went to the bathroom, I noticed that there was no water in the toilet bowl or in the sink when I tried to run it; just the sad creaking of pipes and ceramic. The infrastructure and planning here were already struggling, and it's even worse now that the city is so big. More than seven hundred thousand people live in the northern capital, compared with just twenty thousand in 1950. The climate crisis is not Tamale's only problem.

Sadik Shahadu is a jack-of-all-digital-trades, but he's especially well known for his shepherding of the Dagbani Wikimedians User Group. This is a group of like-minded, highly educated Tamale youth, several with master's degrees, who get together to spend hours committing local language, history, and knowledge to Wikipedia. Today, nearly thirteen thousand articles have been written in Dagbani, and plenty of the volunteers are multilingual with smaller languages like Kusaal, Dagaare, and Gurene for which they have also begun to write articles.

The volunteers have done this because no one else has; I witnessed for myself that the bureau was poorly digitized, and as a mainly oral language in which speakers have had historically low literacy rates, Dagbani has not had web users pumping out materials in the way other languages have done. The languages that do saturate the internet tend to reflect prestige and privilege rather than speaker number—more websites use Norwegian, which has four million speakers, than use Swahili, which has two hundred million. Swahili, like every single other African language (there are at least two thousand of them), appears on less than 0.1 percent of websites. Couple this with the dominance of colonial languages in the continent, low disposable income to access internet services, and connectivity gaps, and it becomes easier to understand why many African languages, and the knowledge held within them, have gone largely unwritten on the internet. For all the Dagbani speakers who have not learned a colonial language, like English, their chance of being able to understand much written content online is next to zero.

Elsewhere in Ghana, many seem complacent about the status of the Dagbani language; here, the room was awash in anxiety about it. Alhassan Mohammed Awal, who was one of the first people to sign up, told me: "Any time I went online to search about any materials about the Dagbani language, I couldn't find any." A colleague of his added: "If we don't make conscious efforts to digitize this language, someday, somehow, it'll also be at risk of extinction [. . .] we need control efforts just to keep it active and alive."

I found it moving that—on top of newsier items, like making sure politicians have Wikipedia articles about them—so much of the content the volunteers have uploaded are folk tales, parables known as salima-yila that are often retold by drummer narrators who, until now, have essentially been Dagbani Wikipedia themselves, memorizing their community's history not on the internet but in their heads and hands. Many of the stories that the volunteers have put on Wikipedia appear to be cautionary tales for naughty children, such as the one about the child who insists on playing with a small climbing spider—Kpatiŋdarinŋga—despite his mother's warning. Pumpuŋɔ, pumpuŋɔ, the spider says onomatopoeically, drumming his eight masterful feet on his web, slowly approaching the boy. The web engulfs him, entrapping him, until the villagers discover him and free him from the spider, teaching the child an important lesson about not disobeying your elders. It made me think of Kurdish folklore and about how repetition could enable you to remember a story and retell it.

Several of these proverb-laden stories encourage conflict resolution and peaceful cohesion. One suggests God loves those who belong to a group, another says one finger cannot pick up a stone, all expressions emphasizing the value that the Dagomba place on unity and community support. I learned in my research about Ghanaian proverbs that a frequent deployer of them is considered wise, and even cunning, so much so that there is even a meta proverb about people who use proverbs: ŋaha ŋaha.ra nyɛla vubɔ.ra—"a person who uses proverbs is a troublemaker." If someone ever says this to you, here is your response: ŋun wum li ka baŋ digbini gba nyɛla vubɔ.ra—"The one who hears and understands it is also a troublemaker."[10]

Wikipedia's defining feature is collaboration: It is compiled entirely from the often unacknowledged work of internet volunteers around the world. A fairly recent attempt to see how it has been used by Setswana- and Punjabi-speaking editors has established that it has been "crucial" for the preservation and promotion of these languages,[11] but that community engagement and content quality were distinct challenges. As any fellow English-language editors on Wikipedia may know, the rules behind editing are famously strict so as to maintain its usefulness and credibility among a sea of different writers and, potentially, bad actors. This can be a major obstacle for countries and cultures with barely any Wikipedia presence; for this reason, the rules for writing Dagbani articles aren't nearly as strict as those placed on larger languages. Another problem is that Wikipedia heavily relies on citations, but what do you do when a language has very little textual output and all the knowledge is transmitted orally? Well, you still cite from trusted sources, but you reconfigure how you platform them. Researchers working with the Ovaherero people of

Namibia smartly tried to navigate this by holding interviews with members of the community in open or semipublic settings, ensuring that speakers could essentially be live fact-checked and peer-reviewed as they gave their retelling of, say, a historical event; these were then recorded and uploaded to Wikicommons.[12]

The Dagbani Wikimedians User Group has tried to make sure that their ancestral knowledge and language can be preserved through a similar intervention; they take photo walks in which they capture first-of-their-kind photography of local practices, before uploading them to Wikicommons where they may be used as references. One of these photo walks took the Wikimedians to the Yoggu village in Tolon, east of Tamale, who are known as great blacksmiths and where metalwork has gone hand-in-hand with gunmanship. They recorded a funeral in which warrior dances are performed and where a young man shoots a long rifle, whose gunpowder explodes in a spray of sparks as if it were a firework. In another dance, Sonaa, the chief blacksmith, jumps around on a naked flame, a unique ability only he as chief possesses. Evidence of the intricate metalwork that generations of Dagomba have mastered is otherwise nonexistent on the internet. Aside from its great cultural significance, these practices also serve as a lesson to more wasteful societies. An American anthropologist, Wyatt MacGaffey, has written in the past that the trash heaps of Tamale look barren compared to those in Accra, where junk abounds; in Tamale every crumb of food is eaten by people or by their much-cared-for livestock, and every scrap of metal is refashioned by the blacksmiths.[13] Tamale itself has a machelefong, a "blacksmith district," which has contributed to the city's fast economic growth. Almost all the words for the craft actually come from Hausa, best known as a Nigerian language, revealing that at some point in the past there must have been close cultural contact between different groups practicing the craft, long before European colonial powers drew borders between kingdoms and communities. Some of the household items created by Tamale blacksmiths betray loan words Dagbani later received—a cookpot, for example, is a krookpoti.

As speakers may disperse across the country, and as the need for more and more Dagbani text grows, language activists like Wikipedia volunteers act as the defensive wall, ensuring their language has a presence in wider Ghanaian life. AI tools, for example, cannot operate in a language unless there are millions of data points at hand; if the information of the future is held only in English and a smattering of prestige Ghanaian languages, Dagbani risks disappearing. When I tried to learn more about the Yoggu village, I found a TikTok video of a local dance being performed. The comments section was filled with remarks in English saying, "Please let's protect these cultures for the coming generations," "Some of us are no more Dagombas, cos we don't know our culture," and "I'm pure Dagomba and I must be frank: I don't know the [dance's] name."[14]

What the Wikipedia language activists have demonstrated is that where there is a will to change and enough awareness around language endangerment, members of the community can be activated to lend a helping hand. In contrast to the insistent textual demands of the bureau, the Wikipedia group also shows that language revival does not necessarily need to come at the cost of total submission to the expectations or practices of Western epistemology. Images and audio can also be part of extending a language's presence in our lives.

And this knowledge is more vital than ever. As scientists back in Kumbungu are discovering, knowing the meaning of a word can be the difference between surviving the climate crisis or surrendering to it.

■ ■ ■

On December 26, 2004, an eerie silence fell across the waters of Mo Ko Surin, an archipelago of islands in the Andaman Sea. The indigenous people who live there—the Moken—are so expert in the ocean surrounding them that they are called "people of the sea" in the languages of their closest neighbors. Young Moken are twice as good as European children at seeing underwater, naturally adjusting their pupil size to spot the sea cucumber and clams they harvest; almost all their trade relies on the Moken's ability to free dive and forage. So when the cicadas stopped singing and the tide receded, as if it was taking a deep breath, the chief of the Moken, a man named Salama, started shouting that this was laboon. Those who heard him immediately understood what was happening; they had heard their whole lives about the great wave that could wipe out humanity. They sought out high ground and waited. The Indian Ocean tsunami that would claim the lives of more than twenty-two thousand people engulfed the Moken's villages, its waves reaching up to thirty meters. It was one of the deadliest natural disasters in world history. But not a single member of the Moken died.[15]

Indigenous knowledge and language are tightly linked, and as the latter wanes, as we've seen in every chapter of this book, the former does, too. The prescribed fires of the Karuk that have helped the tribe manage the California wildfires are part of a broader idea of land stewardship named pikyav, which loosely translates to "fixing" in English. That the Ṣhehrɛt name the delicate heart of the frankincense tree shows that they care about it. Languages don't necessarily shape how we think—what linguists call determinism—but they do reveal what we prioritize. We don't have words for things we don't care about. When I was doing my interviews about Ṣhehrɛt in Oman, Miranda Morris directed me to her work on Bathari, a nearby language of a people on the Omani coast. Their seasons' names reveal the rising and setting of certain stars and the detail of the winds blowing in that particular time, all useful information for fishermen that use it to understand what fish may be available and when.[16] Bathari is nearly extinct, and many of these traditional ways of life have long vanished, preserved only in old songs.

Lose the practice and you lose the words; lose the language and you can only prove the practice ever existed at all if you document the words or find translated words to talk about them. We have already observed how slim this archive is for a language like Dagbani. Its narrowness worries Emmanuel Attoh, a researcher at the International Water Management Institute. "I've seen people who migrate from the north, and they cannot even tell you one word in their language," he told me on a video call from Sri Lanka, where he now lives. He's from the melting pot of Accra, where he witnessed lots of northerners speaking Twi over their local languages.

As for what these northerners have left behind, Attoh knows it very well. He is a hydro-climatologist, researching water insecurity and climate risks. His work took him to Kumbungu, the same place I had met the rice farmers. It quantified what the farmers have said about the inconstant rain:[17] that the rainy season seemed to be getting shorter and that the number of especially hot days seemed to be increasing. Livestock was more likely to die, pests were multiplying, and there were more wildfires. No wonder so many seem to be deciding that they can no longer farm there.

When I asked Attoh whether he thought Dagbani language loss in a faraway city could have an impact on those left back home, he answered rapidly, as if he'd already been dwelling on it for a while. "The first thing they lose is their beliefs," he said. "Then you lose the culture. In Kumbungu, there are some birds that are so special that they don't kill it. They are special in a religious sense, but they also help you to predict the weather. The birds have local names, they're not appreciated in English. So how will I refer to that bird, if my child doesn't know the name?"

The farmers who can understand how to read these birds only acquire such knowledge with experience; some farmers who are recognized as seemingly having a divine gift for rain prophecy are called sabanda, "bearer of rain knowledge."[18] Signs like the coucal bird's singing or the noisy movement of a large number of hornbills can all mean the onset of rain. A quantitative study found that bird sound was one of the most reliable rainfall predictors that the farmers used from among their assortment of traditional knowledge, with other methods including monitoring how painful mosquito bites are or assessing fog density. Farmers in this research project were about as accurate as the Ghana Meteorological Agency themselves at predicting weather, anticipating one in three rainfall events. This is a legitimately powerful tool to have when weather forecasting in Africa is nothing like it is in the rest of the world. Over the course of modern history, it's been just as ignored and undersupported as its indigenous languages; while North America had 291 radar stations as of 2024 to follow weather patterns, the entire African continent had just 37.[19]

Indigenous methods like these can work in tandem, rather than in opposition, to Western technology. Given the privilege of extra information and knowledge, the idea is that more farming families will be able to stay and adapt to increasingly erratic weather patterns rather than having to leave their ancestral lands *by force*; they might not be able to delay climate change, but longer-term adaptation may offer greater resilience. For farmers with low literacy, indigenous language radio is one of the first ideas that has been deployed, allowing them to access real-time weather information and proving that you don't always need to make new tech for new problems. But some of the funding that could support projects like this one risks being as precarious as that of Ghana's language bureau. The fate of Ghana's language diversity does not only hinge on language protection from language workers; if it survives, it will only be because the world starts to care about those who are most harshly affected by the climate crisis, the government takes notice of what its linguists are saying, and big businesses and foundations take an interest, due to either compassion or financial incentives. It is an imperfect layer of defense.

Attoh himself couldn't remember what the birds were called in Dagbani. The study he had sent me called them all an alacheyu, which a Dagbani dictionary I found online says is strictly only a particular large bird that feeds on grasshoppers. As I read the dictionary's words for birds, a sea of definitions with no English translations, I could see an etymological color that has been hardly revealed, its own knowledge-within-knowledge, like the ŋmaanchee bird, named for its constant pursuit of *ŋmaansi,* monkeys. On the hunt for other bird words, my internet journey happily, and perhaps unsurprisingly, led me back to Wikipedia, where I finally found the word for the singing coucal in Dagbani—baɣimpiɔŋ. *A bird that hides and moves carefully,* the entry says. On Facebook, I found a Dagbani speaker who cited a proverb about them: Baɣimpiɔŋ nimbila yi zaɣ'sira, di borila dooibu.

I messaged it to Sadik. "When the coucal's eye itches, it's about to fall off," he wrote back, unceremoniously. "It means when someone is going to be harmed, they usually go closer to dangerous places." Dagbani proverbs deliver many warnings; whether they are heeded is another story.

THE STORY OF DIALËT

paciugh: originally meaning a muddy or messy mixture, it is
used affectionately for a mischievous child

I was very well acquainted with Nonna's carpet; it had faded to
a color somewhere between gray and green, like pondwater. I
had spent years crawling around on it, rough against my knees
and palms, first as a child and then as a teenager, chasing my old
Yorkshire terrier between the legs of the coffee table when she was
feeling mischievous. Today I was sitting on the carpet, a pad of
paper in my lap, as I studied Mum and Nonna opposite me on her
small sofa.

"Ho paura del cane," Mum said. "G'ho paura del can."

"G'ho paura del can," I repeated, writing it down. I said paura as
I would in Italian, morphing the vowel sounds to stress the *u. I am
scared of the dog.*

"G'ho pa-u-ra," she corrected, emphasizing a *u* that comes far
closer to the front of the mouth with force behind it. That *u* and the
strong nasality of can are the kind of sounds that would alert a
knowledgeable listener to the fact that the speaker came from near
Piacenza. There are far more vowels in this language variety than
there are in Italian, and many of them are a lot closer to sounds you
might have heard in French. The same goes for many of the words;
tir-buson, our word for corkscrew, is much closer to French's tire-
bouchon than Italian's cavatappi.

"Il cane," Nonna muttered, thinking.

"No, we're doing al dialët, Mum," Mum said. "First we're saying it in Italian to get the feel of it and then in dialët." She asked me for the next phrase.

"The women are scared of the dog," I read out.

"Le donne hanno paura del cane," she said in Italian, before switching to dialët. "I donn' g'hann paura del can. Mum, how do I say 'the women'?"

"*I* donn'," Nonna confirmed.

"Yesterday, I was scared of the dog. I am not scared of the dog," I continued.

"Ieri, avevo paura del cane. Ier, g'hav paura del can. Non ho paura del cane; g'ho mia paura del can."

If you're eagle-eyed, you will have spotted there that negation is completely different. In Italian, it comes before the verb, whereas in dialët it comes after it. While it sounds different to French, pas as in je n'ai pas also goes after the verb, originating in the old French "not a step," meaning "not at all." Once upon a time in old French you could also say mie instead of pas, meaning "not a crumb." Eventually, it got grammaticalized in French—and mie, becoming mia, likewise entered the grammar of speakers in Piacenza. Etymologically, it's as if we're saying, "I don't have a crumb of fear of the dog."

The sentences I was reading out are designed to paint a basic picture of grammatical structures in a language, the slight variations of phrases revealing gender agreements, tenses, and negation. They came from the Language Sustainability tool kit, a list of questions that was created by two nonprofit US organizations that robustly preserve and defend languages at risk of disappearing—the Living Tongues Institute for Endangered Languages and Wikitongues. For low-resource languages, and especially those that are vulnerable, this is a way you can gather the kinds of words and phrases—known as forms—that can help a linguist conduct further research or help a learner to build their own resources.

The program's cleverness emerges as you move through it; gathering words about everyday domains like the body, nature, numbers, and daily life before working out how to be scared of a dog in the past, present, and future tense. Once completed, these sentences give a very thorough sense of a language's grammar; in fact, it wasn't until we started this exercise that I understood how to conjugate "to have" in dialët. There are massive lexicon lists to collect, to the point that the authors believe it could take four to eight hours with a speaker to retrieve them all, although I could see that I would need far longer with Mum and Nonna. It was hard work for Mum, and basically impossible for Nonna, who at ninety-four could easily speak spontaneously in dialët but kept pivoting to standard Italian when we asked her for specific vocabulary. Although her words were there, her ability to retrieve them on command was cloudy. I could see, however, that with every new word Mum was beginning to find a rhythm, first searching for the word in Italian and then dialët, as if Italian was the key she needed to open and walk through her impressive, triglossic memory palace. This is apparently a common tactic that multilinguals deploy when they try to remember a term.

As Mum carried on, I began hearing where the words mimicked each other or diverged. It felt like a camera pulling into focus as I started spotting what meant singular or plural or how present tense gave way to past. But the kit had warned me that I might find it hard to write down words if I wasn't familiar with the language's writing system, and it was right. Without knowledge of the International Phonetic Alphabet I had to improvise, using only the sounds and writing methods in my arsenal. But I hoped that my scribblings, along with my recordings, would work together one day when I did learn how to write our language.

I had great ambitions for this tool kit. Having seen some of the lexicon lists that now bolster the research in fast-disappearing languages like those I found for Śḥehrɛ̄t and Karuk, I've witnessed how they become survival tools for speakers who might otherwise be the last in their line. When I came across it, it felt like a treasure map. I thought that every time I came to see Nonna, especially if Mum came, too, I could use the two of them to retrieve vocabulary together. I'd have my own family lexicon to read, and perhaps compare with other Emilian varieties when I got the hang of things. I had never expected to suddenly become fluent in our language, but I hoped an increased knowledge of how it worked would help me understand Mum and Nonna's conversations more. I didn't want to do it as some grand contribution to language scholarship; I wanted to do it because my gut told me it was important. This also meant that there were some words in the list I felt like I could safely skip—would I ever really need to know our dialect's word for a tribe or a shaman? The list was originally created for the Munda languages of India, Bangladesh, and Nepal, and some of the questions naturally reflect their cultures. All I had to do was adjust them to my own family's context; I could have easily replaced them, maybe with vocabulary about the Catholic Church. An even longer set of questions can be downloaded if you are seriously brave, and have the luxury of time, to draw out even more words and forms.

But after just a couple of sessions in my nonna's house documenting her wisdom and her stories, and a few more stolen moments I recorded when she and Mum were in lively conversation, my growing lexicon would come to an abrupt halt. One bright summer morning, Nonna was carried out on a stretcher by paramedics, past the terrazzo that my nonno had laid down another lifetime ago, past her roses in abundant bloom and out of the street she had lived on longer than any other resident there. Nonna would never go home again, and when I first went back there months later, to the garden's long grass and her silent kitchen, I wondered if I ever would, too.

■　■　■　·

When I began writing this book, with my nonna already ninety-three and long housebound, I was aware that time was precious. It is why when she would be making tea or would sit in front of the TV with me, I would sometimes quietly begin recording what she was saying on my phone as a Voice Memo. It has left me with a small artifact of the time and place she came from, a context that survived well into the twenty-first century despite its firm roots in centuries before. My mum's cousin thinks Nonna and her sister Zia Elvira sometimes said things she'd never heard anyone else say, as if La Serra had fostered its own unique language variety. Maybe that was true; it would have taken a skilled linguist to travel there in the 1930s and 1940s to determine, village by village and, in their case, isolated building by isolated building, how language twisted and turned between them.

Much of Europe was busy with languages and poor then; in that sense, La Serra was not unique. So we will only ever know such language distinctions by word of mouth, something that feels more powerful to me in this case than a scientific paper ever would be. This has now become a personal story that I cannot detach from loss, a reality I always dreaded; I feel its sadness deep in my chest. I heard recently that grief is the last act of love; so, too, is writing this.

A few months after Nonna's death, I realized how much I still had to learn. I wasn't just at a loss when it came to finding the right words of Nonna and Mum's language, transported to north London from the Piacenza Apennines, but even for its actual *name*. They had only ever called it dialët—the dialect. Both Nonna and Nonno came from the very eastern edge of Piacenza, with Nonna's isolated farmhouse hovering right on the border with Parma. Both provinces are in the region of Emilia-Romagna, where language indexes state that two languages, not dialects, are spoken—Emilian and Rumagnol. I had never been told that our dialët could be a dialect of a language other than Italian—or even a language in its own right. Mum and Nonna didn't know, either. If we spoke a dialect, where was it from—

Piacenza? Our comune? The exact paesi they come from? How was I going to learn this language if I didn't even know what it was called?

It is challenging to fully identify Italy's so-called dialects, which most of the time actually refer to languages that are unrecognized. The Yiddish specialist Max Weinreich is regularly cited here; at one of his lectures in the 1940s, an attendee once told him that he believed "a language is a dialect with an army and a navy." Yiddish is, in fact, the language Weinreich quoted it in himself—a shprakh iz a dyalekt mit an armey un flot—and he dedicated much of his career to gifting Yiddish the status it so rightly deserved, following centuries in which it was dismissed as simply a dialect of German and even as zhargon—jargon.[1] The key difference for linguists between dialects and languages is differentiation, though this is almost always subjective and there is no universally accepted criterion measuring one from the other. If a standard way of speaking diverges for a particular group of people, that tends to become known as a dialect because the core elements of the language broadly remain similar. Liverpudlian English might sound incomprehensible some of the time to a Londoner, but they ultimately still speak the same language, just with variation. Their distance is low. But take Scots and English, both daughters of Middle English, instead; these languages grew apart for a very long time, and their distance is substantially higher. Once you've added in the firm political divisions between national identities, you end up with a clearer image of two different languages, without one being a dialect of the other.

Shortly after Italy was unified following the hard-won wars of independence, the Italian statesman Massimo d'Azeglio said, "L'Italia è fatta. Restano da fare gli italiani." *Italy is made. Now we must make Italians.* Italy has always been a peninsula of several indigenous languages, and, not so long ago, your mother tongue was the language of your village or your city; standard Italian, a Tuscan language variety, was transported across the country from the medieval period as a literary language thanks to Florence's powerful influence and figures like Dante Alighieri. But people would still have spoken their local variety to one another in the street. Italian wouldn't become an official, national language until unification in 1861. Before then, Italy had been a miscellany of papal states, kingdoms, and duchies, frequently under foreign control; at different points after the fall of the Western Roman Empire, various parts of Italy have been ruled by—deep breath—the Ostrogoths, the Byzantines, the Lombards, the Franks, several popes, Arabs, Normans, the Spanish, the French, the Bourbons, and the Austrians.

It is little wonder, then, that the spirit of campanilismo is so strong in Italy. A campanile is a bell tower; in this, campanilismo shares a similar root to English parochialism, from the Latin parochia, or "parish," although they don't really mean the same thing. Parochialism in English normally stands for small-mindedness, but in Italian, campanilismo is the deep attachment an Italian feels to their birthplace. If your city-state was always at war with other city-states nearby, or your hometown was swapped between foreign noblemen every other century, it's not surprising that you would have felt a stronger connection to what, and importantly *who*, you knew within close environs, rather than your region more broadly. Those who shared your local church also shared family, culture, and language with you. This was even more true if you were illiterate, and at the time of the unification of Italy in 1861, it has been estimated that only around 20 to 25 percent of the adult population could use the parole di carta, "words of letter-writing,"[2] in which Italian was becoming a standardized language.

As access to education expanded across the twentieth century, people of wider socio-economic backgrounds could now speak the language of their country alongside the language of their campanile. But the local language and the national language never shared equal value, at least not at the level of the Italian government. Regional languages, which were by and large used orally, were never a language of instruction in schools and by the fascist era were heavily discriminated against. Italian was "purified" under Mussolini and the country went through a forced Italianization. Surnames with any hint of foreignness were relieved of it—Rusovič was changed to Russo—and a book published in the 1930s recommended word changes in every corner of Italian life, even suggesting a croissant should only ever be called a cornetto. Italian became the exclusive, mandated language spoken across schools, newspapers, and broadcasting. In a shift that is by now very familiar to us, regional languages were becoming associated with provincialism and the past, while Italian was fully established as the language of Italy, unity, and the future.

As a result, most of us today have no idea that Italian is one of around twenty-seven indigenous languages, all of which have an undetermined number of local varieties within them, each as individual as the many church bells that ring out across them. It took Italy nearly half a century to formally roll back its antagonism toward its regional and minority languages; in 1999, the country conceded to EU pressure to protect minority languages with Law 482, which on the face of it looks like one of the most progressive language planning policies in the whole of western Europe. Within it, the state assures a yearly fund toward the protection of historic minority languages and stipulates that the Italian public service broadcaster can work with regions to help supply programs in languages other than Italian. However, it has been poorly enacted—plenty of languages go without TV programming or much protection—and the law acknowledges only twelve languages in the first place: French, Occitan, Franco-Provençal, German, Ladin, Friulian, Slovene, Sardinian, Catalan, Arberesh, Greek, and Croatian. The majority of Italy's linguistic past—and present—is missing from this list.

The lack of attention given to Italy's many languages—the "decades of hostility" and "opaque ignorance" that the famous linguist Tullio de Mauro identified—has meant many indigenous languages are now fast disappearing. Italy's national statistics office, Istat,[3] reveals that the bilingualism between Italian and local languages that existed for a brief window after unification has been short-lived. In 2015, only 14 percent of Italians mainly spoke in dialect, down from 32 percent in the 1980s. Thirty-two percent spoke a mixture of their dialect and Italian and 46 percent spoke mainly in Italian. A whopping 80 percent of Italians under the age of thirty-four are bilingual—except it's with another foreign language that is usually English. The north is where regional language diversity is disappearing the fastest and where bilingualism with a foreign language is the strongest. Languages like Neapolitan and Sicilian, on the other hand, retain a lot more vitality, probably due to their previous existence as unified kingdoms, compared with the much more politically divided north. The south is also traditionally less economically developed than the north, which may be why foreign language adoption is more limited. The north, on the other hand, is where bilingualism with a foreign language is the strongest and regional language diversity is disappearing the fastest.

My nonna's language, whatever it was called, came from the heartlands of the endangered north—as it turns out, not so far from where Professor Marco Tamburelli comes from. The director of the International Research Network on Contested Languages at Bangor University, he knows Italy's linguistic amnesia intimately because he's from Lombardia, even farther west toward the French border. He feels ambivalent about identifying himself as an Italian. When he sees Italians described as Mediterraneans, he thinks about how he's from a place far closer to the Swiss mountains than to the sea, or how his mother always cooked with butter rather than olive oil. "If being Italian means sea and sun, pasta and pizza, then we are not Italian."

He spoke both Italian and lombard growing up, alternating between the two depending on whom he was speaking to, like many across the entire country still do today. He only really considered that he might in fact speak two languages rather than one when he was studying linguistics at University College London, in the middle of a phonology class. "They were talking about *u* and *e* and front-rounded vowels," he said, and as he pronounced them I heard the echoes of how my mum sounds when she speaks: they were identical. "And I said, oh, yeah, I speak a language with those sounds." When Tamburelli said that it was Italian, the lecturer replied, "No, Italian doesn't have those." That's when he started to wonder what was going on; how could he, an Italian, not be producing Italian sounds?

Despite linguists clearly establishing Italy's indigenous language diversity, Tamburelli has to push back against the majority of Italians who describe such languages as dialects and not languages in their own right; according to him, it is still challenging for academics within Italy to question this. In the 2010s, linguist Francesco Screti analyzed articles from *La Repubblica*, a popular Italian newspaper, to investigate how the media props these views up. Italy's dialetti, he found, were presented as being historic relics of a pre-unification past, while Italy's unification was described as a "challenge to the country of a thousand belltowers and as many dialects," as if they were a problem to be solved. Italy's divisions were blamed on differences of "accent, dialect or origin," and Italian was portrayed as clear and straightforward, unlike dialetti, which are "unintelligible" or "immutable." This dismissive attitude is part of the reason that many still call their languages dialects, like Mum and Nonna. Apart from it not being true, it means my nonna and mum were entirely unaware they were in fact trilingual, not bilingual. For a country with the highest number of heritage sites in the world, Italian cultural memory seems surprisingly selective.

Linguists like Tamburelli are now trying to conduct the kind of analysis that should have been done decades ago, establishing the true variety of Italy's many languages. "We define languages from the point of how different they are," he explained, and try to ignore any other bias. It's the linguistic equivalent of DNA analysis, where researchers use something called the Levenshtein distance, used to measure the difference between two sequences. So, taking Italian's cane and Nonna's can, you would use the loss of the *e* and the change of the *a* vowel to help calculate the Levenshtein distance between them, which, on this occasion, would be quite low given how similar the words are. Linguists may also use word lists that are sets of basic vocabulary that most languages have—body parts, family words, numbers—and compare those. Using these methods, Tamburelli and his colleague Lissander Brasca revealed something brand new about languages like my nonna's in the north. They firmly established that Gallo-Italic languages like those spoken in Lombardia and Emilia-Romagna were not dialects of Italian—they were out on their own branch of a family tree that was actually far closer to French.[4] In fact, they are closest to languages like Occitan and Franco-Provençal.[5]

All these languages are descendants of Latin, but they aren't all valorized in the way that, say, Italian and French are. Perhaps this is why it's not been a Western government, but a cultural heritage organization—UNESCO—which, internationally and politically, has done a lot in recent years to legitimize Italian languages' existence. For Tamburelli, prestige is at the heart of a language's place in the world; people are told to value a language like French, and so they do. I asked him what he says to people to try to persuade them that every language deserves it. "If you think that it's just about making money and eating and sleeping, then, sure, you use another tool in the toolbox," he explained. "But is that a way to look at the world? Why don't you just eat pills—why do you make lasagna? There is more to food than just giving me energy. Look at France—why do you want all these wines, all these cheeses? Just keep one cheese and, suddenly, we feel poor."

I imagined Italy, with all its DOP prosciutti and DOC wines, which denote protected areas of origin, having an equivalent system for its many languages, like a protected or controlled origin that gives people regional pride. Linguists have something like this—glottocodes, which are unique character codes for distinctive language varieties—but I wonder if there could be something more accessible for the general public. If it is true that a wine will taste different because the grapes face south on a mountainside, or have slightly more minerality in the soil than exactly the same grapes twenty-five kilometers away, why do we assume that language may not alter so rapidly, too?

It was a lesson I had begun to learn the hard way in Bologna when I tried to find resources on Nonna's language. Given that Bologna is the capital of Emilia-Romagna, I had hoped I would find lots of emiliano books there. I found that there were none on emigliän in general, but there were a few on bolognese, the city's variety of it. I started taking pictures of different pages, sending them to my mum so that she could have a look at the words. "No. No, that's not us," she wrote back after every image. Bologna is about as far away from where Nonna grew up as New York to Princeton—far away enough in Italy for a language to meander. "Flux is the natural state of language," Tamburelli reminded me when I told him about my quest. We've effectively domesticated lots of languages, taming them into what we now see as normal and fixed. Clearly, Nonna's was still running around wild somewhere.

After we spoke, I rang my mum because I was excited to tell her how similar dialët was to French, which had blown my mind. "Well, we knew that," she said matter-of-factly. My mum isn't one to philosophize; if there is an opportunity to state the obvious, she'll take it. She has also often found it quaint, and even confusing, that I'd care about our dialect in the first place. "I suppose the language becomes endearing," she finally said. "We think about the family that we have lost."

She was leaving Nonna's as I had rung her, the now quiet house empty without its custodian. Mum had been watering Nonna's plants even though it had been a long time since the doctors told her Nonna wouldn't ever go home again. "You won't feel it, but I will," she said. Feel what? Did she mean the loss of language itself, or more the loss of speaking it with Nonna? I wanted to tell her that of course I felt it, but obviously in a different way. I thought about Mum no longer speaking dialët every day, and how I wished I could speak it with her. If only I could get my hands on some tools or resources that could help. The internet's resources on emigliän were limited; not as bad as Dagbani, but not miles better, either, which was why I was hunting for tangibility: books, recordings, anything that might have once come from the same analog time my nonna had been born into.

We ended the call and I took a walk through my local park, thinking about the language I never knew, that I had heard the familiar music of in my conversation with Tamburelli. And I thought about the long succulent growing across Nonna's hallway, its leaves browning at the edges. Somehow, they were still green with life, despite Mum's protestations that she couldn't save it.

■ ■ ■

When a linguist tells you to go into the mountains, you listen to him.

Bologna did not have what I needed, and nor did the internet—I needed to go back to the very beginning. To Piacenza, where Nonna and Nonno's lives began—a peripheral province at the end of a long Roman road, at the juncture of mountains where people become outnumbered by oak trees and wild boar. The region of Emilia-Romagna was only formed in the 1970s, an irrelevance all the way in the mountains. I never heard my parents mention either Bologna or Emilia-Romagna; just La Serra and Castelletto. All I knew was that we were from the province of Piacenza, which meant we had a natural, blood-born rivalry with Parma next door—who, of course, we speak differently from. A friend of my mum's who comes from our parts told me a joke to highlight this, where two dogs are talking to each other, one of them from Parma and the other from Piacenza. One of them is holding a bone in his jaws; the other, a boneless dog, asks him, "A dove venat?" Where are you from? "Me a summat Paaaaaarma," the dog replies; I'm from Parma, with their trademark elongated vowels, which make him drop the bone. The Piacentino dog rapidly picks it up, and the Parmense dog returns the question. "Me-a-summat-Piaseinsa," the dog replies, through gritted teeth and without dropping the bone, because his vowels, like a good Piaśintein, are far more restricted.

Piacenza is both the name of a city and the wider province it finds itself in, and within either the city or the countryside where Nonna grew up I hoped I would be able to find some books. According to Tamburelli, the more remote I would go, the more speakers I would find. He is noticing that he has to go "deeper and deeper into the mountains" when he conducts fieldwork to find speakers who are fluent enough for his research. "Give me another generation, and we'll go up the valleys, and there will be no one left," he said.

On my last trip to Italy, I'd made a mistake in thinking a random bookshop in Bologna would have my nonna's language in it. This time, I began my search within Piacenza's city borders, and in a library I struck gold: *Dialetto piacentino da tradursi in italiano dagli alunni delle scuole rurale—Piacentino dialect to be translated into Italian for pupils in rural schools*. Within it, I saw a far more accurate representation of how Nonna spoke than what the bolognese books had been showing. Along with a small vocabulary list, it was full of translation exercises that would have been given to schoolchildren to encourage them to learn Italian, converting their existing dialët into literary Italian. It is a strange irony of history that this book that was once used to eradicate rural schoolchildren's mother tongue could now be useful to me as someone trying to learn it. The name made sense, and explained why, even though bolognese is also emigliän, it wasn't accurate enough; I needed to be narrowing my search to a city-by-city level.

Online, I started finding more specific content under piacentino or piaśintein, its endonym. Of course, to me, it'll always be what Mum and Nonna called it: dialët. Right at the end of Emilia-Romagna's borders, piaśintein carries enormous influence from lombard to the point where it's sometimes been classified as part of the lombard superstratum rather than the emigliän one; speakers from the Apennines, like my nonna, will also have come into contact with the local language of Liguria. No wonder it was so different from bolognese.

The resources I began to find online largely, but not totally, illustrated my nonna's variety of piaśintein because this hyperdiversity means that the city piaśintein—where books have mainly been published—is different from the rural one. The city's specific dialët is known as piaśintein dall sass, the language of "the stone." Nonna's provincial dialët is different enough to be called piaśintein arius, "of the air"; the origin of these names probably has to do with Piacenza being paved or built on stone compared to the dirt roads of the mountains. In order to get to Castelletto, where my nonno was from and which was one of the closest villages near Nonna's old house, I had to go through the city, and while I was in Piacenza I went to a free language class so that I could hear some piaśintein dall sass for myself.

The organization that runs courses is called La Famiglia Piasinteina, and I was happy to learn that they put on plays and poetry competitions, all in dialët; over lunch, the president, Danilo Anelli, proudly told me, "They don't have anything like us in Parma." But as I was sitting trying to imbibe everything the teachers said, it occurred to me that it was more of a history lesson than a language lesson; our teachers spent two hours mostly talking about old-fashioned games using wooden sticks and cards that previous generations used to play, spending as much time explaining ideas in Italian as in dialët. There were at least twenty people in the room, with a healthy gender and age mix; it made me happy to see that a fairly diverse group of locals were interested in the evening. But it reminded me of the many bookshops I had gone to, where I had only managed to find books on Italy's languages not in the languages section but in the local history corner.

This is where many such languages have already been relegated to: historical appreciation rather than language revival. I have accepted that this is the same role our dialët will play in my own life, too—but it was eye-opening seeing the same historicizing happening in front of me by people who were still very capable of speaking it. Throughout Italy there are speakers of other languages who are trying to resist being relegated to the history books. For instance, Sicilian politicians are trying to get Sicilian—which has millions of speakers—included in Italy's list of protected minority languages. When a group of linguists and teachers signed a letter in support of the move in 2025, one of their reasons for doing so was because le comunità parlanti chiedono strumenti, non musei[6]—"speaker communities want tools, not museums." They wrote that they'll no longer accept being an object of study and instead want to be seen as citizens with language rights.

With a higher volume of speakers and a powerful regional identity, it will be fascinating to see if Sicilian successfully disrupts the Italian status quo. After it, other Italian languages would surely follow but only if their speakers, and the politicians representing them, are interested in maintaining them in the first place. Danilo told me that most young people in Piacenza do not care about saving dialët, and in any case birth rates are so low that the only young people around are from migrant families who bring other heritage languages with them. Perhaps this was why there seemed to be so much historicizing here in Piacenza. It was because many had decided, or perhaps accepted, that piaśintein has already become something to remember rather than speak.

I wondered if this would be the same when I ventured toward the land of piaśintein arius and its misty forests. I took another train, this time to Fiorenzuola d'Arda, the lowest point before you head into the looming fog of Piacenza's mountainous valleys. I had set up a meeting with Fausto Ferrari, a local historian who fell into documenting the history of the valley he calls Valtolla after his retirement—although it didn't take long to realize that he is also the brother-in-law of a dear friend of my mum's. Thirteen hundred kilometers from home, I was meeting more people I had a direct connection to in a matter of days than I ever did in overcrowded, everywhere-and-everyone-is-an-hour-away London. I met Fausto in a bar where he ordered a white Ortrugo wine, unknown outside Italy but light and slightly fizzy. "We make the best wines," he said, marveling at the glass in his hand. "In Piemonte they get a lot heavier, and a lot more still."

Through his writing (including his blog, *The Brigand of Valtolla*), Fausto wants to raise awareness "of my valley, the Val d'Arda, and the valleys whose rivers flow like a scallop shell, all toward the Po," the river that flows through Piacenza. Valtolla is the valley's old name, the Tolla being a mountain whose name has long shifted to Moria, but it clearly represents a time as much as a physical place to Fausto. The Lombards founded Valtolla over a thousand years ago, where they built monasteries of extreme strategic importance in a volatile corridor between them and their enemies the Byzantines, who held the other side of Italy at the time. Fighting monks were stationed on hilltops that became mini-fortresses, hence why my nonno came from Castelletto, "little castle." War has never been far away here; the people of the valleys were responsible for a massive rebellion against Napoleon, as well as being renowned partisans, including my own family members, during the Second World War. The reason Fausto wanted to raise awareness in the first place is because he feels that much of this knowledge is otherwise forgotten. I asked him why.

"People are ignorant, in the sense that they ignore it, not that they're stupid," he told me in Italian. He told me about the Pietra delle Mole, translated from the dialët "al sass dal lisson," which is hidden in the woods here: a millstone, carved out of the rockside, with which locals used to grind olives, producing oil for gaslights, as well as sharpening farm tools and weapons. The rock that is left in the forest is from the last stonecutter here, who was presumably preparing new grindstones before he stopped working or passed away. For years, nobody knew it existed; now, Fausto organizes hikes for locals to see it. "We helped the local people of Castelletto rediscover this place—which was only five hundred or six hundred meters [away] in a straight line! And yet no one knew it existed. Why? Because their fathers hadn't passed it down. They were busy with livestock, woodcutting . . . they didn't care about this kind of thing. But it's a beautiful thing to preserve."

Saying that people didn't care is an oversimplification; many here were too busy trying to survive. The only way to escape la miseria, for many, was to emigrate, like my family did. According to Fausto's own research, by 1951, five out of eleven comuni in the region didn't have a telephone or telegraph in the community, a quarter of the population had no electricity, and there were only fourteen radios, whereas the average for Italy at the time was forty-three. The average person would eat only ten kilograms of meat a year. Not too far from Castelletto, there is a small prayer chapel dedicated to a cholera outbreak in the late 1800s. Young girls chopped off their plaits and framed them, gifting them to the Virgin, who still watches passersby from behind a metal grate under the emblazoned metal letters P.G.R.—per grazie ricevuta, "for received grace." The girls who had survived the epidemic had offered their hair in gratitude. Life had clearly been difficult here for a very long time.

There was a different church I particularly wanted to visit, at the top of Castelletto, which promised a good vantage point over the valley. The church was old and being renovated, and Fausto was of course involved. I still wasn't sure whether I would visit Nonna's La Serra; I knew I was nearby, but it also somehow didn't feel right for me to go there by myself, without Mum, in a car with a taxi driver to whom I'd have to explain everything. I was worried I would get emotional. The church felt like a middle ground; somewhere I could look over all the different places my relatives had lived in one glorious panorama. When I told Fausto that I had booked a driver to take me there the following day, he said, "Don't be silly. Let me ask Maurizio—he is the pro loco of Castelletto." That meant he was responsible for organizing local festivities, promoting what the village offered its residents. Within half an hour, Fausto had restructured my day. I would not do it alone; even better, I could ask questions of the man who knows everything that needs knowing about my grandfather's home.

When I told Mum that I was going to visit a picturesque church in Castelletto and that I'd get a good view of the valley from it, she went a little quiet. "I wonder if that's la cèsa vècia," she said, using dialët for the "old church." "In Italian they call it la antica chiesa," I replied, "so it must be."

"You know that's the church that is on Nonno's tombstone?" she said. Apparently, Nonno had even once tried to buy the plot of land that the abandoned church was on to build a house there, but the local priest had said no. I pictured his tombstone in my mind: an illustration of a tall bell tower atop a simple building, with a winding path below it as though it was on a hill. His cemetery plot was, of course, now shared with Nonna, though he had been there since 1984. "It's supposed to be la cèsa vècia. We picked it because it reminded us of Castelletto."

"Isn't it spooky you want to go there?"

I might never have learned about the old church and my family's connection with it had I not gone on this linguistic journey, yet another one of countless family stories I had lost a link to. La cèsa vècia is a name for it that is nowhere to be seen on Google Maps, and which every speaker of dialët would probably spell differently. But it's the name my family carried over thirteen hundred kilometers, a name with a feeling of home so powerful that its image adorns their final resting place.

■　■　■

Maurizio had given me a choice: coffee, white wine, or a brugnolino, something I had never heard of. The wine, which he made himself, had a crown cap on it like a bottle of beer and hadn't been opened, but the brugnolino looked as if someone had already been at it. It was 10 a.m., but, curious, I figured it was also 5 p.m. somewhere and went for that. He gave me an approving nod, as if I had passed a test, and gave me a tiny thimble of a glass that his parents had passed down to him. The brugnolino had a warm, dark taste that reminded me of Amarena cherries. But it didn't have cherries in—it was made from sloes. This elixir was about twice as alcoholic as sloe gin, and Maurizio had picked the berries himself, just as he had foraged all of the mushrooms that were now in the village freezer, lying in wait for a polenta festival in the summer. When he wasn't foraging, he was rebuilding a stone wall here, carving out a new Virgin Mary sculpture there, or sorting through the village accounts. Climb up and down a few family trees and Maurizio and I are somehow related, because almost everyone in Castelletto is, too.

Maurizio had a head of short gray curls, a smart lilac sweater and shirt, and a morning free for me before he had to take care of personal business down in the valley. After our brugnolino, he took me around the village with great pride. In the center of Castelletto was what I assumed must be the *new* church, which sits between a stone square with a monument to the fallen of the Second World War, a football pitch, and a big square of tarmac that is lined with long tables during the polenta festival. He said a thousand people can turn up when they have a big celebration, and in the summer emigrants returning for the holidays fill the village with life; otherwise it's sleepy, with about thirty permanent residents. I went up to the stone crucifix, which had a memorial at the bottom, and recognized the face of my great-grandfather that must have been taken in the early 1900s. It's a distinctly Victorian portrait: He gazes straight back, no smile, as if he knew it needed to be somber.

I followed Maurizio gleefully down the different paths he was taking me, relishing the local knowledge and the chance to imbibe it for the first time in my life. I am not sure how interested I was in all of this when I came here as a child; I remember La Serra well, but not Castelletto. Maurizio, just as Fausto had done the day before, spoke to me in Italian because that's all I could speak to them, switching to dialët when referring to something very specific, usually a place name or a kind of food. They spoke in fluent dialët to each other and generally among their friends, but, within their respective families, they told me they only spoke Italian; both have children who have gone to university in big Italian cities, moving far away. Fausto told me that he thought thirty- and forty-year-olds were probably the youngest generation here who could speak it, or at least understand it.

Fausto hoped that people would be interested in studying dialetti again one day. "When things are almost lost, you try to recover them," he said. Maurizio was a bit less sanguine about dialët; he was proud of it, but grudgingly—and I think fairly accurately—pessimistic about its survival. I told Maurizio a story about how my mum and nonna laughed one day when I told Nonna I was moving in with Luke, my now husband. Nonna's face furrowed slightly when she heard his name, confused yet also smiling about something. "Un luc is an idiot in dialët," Mum had explained.

"Simple," Nonna concurred, her long, elongated "seeeehm-ple" making us laugh even harder. I took great pleasure in explaining this to Luke afterward, who took being the butt of a bilingual joke very well. Maurizio grinned, too.

"Do you know what it comes from?" he asked me. I shook my head.

"It's from the husk around a grain of rice. The shell is cast aside, because it's useless. So un luc is useless."

As we approached la cèsa vècia in the car, I saw it was also a husk of sorts. The site dates back to the Lombard monks. The first time it started falling apart was five hundred years into its life in 600 CE, and even though locals were told to pray in a nearby (and safer) church instead, the residents of Castelletto stayed put and rebuilt it. It would be widened periodically until 1945, when the population of Castelletto reached five hundred, and it was decided that it was too small. The church was deconsecrated and repurposed into a barn, gradually becoming dilapidated. Fausto and Maurizio were both catalysts of an association of locals, set up in the nineties, to try to reverse its fortunes once more. It deserved to remain standing, they felt. Apart from it being a connection with an almost ancient past, most residents in the village today had parents who were baptized there. Even my nonno probably was.

We were driving up one of the long, meandering mountain roads Mum told me would make me carsick, but I was focusing so hard on my conversation with Maurizio that I felt fine. "You need to look at that," he said as we pulled up. A solitary miniature purple orchid was bursting through the grass. But what was behind it was just as spectacular: the outline of a roof and a bell tower, thoughtfully re-stored not as a functioning church but a preservation of its skeleton. The roof collapsed a long time ago, and rather than replacing it, it has been left open to the elements, with a single stone barrel vault arching over its walls as the roof's sole reminder. Ruins in the church's gardens were leveled and reinforced with cement, and they form the foundations of open-air celebrations throughout the year. The origi-nal church bell is long gone, and a modern crucifixion is depicted above its simple altar; it was as if the past had been brought back to life without pretending that life had stayed the same since. I thought about Maurizio's dialët, and Nonna's, and whether I could build a dialët like the reconstructed church; a relationship with the language that doesn't pretend I ever acquired it as a child but acknowledges something precious that demands preservation.

For Maurizio, it has become his life's work to preserve local history, and I could see why he was such good friends with Fausto. Back down the hill, in Castelletto's newer church, he's smothered the walls of one of its halls with photographs of residents alive and long gone, local flora and fauna and craftsmanship, and by each photo wall is a whiteboard where he has tried to write down everything he can identify in each photo, like exhibition labels in a museum. I was happy to find dialët I understood on a wall dedicated to mushrooms; spinarö dall'inveren, the thorn-bush mushroom of winter, tells you more than its Italian name—prugnolo—which only tells you about the blackthorn hedges near which it appears. Nonna had always talked about mushrooms and how she knew which ones to pick or not, depending on their color and texture. Maurizio confirmed a story she had told me about checking the underside of a mushroom for spongy pores to work out whether it is a porcini or not.

As we were about to head out, I saw a book on a table by the door called *I Lèver al Castlët Sùlàca e Ucmèr*. "Dialët!" I cried out, pointing at it. Maurizio handed it to me, and said: "Keep it." Finally, after all those bookshops and libraries, all that trailing around trying to find a single place where I might discover Nonna's language written down, here it was: a random mushroom caption on a wall and a local book by the door of the church.

As Maurizio locked up the church again, I stood in the square and opened the book. The Val d'Arda claims a writer and horticulturalist, Arturo Croci, as one of its most famous exports, and it turned out this was one of his poetry books about his birthplace, which, marvelously for me, has been published bilingually, meaning I can directly compare the dialët with the Italian I understand better.

Croci begins it with a statement on why he has written it in dialët. "La parola acmè l'è dita l'è cuc trasmëta l'emuzion e la disa bòta pusè ad la parola scrita," he says of his mother tongue—the spoken word transmits more emotion than the written. He says dialët represents a story of mountain people, pùvrët ma con un gran cöer, poor with a big heart, with wisdom, and good sense even though they hadn't studied, simply trying to do their best. Most, he writes, have left to look for their fortune and a better life. And then his last line cut through me: Sì incò l'è mèi ma dal vòt am dùmand: umìa dabön imparà a vìv, a es ricunusseint e a vurè ben? Yes, today is better, but I ask: Have we really learned how to live, to be seen, and to love well? I put the book in my bag, still somehow successful in my mission not to burst into tears in front of Maurizio, feeling incredibly fortunate and grateful, not only for this writer putting this bilingual book together, but for the generosity of everyone I had met— Maurizio, Fausto, everyone—who cared enough to give me their time and insist that, even though I was languages, countries, and generations away, I could find meaning here, too.

The sense of recognition filled me with a great sense of warmth but also of profound loss. However wonderful it was that I could now read this book, and find myself understanding more and more dialët, I can't speak it with ease to anybody. And it has all come too late. All those days with Mum and Nonna, sitting on the sofa next to them, half in their world and half out of it. I can never recover what was never understood, what I was never a part of. Without a deeper saturation of language revivalists in places like Piacenza, my personal journey with dialët will not be one of revival or reclamation. It is palliative care.

As I stood in the ever-emptying village of Castelletto, I felt that the best I can do for our dialët now is not some unlikely prodigal return to Piacenza, where it has already become a language to memorialize. But I must honor it and what it represents. It can empower and enlighten my understanding of other endangered languages; it can be a lesson for those with languages that still hold life. There will certainly be individual speakers—many of them in the city, working with La Famiglia Piasinteina—who will carry this language forward into the second half of the twenty-first century. But by the end of it, in the absence of a groundswell, interest, and even faith from the last people who'd be capable of passing it to their children, piaśintein—of the stone and of the air—will disappear. It will be a happy pastime for hobbyists and historians; it will be the memory of a granddaughter.

It was time to leave Castelletto, but not before we made one final stop. While Maurizio was driving, he said my nonna's maiden name and asked: "Was that it?" I nodded. "Yes, I remember now," he said. "It was only a few months ago? We rang the bell for her."

He was right; it had only been a few months since she died. Mum hadn't said anything about a bell here. "What do you mean 'the bell'?" I said.

"When someone dies abroad, we ring the church bell for them," he said. "I see all of their names." It's been seventy years since Nonna moved to the UK. I was speechless and wondered if Nonna was aware that this would happen after she died; that there were people here who, even if they didn't have a clue who she was, marked her passing. Maurizio made a turn onto our final road. "We still call this road 'Road of La Serra,'" he said. We pulled up to it, and perhaps because of how helpful and cheerful Maurizio had been, as I saw its large brick walls emerge from over the hilltop all I felt was profound joy. I got out of the car and looked at the farmhouse whose stories had been passed to me in English, that I was now meeting, again, hearing them in Italian.

"My father took me to pick spinarö," he said, pointing at the grass in front of the house, deftly inviting dialët back into our conversation. "Lots of them grow around here." He gestured toward different flowers, telling me what they were called, once in Italian and then in dialët, if it was something different. I imagined a young Nonna, surrounded by nature, walking with her little sheep—la pegra—and singing her songs to them. Like our language, the farmhouse has become a relic. Its name—La Serra—comes from a word for a tree related to the oak that once dominated the ancient forest here, the same one that surrounded the Lombards as they built their warrior monasteries. The industrial revolution, and the railways that guided its blood flow, put a swift end to these trees, but in La Serra's name they remain. In the coming years, La Serra may be knocked down; new owners may decide it can serve a different purpose, although apparently it's been hard to find a buyer. Nearly a century after it was built, it remains isolated, on the edge of a great arboreal wilderness Maurizio tells me only the most experienced locals would walk into.

A long rose bush trailing above the front door was verdant, its patient buds yet to open. The sun had been bright all morning for us, and I took in as much as I could before we got in the car. As we started down the hill, I turned around to get one more glimpse of La Serra, as though scanning it longer would imprint it more deeply in my memory. But the fog of the mountain had already descended, the mist bidding us to drive on.

CONCLUSION

The Welsh language should be dead by now, at least according to an end date given by the politician and intellectual Saunders Lewis in 1962. "Welsh will end as a living language, should the present trend continue, about the beginning of the twenty-first century," he announced in a now famous radio lecture he gave, called "Tynged yr Iaith"—the fate of the language.

Welsh is the oldest living language of Britain, a Celtic survivor of the Anglo-Saxon onslaught that felled its neighbors, Cornish and Cumbric. Welsh language vitality withstood even the political union with England in 1536, remaining the majority language in Wales until somewhere around the beginning of the 1900s. From there, however, came significant linguistic collapse, as would be revealed in census results that came out shortly after Saunders Lewis's lecture: Just 26 percent of Welsh people could still speak the language. Within a century, the proportion of total Welsh speakers had probably disintegrated by more than half.

Linguicide was not a word back then, but Lewis's speech—a long diatribe on how the English had oppressed the Welsh by excluding their language from legislative and political life—seems to have anticipated it. He quoted the Englishman Matthew Arnold, the poet and inspector of schools, who said in 1852: "It must always be the desire of a Government to render its dominions, as far as possible, homogenous . . . Sooner or later, the difference of language between Wales and England will probably be effaced . . . an event which is socially and politically so desirable."

By the end of his lecture, Lewis had made a long list of demands for raising Welsh once more as a language of government, of the courts, and of the nation: He would begin with making it impossible for the Welsh government to continue without using Welsh. "I do not deny that there would be a period of hatred, persecution and controversy in place of the brotherly love which is so manifest in Welsh political life today," he acknowledged. "It will be nothing less than a revolution to restore the Welsh language in Wales."

The lecture could have fallen flat and Saunders Lewis's prediction of Welsh's death would have come true. Instead, it proved to be one of the most important broadcasts in Welsh political history. A Welsh Language Society was set up; schools and even ulpanim to mimic Israel's success with Hebrew were established; laws, political positions, and the creation of a Welsh language broadcaster were all initiated, galvanized by Lewis's call to arms and the efforts of the language activist peers alongside him.

He was not alive to see it when, in 2011, Welsh was finally recognized—and therefore protected—as an official language in Wales. We are still watching the Welsh language revolution today. Their government has a target of one million Welsh speakers by 2050, and it is not willpower that stands in its speakers' way, but funding, teacher recruitment, and the great force of English.

Welsh, Hebrew, Hawaii'an, Basque, Māori: There are many languages that have resisted linguicide so successfully that they have far outlived their death dates. The last few centuries may have decimated the world's language diversity to an unprecedented extent— but in the last few decades we have also witnessed astonishing, fate-reversing language revivals. Most of these languages aren't completely safe, but they are far stronger than they would have been without rallying cries from activists like Saunders Lewis. Calls for language rights have always been linked to demands for greater sovereignty, equality, and diversity. With Welsh language rights, Welsh nationhood, too, has been strengthened, within a United Kingdom it remains very much a part of. The British poet W. H. Auden allegedly wrote once that "civilisations should be measured by the degree of diversity attained and the degree of unity retained." Māori lives within Aotearoa New Zealand; Welsh within Britain; Basque within Spain. Language rights, intimately tied to minority rights more broadly, don't have to come at the expense of another language or identity, as many speakers in this book have demonstrated. Jacky speaks Greek and Ladino, plus many other languages. Martha speaks fluent Kichwa and Spanish. My mum speaks English, Italian, and dialët. Even now, none of their children can say the same.

To achieve that diversity-within-unity, this book has exposed the criteria that societies all too often deprive their populations of: tolerance of multilingualism, minority rights, state recognition, and power.

A language's health is unequivocally tied to the tolerance and encouragement of multiculturalism, and these are values that, as the far right surges globally, are increasingly under threat. From the United Kingdom to Oman, Italy to the United States, the languages of our grandparents are quirks of family history and problems to solve, threatening unity because we presume that togetherness means being identical to each other. Even in countries where there is greater state infrastructure around language diversity—Ecuador and Ghana, for example—language activists are quick to point out that recognition and the accommodation of multilingualism is not enough; without strategies that lift entire communities and improve equality for all, there will always be inequality in their linguistic world, too.

Second, language rights are inseparable from a community's other rights: to land, to religion, or to simply exist. In functioning, peaceful democracies, some communities are waiting for equality before the law and a recognition of the same protections offered to their countrymen. In other scenarios, the revival of a language will only be possible with a fulsome return of what was theirs. Ukrainians in Russian-occupied territories do not want minority rights to protect their language—they want the Russians out. Many of the forty million Kurds want a state of Kurdistan. The Karuk have only just got some of their land back in California, but they've already lost at least 90 percent of their original speaker population. It is hard to believe a full reversal of linguicide is possible in these places, but that doesn't mean the damage can't be limited or stopped from getting worse.

Third, states must acknowledge the languages they have killed and the speakers they have failed; they must recognize languages' role in the identities of their citizens and give children and adults alike the chance to experience the world through a multitude, not monoculture, of languages. Some countries may benefit from state commissioners as seen in Ukraine where government sponsorship can defend against overt linguicide; all countries would benefit from some kind of international monitor that could track linguistic discrimination and preservation over the long term.

Finally, at the heart of all of the various solutions we have seen—better documentation, laws, policies, funding, schools, research—is not language itself but power. Communities wishing to maintain a language will need to claw back autonomy before they make a single grammar book. The linguist David Crystal argues that language revitalization is only possible for endangered languages if their speakers increase their prestige, wealth, and legitimate power in the dominant community. Languages are powerful because they are testimonies to a community and culture taking up space and making meaning of the world. This will always be threatening to those who wish to seize power and cling to it long enough for everyone to forget what they were fighting for in the first place.

Native English speakers enjoy a cultural dominance so ubiquitous we hardly notice it. I hope this book has disturbed any sense that this is a good or inevitable fact. If you are from a developed country and are monolingual, above all in English, you should question why this has become the status quo. Bloated and greedy, our language siphons off the words of many of our speakers, benefiting from what multilingual immigrants contribute to our countries but stripping them of their own language within two generations. Languages changing and adapting is inevitable, but the great tragedy of linguicide is that a community finds it has lost an entire language it never chose to part from, through a change it did not author. Many that have already lost them did so because they lacked the power, voice, or opportunity to say that their languages, too, were worth keeping.

■ ■ ■

To return to a familiar question: Wouldn't it be easier if we all spoke the same language? This is a question I hear all the time, usually from monolingual English speakers who would, of course, benefit the most from a monolingual world. Suggest to them that, yes, it would be good if we all spoke Mandarin, which already has the highest number of native speakers of any language in the world, and they may change their mind. Politics is increasingly polarized in countries like the UK and the US, where everyone speaks the same language; a common language alone does not unite us or solve the world's problems. However, something that does help our communities stick together—gifting resilience, ethnic ties, encyclopedias, cultural bridges, and even health-care interventions—is language diversity. Monolinguals are often ignorant, understandably, about the multilingualism that shapes the world around them. In our pursuit of a select few powerful languages, in our insistence that a common language can unite us, we forget that multilingualism is—like all biodiversity— a connective tissue in the grand scheme of our existence.

Saunders Lewis was half right in his prediction: This is the century that will make or break the future of languages around the world. We haven't lost Welsh yet, but we will probably lose thousands of others. In Australia, a single language out of 358 known indigenous languages is safe;[1] 220 are already extinct, dormant, or "awakening," to use the noctambulant language of Ghil'ad Zuckermann and his sleeping beauty languages. In Eurasia, 200 languages are also basically gone; in Africa, 86; in Oceania, 61; in North America, 182; and in South America, 200. An extremely small portion of those languages will be kissed back to life. Around 693 languages worldwide hover between critical and severe endangerment. Some of their speakers, like Jacky and his Salonikan Ladino, bear the unfathomable burden of being the last in their line and are incapable of the large grassroots groundswell of a whole nation like Wales. Ukrainians in Russia's occupied territories and Kurdish speakers face unrelenting, state-sponsored assaults on their linguistic integrity and a lack of linguicide monitors or human rights instruments to do much about it. Barriers to opportunity continue to force many people worldwide to learn English as the only path to adult prosperity, meaning in some cases that they can speak to their boss more easily than their parents. Despite all the technological leaps that the world has seen in the last half-century, and the research that proves language learning's immense cognitive benefits, children across the planet are still not entitled to schooling in the first language that they speak at home.

In the face of so many obstacles and so much willful neglect, we've seen time and again that it's speakers who pick up the slack where governments fail. It's the Italians setting up their own supplementary schools in London; the foreign linguists in Oman trying to give an ancient language its first writing system so that it can withstand the force of Arabic; the Kichwa midwives whispering words of encouragement; Sadik rallying his Dagbani Wikipedia comrades. It's Kareem's years-long attempt to get Bakhtiar Ali's Kurdish novel translated, or Maymi's daily grind studying Karuk in the hope that she will be able to pass it to her three children while an elder can still help her. Such voluntary work is admirable, and a necessary part of the ecosystem, but alone it is not sustainable. Everyone I interviewed could do with more funding, and as I write amid the second Trump administration it is funding that is scarce; the president has gutted the National Endowment for the Humanities, which helped to fund organizations like the Living Tongues Institute for Endangered Languages, which supports communities around the globe. Their founder told me they had about six months of money left before they would have to "reassess their options."

There is one small action that anyone can take to resist glottophobia, or the discrimination against other people's languages or accents: learning a second language yourself. Research shows that acquiring foreign languages, even as adults, gives us a deeper understanding of how language works, improving our communication skills. For every LinkedIn bro recommending you get this AI agent or that expensive course to communicate better, there is a (far cheaper) language textbook waiting for you to open the first page. Languages are skills we get the privilege of working on our entire lives. But, apart from helping ourselves, it also helps us appreciate all the language diversity out there, the languages we don't get a chance to learn as well as the ones that we do. Children are more likely to want to learn languages if they've been exposed to multilingualism. We must see it to believe it—and the more high-profile multilingual voices, the better. I don't believe it's a coincidence that footballers who speak multiple languages often go viral. We admire them for it—and we rightly assume that, within their international teams and careers, it makes them better players. Wouldn't you be a better player, too—on your figurative football pitch—with more languages at your disposal and more teammates feeling proud about the languages they already speak?

I never thought I would learn languages beyond Spanish and

Arabic, back when I was in my early twenties. But inspired by the language activism I have witnessed, I've not only been learning Italian: I've also started running a Language Bar in Clerkenwell's old Italian social club in London, the same one my mum grew up going to. Once a month, people come to practice their Italian over £3 glasses of wine; there's so much demand that we now regularly sell out tickets. More and more heritage learners are turning up, speaking alongside university graduates in Italian and native speakers. I don't think it is a coincidence that I'm returning to the same community spaces of my mum's childhood, where it is now members of her generation who are trying to keep a distinctive London Italian heritage alive. It is not what it once was, but that doesn't mean it can't be something new again, celebrating not just a century-old migratory wave, but a contemporary one, too. At our most recent Language Bar, we welcomed Arif, whose Bengali family raised him in Rome before he moved to London; now he is one of the native Italian speakers helping me rebuild an attachment to the language. In the other direction, I have started traveling back to Italy more than I have ever done before, accepting any work opportunity that might take me there.

My relationship with Italian is repairing. I say this not to let my governments off the hook, but, rather, to remind any reader what is possible with commitment, the privilege to spend your free time learning, and resistance. Without learning Italian, I wouldn't have been able to conduct several interviews for this book or write any of the last chapter. Even more stories about my family's life would have been lost to the void of family history; the stories you can't read on the internet or ask an AI agent to summarize. I'll never be able to fully quantify what I personally lost; but in the face of linguicide, there is much yet to salvage. I'll never speak al dialët like Mum or Nonna, but I have begun to speak Italian—and now it is helping me thrive in contexts I never imagined, on top of accessing dialët materials for the first time. Learning a heritage language is not a promise of return, but it is a reminder of what was and what still can be.

． ． ．

On Nonna's ninety-fifth birthday, some of her closest family members gathered around her hospital bed, where she decided to put on a show for us. Despite a stroke, a COVID-19 infection, and, now, a doctor's news that Nonna would leave us soon, her happiness at being surrounded by those she loved meant she spontaneously started singing. I looked at Mum, who looked at her cousins, who looked back at me. None of us had a clue what she was singing. She could enunciate barely any of it. It wasn't "Vola colomba," and it wasn't any of the other folk songs she had shared with me. I filmed her, somehow aware this would be the last time I would hear her sing, and when we went home I got out a notebook and pen and tried to write down the words I could distinguish to then search for them on Google.

With so much Italian music available on YouTube, I was—gratefully—able to track the song down: "La sera dei baci." The evening of kisses; a song from the First World War, in which a woman remembers falling for an alpino soldier who goes on to die in the mountains at just twenty. Nonna must have learned it at La Serra, and whatever was going on in her mind had brought her back there. "These were songs to sing, not to dance to," Nonna had once told me; she thought modern music was all about dancing. "These songs are about love, about soldiers." Clearly, this song was what she was thinking of. I wondered why she'd never sung it with us before. I committed it to memory, as I had done all of the other songs she liked, something that is a lot easier now that my Italian has improved. Singing in Italian feels less like remembering and more like speaking anew.

A couple of months later, I sang it after the funeral directors lowered her coffin into the grave. I had been having anxiety dreams for several months about singing at her funeral, terrified I would be too upset to perform. In the moment, faced with her tombstone and the cold silence of January, the first line came out and my voice slipped. I looked at Mum and nodded—*I'm trying again. Ti ricord . . . ti ricordi la sera dei baci.*

I slipped into a sort of dream state I can only access when I'm singing, letting my body take over what I've trained it to do. The song ends: Non c'è al mondo più grande dolore / Che vedere il suo bene morir, "There's no greater pain than to see your loved one die." As soon as it was over, I crumpled and the cemetery workers closed in, eager to get to work. Mum took my arm and we started to walk back to the car. "What song was that?" she asked. "La sera dei baci," I said to her. "It's the last song she sang. Do you remember?" She smiled, nodding. An unfamiliar song to Mum, it was the last thing Nonna passed down to us.

Right at the end, it was as if Nonna and I had our own secret language.

Two things can be true at the same time: that the speakers of living languages must be vigorously supported, but also that languages long gone may be laid to rest and that speakers may continue to find identity and connection in what remains. Our homes and nations hold many ghosts of languages past. But not all ghosts need haunt us.

Each time I tell Mum bon giuran, or I read one of my dialët poetry books, or try to sound out a phrase, Nonna is there, along with the home she once knew and its lost world that she shared with me. In an age that forces impermanence and monoculture, and offers a million reasons to forget, she is as good a reason as I can think of to remember. And I feel her love that, just like language, defies seas and borders, life and death.

NOTES

Introduction

1. United Nations, Department of Economic and Social Affairs, Indigenous Peoples, *Indigenous Languages* (New York: United Nations, 2018), https://www.un.org/development/desa/indigenouspeoples/wp-content/uploads/sites/19/2018/04/Indigenous-Languages.pdf.
2. United Nations, Department of Economic and Social Affairs, "Indigenous Languages Are Critical for Sustainable Development, Belonging and Identity," *Development,* accessed September 16, 2025, https://www.un.org/development/desa/en/news/social/indigenous-languages.html.
3. Camilo Mora, Derek P. Tittensor, Sina Adl, Alastair G. B. Simpson, and Boris Worm, "How Many Species Are There on Earth and in the Ocean?" *PLoS Biology* 9, no. 8 (August 23, 2011): e1001127, https://doi.org/10:1371/journal.pbio.1001127.
4. David French and Eugene S. Hunn, "Lomatium: A Key Resource for the Columbia Plateau Native Subsistence" (unpublished monograph, 1981), accessed September 14, 2025, https://faculty.washington.edu/hunn/vitae/Lomatiums_NWS.pdf.
5. Eugene S. Hunn and Cecil H. Brown, "Names, the Foundation of Linguistic Ethnobiology," in *Linguistic Ethnobiology,* ed. E. N. Anderson, D. Pearsall, E. Hunn, and N. Turner (Oxford: Wiley-Blackwell, 2011), pp. 319–34.
6. Tristram R. Ingham, Bernadette Huatau Jones, Meredith A. Perry, Andrew Sporle, Tom Elliott, Paula Toko King, Gabrielle Baker, Barry Milne, Tori Diamond, and Linda Waimarie Nikora, "Māori Health, Wellbeing, and Disability in Aotearoa New Zealand: A National Survey," *International Journal of Environmental Research and Public Health* 22, no. 6 (May 23, 2025): 829, https://doi.org/10:3390/ijerph22060829.
7. S. Harding, P. Jones, J. Kiaputa, and W. A. Peterson, "Language Improves Health and Wellbeing in Indigenous Communities: A Scoping Review,"

Language and Health 3, no. 1 (June 2025): 100047, https://doi.org/10:1016/j
.langhea.2025:100047.

Emigrate:
The Story of Italian

1. Robert Phillipson and Tove Skutnabb-Kangas, *Papers in European Language Policy. ROLIG-papir 53*, Roskilde University Center, September 1995, ERIC, ED 388 092, https://files.eric.ed.gov/fulltext/ED388092.pdf.

2. British Council, *Language Trends England 2024: Language Teaching in Primary, Secondary and Independent Schools in England,* survey report by Ian Collen and Jayne Duff (London: British Council, 2024), https://www.britishcouncil.org/sites /default/files/language_trend_england_2024.pdf.

3. Richard Ruíz, "Orientations in Language Planning," *NABE Journal* 8, no. 2 (Winter 1984): 15–34, https://doi.org/10.1080/08855072.1984.10668464.

4. Nicola McLelland, "The History of Language Learning and Teaching in Britain," *Language Learning Journal* 46, no. 1 (2018): 6–16, https://doi.org/10:10 80/09571736:2017:1382052.

5. Andrea Sander-Montant, Rébecca Bissonnette, and Krista Byers-Heinlein, "Like Mother Like Child: Differential Impact of Mothers' and Fathers' Individual Language Use on Bilingual Language Exposure," *Child Development* 96, no. 2 (March–April 2025): 662–78, https://doi.org/10:1111/cdev.14196.

6. Malwina Gudowska, *Mother Tongue Tied: On Language, Motherhood & Multilingualism* (London: Footnote Press, 2024).

7. Richard B. Cox Jr. et al., "Shared Language Erosion: Rethinking Immigrant Family Communication and Impacts on Youth Development," *Children* 8, no. 4 (2021): 256, https://doi.org/10.3390/children8040256.

8. YPF Trust, "Supplementary Education—The NRC," National Resource Center for Supplementary Education (England), accessed September 14, 2025, https://supplementaryeducation.org.uk/supplementary-education-the-nrc/.

9. SIAL.courses, *SIAL Progetto 1 a.s. 2024–2025* (PDF), accessed January 8, 2026, https://sial.courses/wp-content/uploads/2024/06/SIAL-Progetto-1-a.s.-2024 -2025.pdf.

10. SIAL.courses, *SIAL Progetto 2 a.s. 2024–2025* (PDF), accessed January 8, 2026, https://sial.courses/wp-content/uploads/2024/06/SIAL-Progetto-2-a.s.2024 -2025.pdf.

11. K. P. H. Sullivan and Annika Egan Sjölander, "Mother Tongue Classes: A Parental Choice, but Does Choice Equate with Parental Involvement and Engagement in Learning?," *Education in the North* 26, no. 2 (2019): 51–65, https://doi.org/10:26203/kk40-gj48.

12. Karen Forbes and Nicola Lupi Morea, "Mapping school-level language policies across multilingual secondary schools in England: An ecology of English, Modern Languages, and Community Languages Policies," *British Educational Research Journal* 50, no 3. (January 2024): 1189–1207.

Build:
The Story of Ṣḥehrɛ̄t

1. Giuliano Castagna, with a contribution by Suhail al-Amri, *An Annotated Corpus of Three Hundred Proverbs, Sayings, and Idioms in Eastern Jibbali/Śḥərɛ̄t* (Cambridge, UK: Open Book Publishers, 2024), DOI: 10.11647/OBP.0422. https://www.openbookpublishers.com/books/10.11647/obp.0422.

2. Fabio Gasparini, Kamala Russell, and Janet C. E. Watson, eds., *Diversity Across the Arabian Peninsula: Language, Culture, Nature* (Cambridge: Open Book Publishers, 2024), https://doi.org/10:11647/OBP.0411.

3. Richard Gravina, "The Vowel System of Jibbali," *Occasional Papers in the Study of Modern South Arabian* 2, no. 1 (2022): 1–22, https://doi.org/10:1163/26670027-00201002.

4. Said Al Jahdhami, "Minority Languages in Oman," *Anglisticum Journal* (IJLLIS) 4, no. 10 (October 2015): 105–112, https://www.anglisticum.org.mk/index.php/IJLLIS/article/view/1189/1578.

5. John C. Wilkinson, *The Buraimi Oasis and the Arabian Peninsula: Society, Economy and Political Development* (Oxford: Oxford University Press, 2023), chap. 9, https://academic.oup.com/book/59730/chapter/507134657.

6. Afaf Al-Issa, "The Language Planning Situation in the Sultanate of Oman," *International Journal of English Language and Translation Studies* 8, no. 4 (2020): 10, https://manahelalkhwairinternational.com/wp-content/uploads/2020/12/Ali-10.pdf.

7. Lindell Bromham and Teemu K. Paxton, "Global Predictors of Language Endangerment and the Future of Linguistic Diversity," *Nature Ecology & Evolution* 6 (2): 163–73.

8. Amalia E. Gnanadesikan, *The Writing Revolution: Cuneiform to the Internet* (Malden, MA: Wiley-Blackwell, 2008).

9. Amir Azad Al Kathiri, Abdulaziz Ahmed Al Maashani, and Omar Said Al Shahri, *Frankincense: Community and Folklore,* trans. Mahfoodh Khalaf Mahmood, n.p.

Occupy:
The Story of Ukrainian

1. Vladimir Putin, "On the Historical Unity of Russians and Ukrainians," Official Internet Resources of the President of Russia, July 12, 2021, https://www.en.kremlin.ru/events/president/news/66181.

2. Atlantic Council, "Putin Vows to 'Actively Defend' Russians Living Abroad," NATOSource, July 2, 2014, https://www.atlanticcouncil.org/blogs/natosource/putin-vows-to-actively-defend-russians-living-abroad/.

3. Mica Rosenberg, "Mayan Languages Enjoy Renaissance," Reuters, August 9, 2007, https://www.reuters.com/article/world/mayan-languages-enjoy-renaissance-idUSN13204436/.

4. "Post-Yugoslav 'Common Language' Declaration Challenges Nationalism," Balkan Insight, March 30, 2017, https://balkaninsight.com/2017/03/30/post-yugoslav-common-language-declaration-challenges-nationalism-03-29-2017/.

5. Laada Bilaniuk, *Contested Tongues: Language Politics and Cultural Correction in Ukraine* (Ithaca, NY: Cornell University Press, 2005).

6. Joan F. Chevalier, "Russian as the National Language: An Overview of Language Planning in the Russian Federation," *Russian Language Journal* 56, no. 1 (2006): 25–36.

7. "Givenchy Uniform for French Academy Immortal Daniel Rondcau," *WWD* (*Women's Wear Daily*), November 2021, https://www.wwd.com/fashion-news/fashion-scoops/givenchy-uniform-french-academy-immortal-daniel-rondeau-1234991491/.

8. Adam Nossiter, "The Guardians of the French Language Are Deadlocked, Just Like Their Country," *New York Times*, March 3, 2019.

9. Dmytro Kremin, *A Violin from the Other Riverside: Contemporary Ukrainian Poetry*, trans. Svetlana Lavochkina (Sandpoint, ID: Lost Horse Press, 2023).

10. "Навіщо Росія створює в Криму медіа українською?" Крим.Реалії, January 24, 2020, https://ua.krymr.com/a/navischo-rosii-v-krymu-nove-media-ukrainskouy-movoyu/30395122.html.

11. "Жовті фіранки та синя скатертина: хто в Луганську чекає на Україну," DW Ukrainian Service, January 22, 2021.

12. "The Number of Protocols for Violations of the Language Law Has Increased by 1:7 Times in 2024," OpenDatabot, October 25, 2024, https://opendatabot.ua/en/analytics/language-law-2024.

13. "Russia vs Ukraine: the Biggest War of the Fake News Era," Reuters, July 31, 2024.

14. Halya Coynash, "Mariupol Only for the Invaders: Russia Changes Street Names to Totally Plunder Ukrainian Owners," Kharkiv Human Rights Protection Group (War crimes section), October 21, 2024, https://khpg.org/en/1608814070.

15. "'Who Else Would They Glorify?' In Occupied Mariupol, Russia Just Opened a Museum to a Key Enforcer of Stalinist Repressions," Meduza, February 19, 2025.

16. *Visit Ukraine* (blog), "Ukraine renamed 327 settlements as part of decommunization and derussification," September 19, 2024, https://visitukraine.today/blog/4786/ukraine-renamed-327-settlements-as-part-of-decommunization-and-de-russification.

17. *Ukraine: Language Wars*, ARTE.tv Documentary, YouTube video, uploaded October 7, 2022, https://www.youtube.com/watch?v=Mgcb0vJjs78.

18. Kateryna Ustiuhova, "surzhyk: Wherever It Was Sowed, It Will Grow," Babel (Medium), September 30 2024, https://medium.com/babel/surzhyk-wherever-it-was-sowed-it-will-grow-1f812e7ac80f.

Expel:
The Story of Ladino

1. Efrat Aviv, "Millet System in the Ottoman Empire," Oxford Bibliographies, last modified November 28, 2016, DOI:10:1093/obo/9780195390155-0231.
2. Mariángela Chatzistamatiou, *Holocaust Songs of the Greek Jews: Ta tragoudia tou Olokaftomatos ton Ellinon Evraion,* English and Greek bilingual edition (Athens: Alexandrea, 2024), 240.
3. United States Holocaust Memorial Museum, *The Holocaust in Greece,* March 5, 2013, https://www.ushmm.org/m/pdfs/20130305-holocaust-in-greece.pdf.
4. Mark Mazower, *Salonica, City of Ghosts: Christians, Muslims and Jews, 1430–1950* (New York: Knopf, 2005).
5. Chi Luu, "Word to Your Mother (Tongue): Can Hip Hop Save Endangered Languages?," *JSTOR Daily,* March 3, 2015, https://daily.jstor.org/word -mother-tongue-can-hip-hop-save-endangered-languages/.
6. "Saving a Language Through Song," University of Sydney—News & Opinion, March 12, 2020.
7. Begoña Echeverria and Heather Sparling, "Heritage Language Revitalisation and Music," *Journal of Multilingual and Multicultural Development* 45, no. 1 (2024): 1–8, https://doi.org/10.1080/01434632.2022.2157006.
8. "Spain Passes Law Awarding Citizenship to Descendants of Expelled Jews," *Guardian,* June 11, 2015, https://www.theguardian.com/world/2015/jun/11 /spain-law-citizenship-jews.

Exploit:
The Story of Karuk

1. Herbert W. Luthin, ed., *Surviving Through the Days: Translations of Native California Stories and Songs* (Berkeley: University of California Press, 2002), http://ark.cdlib .org/ark:/13030/kt1r29q2ct/.
2. "California's Tribal Communities," Judicial Branch of California, Tribal/State Programs, June 2018, https://courts.ca.gov/3066.htm.
3. Sabrina Imbler, "How the Wiyot Tribe Won Back a Sacred California Island," Atlas Obscura, November 15, 2019.
4. "US Indian Boarding School History," National Native American Boarding School Healing Coalition, accessed September 14, 2025, https:// boardingschoolhealing.org/education/us-indian-boarding-school-history/.
5. Rebecca Nagle, "The U.S. Has Spent More Money Erasing Native Languages Than Saving Them," *High Country News,* November 5, 2019, https://www.hcn .org/issues/51-21-22/indigenous-affairs-the-u-s-has-spent-more-money -erasing-native-languages-than-saving-them/.
6. Kari Marie Norgaard, Ron Reed, and J. M. Bacon, "How Environmental Decline Restructures Indigenous Gender Practices: What Happens to Karuk

Masculinity When There Are No Fish?," *Sociology of Race and Ethnicity* 4, no. 1 (2018): 98–113, https://doi.org/10:1177/2332649217706518.

7. D. H. Whalen et al., "Health Effects of Indigenous Language Use and Revitalization: A Realist Review," *International Journal for Equity in Health* 21 (2022): 169, https://doi.org/10:1186/s12939-022-01782-6.

Criminalize:
The Story of Kurdish

1. Kareem, Najat Omer. *Body-Related Idioms in Standard English and Kurdish: A Comparative Study,* MA thesis, University of Koya, 2008, https://eprints .koyauniversity.org/400/1/MA_DENG_2008.pdf.

2. CLEAR Global, "Rapid Overview of Language Issues: Türkiye-Syria Earthquakes," February 2023, https://clearglobal.org/wp-content/uploads /2023/03/Rapid-overview-of-language-issues-Turkiye-Syria-earthquakes.pdf.

3. Amnesty International, "Türkiye/Syria Earthquakes: A Human Rights Approach to Crisis Response," February 23, 2023, https://www.amnesty.org /en/latest/campaigns/2023/02/turkiye-syria-earthquakes-a-human-rights -approach-to-crisis-response/.

4. Tove Skutnabb-Kangas and Sertaç Bucak, "Killing a Mother Tongue: How the Kurds Are Deprived of Linguistic Human Rights," in *Linguistic Human Rights: Overcoming Linguistic Discrimination,* ed. Tove Skutnabb-Kangas and Robert Phillipson, in collaboration with Mart Rannut, *Contributions to the Sociology of Language* 67 (Berlin and New York: Mouton de Gruyter, 1994), 347–70.

5. Mohammad Kareem, "Sèvres Centennial: Prospects for an Independent Kurdistan," *Middle East Centre Blog,* London School of Economics, August 28, 2020, https://blogs.lse.ac.uk/mec/2020/08/28/sevres-centennial-prospects -for-an-independent-kurdistan/.

6. Farangis Ghaderi, "Jin, Jiyan, Azadi and the Historical Erasure of Kurds," *International Journal of Middle East Studies* 55, no. 4 (2023): 718–23, https://doi .org/10:1017/S002074382300137X.

7. Parinaz Azhari and Ladan Golipour, "Why 'Jîn'": Erasure of Kurdish Women and Their Politics from the Uprisings in Iran," *Jadaliyya,* November 1, 2022, https://www.jadaliyya.com/Details/44560.

8. Mohammad Ali Forughi, "Aqalyatha-ye Keshvar," *Yāghmā* 3, no. 7 (1950): 264–7.

9. Marlene Schäfers, "Tracing Connections: Kurdish Women Singers and the Ambiguities of Owning Oral Tradition," in *Diversity and Contact Among Singer-Poet Traditions in Eastern Anatolia,* ed. Martin Greve, Wendelmoet Hamelink, and Ulaş Özdemir (Würzburg: Ergon Verlag, 2019), 77–93.

10. Niko Schmitz, "I Was Told Not to Call a Kurdish City by Its Name. Here's Why," Bianet, May 21, 2024, https://bianet.org/yazi/i-was-told-not-to-call -a-kurdish-city-by-its-name-here-s-why-295617.

11. Esra Çevik, "Kurdish Language Rights and Mother Tongue in Education," CRD (pdf), November 2019, https://crd.org/wp-content/uploads/2019/11 /EUTH-Turkey-Kurdish-Language-Rights-Mother-Tongue-in-Education-Esra -Cevik.pdf.

12. Burcu Karakaş, "Kurdish Pupils Denied Language Lessons in Turkey amid Wider Curbs, Families Say," Reuters, December 4, 2024, https://www.reuters .com/world/middle-east/kurdish-pupils-denied-language-lessons-turkey-amid -wider-curbs-families-say-2024-12-04/.

13. Rawest, Dil Yuvadır (Infographic), September 2019, archived from Rawest website at https://rawest.com.tr/wp-content/uploads/2019/09/DilYuvadir_ infografik.pdf (accessed February 2, 2021, via Wayback Machine).

14. "Kurdish Barometer: 61% of Kurds Want Kurdish to Be Official Language," Bianet, October 24, 2023, https://bianet.org/haber/kurdish-barometer-61-of -kurds-want-kurdish-to-be-official-language-286892.

15. Özlem Belçim Galip, "Kurdistan: A Land of Longing and Struggle: Analysis of 'Home-land' and Identity in the Kurdish Novelistic Discourses from Turkish Kurdistan to Its Diaspora (1984–2010)," PhD diss., University of Exeter, 2012.

16. Martha García González, "Translation of Minority Languages in Bilingual and Multilingual Communities," in *Less Translated Languages,* ed. Albert Branchadell and Margaret West (Amsterdam: John Benjamins Publishing Company, 2005), 105–23, https://doi.org/10:1075/btl.58:10gon.

17. Farangis Ghaderi and Joanna Bocheńska, "Challenging Assimilation and Marginalization: The Case of the Kurdish Language," *Melbourne Asia Review,* Edition 21 (2025), DOI: 10:37839/MAR2652-550X21:7.

Shame:
The Story of Kichwa

1. Marleen Haboud, "Vitalidad del Kichwa en Ecuador: lo feo, lo malo, lo bueno . . . ," ILCLA / STILILLA, 2016, Pontificia Universidad Católica del Ecuador, https://www.researchgate.net/profile/Marleen_Haboud/publication /317030910_Vitalidad_del_Kichwa_en_Ecuador_lo_feo_lo_malo_lo_bueno /links/591fd4b1aca27295a89e6489/Vitalidad-del-Kichwa-en-Ecuador-lo-feo -lo-malo-lo-bueno.pdf.

2. "En Imbabura se desarrollan seis iniciativas para revitalizar el kichwa," *El Comercio,* October 15, 2021, https://www.elcomercio.com/sociedad/en -imbabura-se-desarrollan-seis-iniciativas-para-revitalizar-el-kichwa.html.

3. Buen Vivir and Sumak Kawsay, " 'Good Living': An Introduction and Overview," Alternautas, accessed September 14, 2025, https://journals .warwick.ac.uk/index.php/alternautas/article/view/989/848.

4. Miguel Ángel Carpio and María Eugenia Guerrero, "Did the Colonial mita Cause a Population Collapse? What Current Surnames Reveal in Peru," *Journal*

of Economic History 81, no. 4 (December 2021): 1015–51, https://doi.org
/10:1017/S0022050721000498.

5. Nancy H. Hornberger and Serafín M. Coronel-Molina, "Quechua Language
   Shift, Maintenance, and Revitalization in the Andes: The Case for Language
   Planning," *International Journal of the Sociology of Language,* no. 167 (2004): 9–67,
   https://doi.org/10:1515/ijsl.2004:025.

6. L. Danielle Robinette, "Bilingual Intercultural Education in Ecuador:
   Education as a Means of Language Revitalization," senior honors thesis,
   University of Louisville, 2015.

7. Nicholas Limerick, "Kichwa or Quichua? Competing Alphabets, Political
   Histories, and Complicated Reading in Indigenous Languages," *Comparative
   Education Review* 62, no. 1 (2018): 103–24, https://doi.org/10:1086/695487.

8. Karolina Grzech, Anne Schwarz, and Georgia Ennis, "Divided We Stand,
   Unified We Fall? The Impact of Standardization on Oral Language Varieties:
   A Case Study of Amazonian Kichwa," *Revista de Llengua i Dret/Journal of
   Language and Law,* no. 71 (2019): 123–45, https://su.diva-portal.org/smash/get
   /diva2:1326144/FULLTEXT01.pdf.

9. Grzech, Schwarz, and Ennis, "Divided We Stand, Unified We Fall? The
   Impact of Standardization on Oral Language Varieties," 123–145.

10. Inter-American Development Bank, Loan Proposal: Reduction of the Digital
    Divide in Education in Ecuador (EC-L1282), 2024, https://ewsdata.rights
    indevelopment.org/files/documents/90/IADB-BR-L1590_x2TqiWy.pdf.

11. Haboud, "Vitalidad del Kichwa en Ecuador," 42.

12. "Voices of Resilience: The Importance of Indigenous Women for Language
    Preservation," YouTube video, uploaded December 10, 2024, UNESCO,
    https://www.youtube.com/watch?v=stpZaLfdVko.

13. Natàlia Gorina-Careta et al., "Exposure to Bilingual or Monolingual Maternal
    Speech During Pregnancy Affects the Neurophysiological Encoding of Speech
    Sounds in Neonates Differently," *Frontiers in Human Neuroscience* 18 (2024): Article
    1379660, May 22, 2024, https://doi.org/10:3389/fnhum.2024:1379660.

14. Judit Gervain, "The Role of Prenatal Experience in Language Development,"
    Current Opinion in Behavioral Sciences 21 (2018): 62–7, https://doi.org/10:1016/j
    .cobeha.2018:02.004.

15. Natalie A. Chambers, "Language Nests as an Emergent Global Phenomenon:
    Diverse Approaches to Program Development and Delivery," *International
    Journal of Holistic Early Learning and Development* 1 (2015): 25–38, https://ynlc
    .ca/wp-content/uploads/Language_Nests_as_an_Emergent_Global_Phe.pdf.

16. L. Bouchard, "The Quichua System of Beliefs About Language Acquisition
    and Cultural Resilience in Quichua-Spanish Contact," *Anthropological Linguistics*
    55, no. 1 (Spring 2013): 36–60.

17. University of York and Aarhus University, "Properties of 'Baby Talk' Similar
    Across Many Languages," University of York News & Events, October 10,
    2022, https://www.york.ac.uk/news-and-events/news/2022/research/baby
    -talk-similar-across-many-languages/.

18. "Is Speaking in Baby Talk Good for Babies' Language Learning?," Tiny Happy People (BBC), accessed September 14, 2025, https://www.bbc.co.uk /tiny-happy-people/articles/zs4g3j6.

Sanctify:
The Story of Hebrew

1. Gideon Kouts, "From Sokolow to 'Explaining Israel': The Zionist 'Hasbara' First 'Campaign Strategy Paper' and Its Applications," *Revue Européenne des Études Hébraïques,* no. 18 (2016): 103–146, https://www.jstor.org/stable /26624281.

2. David Tavárez, "Ritual Language," in *The Cambridge Handbook of Linguistic Anthropology,* ed. N. J. Enfield, Paul Kockelman, and Jack Sidnell (Cambridge: Cambridge University Press, 2014), 516–36, https://doi.org/10:1017 /CBO9781139342872:024.

3. "Hebrew: A Holy Language," YouTube video, uploaded by Center for Jewish History, August 16, 2017, https://www.youtube.com/watch?v=XBUt7twJ1uY.

4. "Parvum Verborum Novatorum Léxicum (Excerpt),"Lexicon Recentis Latinitatis, Latinitas Foundation, June 1, 2004, Vatican: Holy See, https:// www.vatican.va/roman_curia/institutions_connected/latinitas/documents/rc _latinitas_20040601_lexicon_it.html.

5. "The Position of the Jews in the Tsarist Empire, 1881–1914," in Antony Polonsky: *The Jews in Poland and Russia*, vol. 2, chapter 1, Yale University Press / Littman Library of Jewish Civilization, https://www.brandeis.edu/tauber /events/Polonsky_vol2%20_%20ch1.pdf.

6. Chen Malul, "Robinson Crusoe in the Languages of the Jews: How the Classic English Novel Spread Throughout the Jewish World and Its Many Languages," *The Librarians* (blog of the National Library of Israel), January 12, 2020, https://blog.nli.org.il/en/lbh_robinson-crusoe/.

7. Elon Gilad, "Word of the Day: Ekdakh: How a Precious Stone Became a Pistol," *Haaretz,* July 21, 2014.

8. Anat Rosenberg, "Katav: How Hebrew Struggled to Find a Reporter," *Haaretz,* June 5, 2014, https://www.haaretz.com/2014-06-05/ty-article/.premium /katav-how-hebrew-found-a-reporter/0000017f-e605-da9b-a1ff-ee6f3e 650000.

9. Ghil'ad Zuckermann, *Revivalistics: From the Genesis of Israeli to Language Reclamation in Australia and Beyond* (Oxford: Oxford University Press, 2020), 9.

10. Zuckermann, *Revivalistics,* 90.

11. Jacques Derrida, *Acts of Religion,* ed. Gil Anidjar (New York: Routledge, 2002), 226–7.

12. "Solving the Crisis in Hebrew Studies," *Jerusalem Post,* February 9, 2023, https://www.jpost.com/aliyah/article-731087.

13. Zach Golden, "How Yiddish Became a 'Foreign Language' in Israel Despite Being Spoken There Since the 1400s," *Forward,* September 11, 2023, https://

forward.com/yiddish-world/560390/how-yiddish-became-foreign-language
-israel/.

14. "Gender" in *Yiddish: Biography of a Language* (chapter abstract) (New York: Oxford University Press, 2020), https://academic.oup.com/book/33481
/chapter/287772297.

Ignore:
The Story of Dagbani

1. Abdulai Salifu, *Names That Prick: Royal Praise Names in Dagbon, Northern Ghana*, PhD diss., Indiana University, 2008, ProQuest Dissertations & Theses Global (3344619).

2. Anastasia Riehl, "The Rising Ocean Will Extinguish More than Land. It Will Kill Entire Languages," *Guardian*, June 28, 2023, https://www.theguardian
.com/environment/2023/jun/28/indigenous-languages-climate-crisis-threat
-pacific-islands.

3. Josephine Dzahene-Quarshie and Sarah Marjie, "Why Migrants Learn Language of the Market," in *Negotiating Language Use in Specific Domains Among East African Migrant Students and Workers in Ghana*, September 2020, Figure/ Table 3, https://www.researchgate.net/figure/why-migrants-learn-language
-of-the-market_tbl3_321750595.

4. Fatawu Amidu and Enusah Manduaya Adam, "Language Distribution and Vitality: The Case of Mampruli Among Migrants in the Sekyere Afram Plains District, Ghana," *Journal of African Studies and Ethnographic Research* 1, no. 1 (2019): 54–69, https://royalliteglobal.com/african-studies/article/download
/22/30/81.

5. Seth Appiah-Opoku, "Indigenous Economic Institutions and Ecological Knowledge: A Ghanaian Case Study," *The Environmentalist* 19, no. 3 (1999): 217–27, https://doi.org/10:1023/A:1026498611175.

6. Bureau of Ghana Languages, "Ghana: Save Indigenous Languages from Extinction," February 22, 2021, Bureau of Ghana Languages website, accessed September 14, 2025, https://bgl.gov.gh/2021/02/22/ghana-save-indigenous
-languages-from-extinction/.

7. Joseph Kofi Avunyra, Xegbee xe dona—A bird speaks its own language—EƲe (PEN Ghana) | IMLD 2023, YouTube video, uploaded March 22, 2023, https://www.youtube.com/watch?v=si-9txGlAI8.

8. Knut J. Olawsky, "Introduction: Some Remarks About Dagbani and Its Orthography," extract from "Application for an Orthographical Survey of Dagbani" (unpublished manuscript, Düsseldorf, 1995), accessed September 15, 2025, https://user.phil.hhu.de/~olawsky/hp-ortin.htm.

9. "Bureau of Ghana Languages Owes Printing Firms GH¢ 0:3 Million," AllAfrica, January 8, 2019, https://allafrica.com/stories/201901090137.html.

10. Abdul-Razak Inusah and Sadia Jomo Issahaku, "The Role of Oral Proverbs in

Dagbani," *International Journal of Language, Literature and Culture* 6, no. 1 (2019): 1–10, https://www.researchgate.net/publication/332180528_1-10_Abdul -Razak_Inusah_Sadia_Jomo_Issahaku_The_Role_of_Oral_Proverbs_in _Dagbani.pdf.

11. Shahid Minhas and Abiodun Salawu, "Wikipedia and Indigenous Language Preservation: Analysis of Setswana and Punjabi Languages," *Frontiers in Communication* 10 (2025): article 1442935, https://doi.org/10:3389/fcomm .2025:1442935.

12. Peter Gallert, Heike Winschiers-Theophilus, Gereon K. Kapuire, Colin Stanley, Daniel G. C. Cabrero, and Bobby Shabangu, "Indigenous Knowledge for Wikipedia," in *Proceedings of AfriCHI* 16: The African Conference for Human-Computer Interaction (ACM, 2016), https://doi.org/10:1145 /2998581:2998600.

13. Wyatt MacGaffey, "The Blacksmiths of Tamale: The Dynamics of Space and Time in a Ghanaian Industry," *Africa: Journal of the International African Institute* 79, no. 2 (2009): 169–85.

14. A link to the video can be accessed here: https://www.tiktok.com /@gbewaamultimediahubgh/video/7521805287808896262.

15. Susan Smillie, "Tsunami, 10 Years On: The Sea Nomads Who Survived the Devastation," *Guardian,* December 10, 2014, https://www.theguardian .com/global-development/2014/dec/10/indian-ocean-tsunami-moken-sea -nomads-thailand.

16. Miranda Morris, *The Modern South Arabian Languages (MSAL), UNESCO International Year of Indigenous Languages* report, in collaboration with Friends of Soqotra, 2019, https://www.friendsofsoqotra.org/Soq_Archipelago/pdfs /2019%20UNESCO%20International%20Year%20of%20Indigenous%20 Languages_The%20Modern%20South%20Arabian%20Languages%20 (MSAL).pdf.

17. Emmanuel M. N. A. N. Attoh, Ruddy Afriyie, Gordana Kranjac-Berisavljevic, Enoch Bessah, and Fulco Ludwig, "Changing Terrain: Evidence of Climate Change Impacts and Adaptive Responses of Dagbani Indigenous Communities, Northern Ghana," in *Routledge Handbook of Climate Change Impacts on Indigenous Peoples and Local Communities* (London: Routledge, 2023), 244–58, https://www.taylorfrancis.com/chapters/oa-edit/10.4324/9781003356837 -19/changing-terrain-emmanuel-attoh-ruddy-afriyie-gordana-kranjac -berisavljevic-enoch-bessah-fulco-ludwig.

18. Emmanuel Nyadzi, Saskia E. Werners, Robbert Biesbroek, and Fulco Ludwig, "Techniques and Skills of Indigenous Weather and Seasonal Climate Forecast in Northern Ghana," *Climate and Development* 13, no. 4 (2021): 551–64, https:// doi.org/10:1080/17565529:2020:1831429.

19. Emmanuel Asiedu Brempong and Shreya Agrawal, "Nowcasting on Search Is Bringing AI-Powered Weather Forecasts to People Across Africa," Google blog (Africa), March 28, 2025, https://blog.google/intl/en-africa/products/explore

-get-answers/nowcasting-on-search-is-bringing-ai-powered-weather-forecasts
-to-users-across-africa/.

Remember:
The Story of dialët

1. George Johnson, "Scholars Debate Roots of Yiddish, Migration of Jews," *New York Times,* October 29, 1996.

2. *L'italiano e il libro: Il mondo fra le righe,* ed. Rosario Coluccia (Italy: Accademia della Crusca, 2024).

3. ISTAT (Istituto Nazionale di Statistica), L'uso della lingua italiana, dei dialetti e di altre lingue in Italia, Anno 2015, Comunicato-Stampa, December 27, 2017, https://www.istat.it/comunicato-stampa/luso-della-lingua-italiana-dei-dialetti -e-di-altre-lingue-in-italia-anno-2015/.

4. Marco Tamburelli and Lissander Brasca, "Revisiting the Classification of Gallo-Italic: A Dialectometric Approach," *Digital Scholarship in the Humanities* 33 (2): 442–455, https://doi.org/10:1093/llc/fqx041.

5. ISTAT (Istituto Nazionale di Statistica), L'uso della lingua italiana, dei dialetti e di altre lingue in Italia.

6. "Lettera aperta sull'insegnamento della lingua siciliana nelle scuole: una risposta accademica e civile a chi parla di 'baratro formative,'" *Il Giornale di Pantelleria*, May 22, 2025, https://www.ilgiornaledipantelleria.it/lettera-aperta -sullinsegnamento-della-lingua-siciliana-nelle-scuole-una-risposta-accademica -e-civile-a-chi-parla-di-baratro-formativo/.

Conclusion

1. Evangelia Adamou, *Endangered Languages* (Cambridge, MA: MIT Press, 2024).

ACKNOWLEDGMENTS

A special thanks must go to all of the speakers, linguists, and custodians mentioned in this book, who shared their expertise, time, and languages with me. For many, it would have been the first time a journalist had ever reached out to them, and I am humbled that they took the time to even reply. Many also made time after our interviews to confirm spellings and translations. I am so very grateful; I hope I have done your languages justice.

I am indebted to two incredible publishing teams, one in the UK and one in the US, who helped me bring this work together. Thank you to Eva Hodgkin at William Collins and Katie Berry at Crown for your wonderful advice, skill, and support, as well as my agent Emma Smith, who magically makes everything come together. Thank you also to Amanda Cook, Penny Simon, Ally Coy, Abby Oladipo, Elisha Zepeda, Freya Alsop, Nicholas Allen, Nicola Webb, and Matt Clacher for championing my work.

How To Kill a Language took years, miles, and languages to write, and it wouldn't have happened without some opportunistic trips taken in and around other projects I was lucky to work on. A European Journalism Center grant took me to Oman, where I covered sustainable travel, and a Lloyds Register Foundation grant took me to Ghana, where I got to make a YouTube documentary on how AI is saving lives and languages, which can still be watched on my channel. There is no way I would have been able to travel to nearly as many countries without a healthy grant-giving environment for freelance journalists, and I am very grateful to have received them. An invitation to speak about my journalism at the Universidad San Francisco de Quito equally meant I could travel to Ecuador—thank you Tania Orbe Martínez for having me. Trips to such far flung places meant I was frequently reliant on fixers, who do an awful lot more than fixing. You kept me sane, on time, and with a full belly and expeditions filled with laughter: Ollie Hancock, Kofi Williams, Gabriel Narh Addo, and Adam Al Ghafri—thank you.

Thank you to the interns and assistants who helped me keep my other work going as I wrote, as well as the studies you found for me and pointers you gave as I dug deeper and deeper into the languages I selected. Suchita, India, Bee, Marta, Giovanna, and all the very bright young minds who I hope will one day write books on language too: thank you.

Then there is "the team": the friends and family who enable and empower me more than they could ever know. Thank you Megha and Seren for always reminding me why it's important to tell stories in the first place. Priya, Alice, Isabella: thank you for guiding me through both book two and a wedding. To Luke, who was promoted from boyfriend to husband throughout this process and who kept me fed, loved, and didn't mind being called un luc: I love you. Thank you Dad, for your proofreading and indeed your love of reading that made me capable of writing books in the first place. Mum—you showed me multilingualism was something to be proud of and to nurture. Thank you for your relentless stewardship of who I am, who I came from, and who I can be. And thank you Nonna. Your love made—and makes—me feel like anything is possible. I miss you so very much.

INDEX

ABOUT THE AUTHOR

SOPHIA SMITH GALER is an award-winning journalist who has reported for the BBC and Vice News around the world. She studied Spanish and Arabic at Durham University, and in 2022 *British Vogue* selected her as one of the twenty-five most influential women in the UK.

sophiasmithgaler.com